Improving Working as Learning

Interest in learning at work has captured the attention of many people around the world, often taking centre stage in policy debates about improving economic performance, prosperity and well-being. This book is about the learning that goes on in workplaces – ranging from offices, factories and shops to gyms, health centres and universities – and how it can be improved. Such learning includes everyday work activity, on-the-job instruction and off-the-job training events.

Improving Working as Learning is the first book to analyse systematically learning at work in different settings by developing and applying a new analytical framework. The Working as Learning Framework (WALF) connects the particularities of work tasks with the way jobs are organized and the wider pressures and constraints organizations face for survival, growth and development. The authors convincingly demonstrate that the framework offers a sophisticated understanding of how improving the work environment – both within the workplace and beyond – can enhance and sustain improvements in learning at work.

Each chapter presents evidence – taken from both private and public sectors – to illustrate how the Working as Learning Framework provides a means by which employers, researchers and policy-makers can:

- improve the conditions for nurturing and sustaining learning at work;
- build appropriate workforce development plans within given constraints;
- recognize that the creation and use of knowledge is widely distributed;
- mobilize existing workplace resources to support learning;
- enhance and extend our understanding of how workplace learning is shaped by relationships at, and beyond, the workplace.

This topical book will appeal to an international readership of undergraduate and postgraduate students, vocational teachers and trainers, human resource professionals, policy-makers and researchers.

Alan Felstead is Research Professor at Cardiff School of Social Sciences, Cardiff University.

Alison Fuller is Professor of Education and Work in the School of Education, University of Southampton.

Nick Jewson is Honorary Research Fellow at Cardiff School of Social Sciences, Cardiff University.

Lorna Unwin is Professor of Vocational Education at the Institute of Education, University of London.

Improving Learning TLRP

Series Editor: Andrew Pollard, Director of the ESRC Teaching and Learning Programme

Improving Working as Learning

Alan Felstead, Alison Fuller,
Nick Jewson and
Lorna Unwin

Routledge
Taylor & Francis Group

LONDON AND NEW YORK

First published 2009
by Routledge
2 Park Square, Milton Park, Abingdon, Oxon OX14 4RN
Simultaneously published in the USA and Canada
by Routledge
29 West 35th Street, New York, NY 10001

Routledge is an imprint of the Taylor & Francis Group, an informa business

Typeset in Charter ITC and Stone Sans by
Florence Production Ltd, Stoodleigh, Devon
Printed and bound in Great Britain by
TJ International Ltd, Padstow, Cornwall

British Library Cataloguing in Publication Data
A catalogue record for this book is available from
the British Library

Library of Congress Cataloging in Publication Data
Improving working as learning/Alan Felstead . . . [et al.].
       p.cm.
   1. Organizational learning.   2. Knowledge management.
   3. Employees – Training of.   I. Felstead, Alan, 1963–.
   HD58.82.I1473 2009
   658.3′124–dc22   2008050126

ISBN10: 0–415–49645–4 (hbk)
ISBN10: 0–415–49646–2 (pbk)
ISBN10: 0–203–87795–0 (ebk)

ISBN13: 978–0–415–49645–2 (hbk)
ISBN13: 978–0–415–49646–9 (pbk)
ISBN13: 978–0–203–87795–1 (ebk)

Contents

Figures

Acknowledgements

Research is always a collective endeavour involving many parties. We would like to thank all those who have made the research project reported in this book possible. First and foremost, our sincere thanks must go to all of our respondents, who generously gave us many insights into their daily working lives and the learning activities in which they were engaged. We hope that in this book, and the other outputs which the project has produced, we have done justice to what we were told, what we observed and what we learned from them. Second, we were very fortunate to receive help and support from a team of researchers who participated, at various points, to plan the project, secure the funds and carry out the work. David Ashton played a key role in preparing the original funding bid and was involved in the early stages of the project. Similarly, Sally Walters was involved both in the preparatory work and early part of the research. Daniel Bishop, Peter Butler, Konstantinos Kakavelakis and Tracey Lee were the research officers for several of the case studies during the main stage of the fieldwork. We also received some assistance with individual case studies from Julian Clarke, Asma Khan, Fiona Shirani and Mike Tomlinson. Jason Hughes, Kate Stephens and Jill Turbin provided valuable contributions to our literature reviews. Third, we were ably assisted by two administrators on the project – Suzie Beazer and Sonia Burton – who provided the repository for all the data we collected, co-ordinated a freelance team of transcribers who dealt with several hundred interviews and helped to manage a very complex programme of work. Towards the end of the project Caitlin Thorpe provided us with additional help in drafting all of the figures shown here. Fourth, we discussed many of the ideas presented in this book with research colleagues at a variety of venues. We discussed our findings with members of our Advisory Group with whom we met every six months over almost five years. At one time or another, the following served in such a capacity: Fiona Aldridge, Steve Anelay, Clare Boden, Patrick Bowen, Stephen Boyle, William Buller, Lynne Caley, Mike Campbell, John Doherty, Joyce Findlaker, Martha Goyder, Clare Hansen, Iain Murray, Maureen O'Mara, Sue Otter, Patrick Watt, Nita Webb and Victoria Winkler. Towards the end of the project we received excellent feedback from a wider audience of researchers and stakeholders who attended a Consultative Research Conference we hosted in Cardiff in January 2008. Last but not least, we owe an enormous debt of gratitude to the Economic and Social Research Council's Teaching and Learning Research Programme for funding the project (RES-139-25-0110A) and to Alan Brown and Andrew Pollard, in particular, for offering us support whenever it was needed.

Alan Felstead
Alison Fuller
Nick Jewson
Lorna Unwin

Abbreviations

ANT	Actor–Network Theory
BPM	beats per minute
BRC	British Retail Consortium
BSA	British Sandwich Association
CAP	Competence Assessment Programme
CHAT	Cultural Historical Activity Theory
CIPD	Chartered Institute of Personnel and Development
CoP	Community of Practice
CR	contract researchers
CTF	Construction Task Force
CVCP	Committee of Vice-Chancellors and Principals
DCSF	Department for Children, Schools and Families
DfES	Department for Education and Skills
DH	Department of Health
DIUS	Department for Innovation, Universities and Skills
DTI	Department of Trade and Industry
DWP	Department for Work and Pensions
ETM	exercise to music
EU	European Union
FIA	Fitness Industry Association
GP	General Practitioner
HE	Higher Education
HEFCE	Higher Education Funding Council for England
HR	Human Resource
IATF	International Automotive Task Force
ILO	International Labour Organization
ML	Manufacturer Label
MPL	Minimum Presentation Levels
NHS	National Health Service

NIACE	National Institute of Adult Continuing Education
NPD	New Product Development
NVQ	National Vocational Qualification
OECD	Organisation for Economic Cooperation and Development
OST	Office of Science and Technology
OTP	Organizational Transformation Project
PCT	Primary Care Trust
PI	Principal Investigator
PIU	Performance and Innovation Unit
PMO	Process Manufacturing Operations
PPL	Phonographic Performance Limited
REPs	Register of Exercise Professionals
RL	Retailer Label
SLA	Service Level Agreement
SSC	Sector Skills Councils
TUC	Trades Union Congress
UKCES	UK Commission for Employment and Skills
USP	unique selling point
WALF	Working as Learning Framework

Chapter 1

Setting the scene

Introduction

This book is about the learning that goes on every day in offices, factories and shops throughout the world. Such activity can take a number of forms, including learning as part of everyday work activity, on-the-job instruction and off-the-job training events. This book is not the first – and will certainly not be the last – to have such a focus. However, it does claim to be the first to analyse systematically learning at work in a range of different occupations and economic sectors using a single, newly developed analytical framework, which we refer to as the Working as Learning Framework (WALF). We argue that such a holistic understanding of learning at work can only be achieved by traversing a series of analytical layers of enquiry. This journey takes us beyond the particularities of the work task itself and into the world of work organization and the wider pressures organizations face for survival, growth and development, or what has previously been referred to as the 'context of learning'. It has become commonplace in the UK and some other countries to castigate and even pathologize employers for their reluctance to invest in workforce development and thereby improve the knowledge and skills of their employees. This book shows that, while some employers can and certainly should do more, both they and the research and policy communities need to develop a more sophisticated understanding of how to ensure that these improvements take effect. As we were putting the finishing touches to this book, the fall-out from the global 'credit crunch' was only just being reported. In these circumstances, more than ever, we need to find innovative ways to help workplaces – in both the public and private sectors – create the conditions in which learning can both flourish and be celebrated.

There have been a number of other endeavours to pursue a similar approach to understanding learning at work. Some have been derived from a collection of essays drawn together by researchers in the field (e.g. Garrick and Boud 1999; Evans *et al.* 2002; Rainbird *et al.* 2004). Others have been the outcome of a network of projects 'each with *its own* small research team, and each with *its own specific* research focus' (Evans *et al.* 2006: xi, emphasis added). Yet others have emerged from case studies carried out, analysed and written up by different country-specific teams of researchers across Europe (e.g. Boreham *et al.* 2002; Nijhof and Nieuwenhuis 2008). Despite their ambitions to produce a common analytical framework, these attempts were in the end limited because they were not based on the collective output of academics, with different disciplinary backgrounds and methodological approaches, 'working as a team on one co-ordinated project' (Evans *et al.* 2006: xi). This placed limits on the ability of these initiatives to produce a common and shared analytical framework that can be applied and used in a wide variety of different contexts. In contrast, the research reported in this book was conceived and designed to provide the means to achieve just such a goal. It brought together an interdisciplinary team to work on a *single project* over a number of years and to carry out research in a variety of fields of economic activity.

Although this book reports on research carried out primarily in the UK, the growing interest in learning at work has captured the attention of researchers and policy-makers around the world. Exhortations for improvements and enhancements to learning are commonplace. Moreover, these calls are made more frequently, more widely and more loudly now than in the past. They can be heard in national and international policy debates, such as those which surround the International Labour Office's (ILO) campaign for 'Decent Work', the European Union's concern over the 'Quality of Work and Employment', and the Organisation for Economic Cooperation and Development's (OECD) interest in enhancing the skills of the workforce (ILO 1999; European Foundation for the Improvement of Living and Working Conditions 2002; OECD 2005 and 2007). A better understanding of learning at work – and the development of analytical, conceptual and methodological tools that can be applied and used in a variety of settings – is therefore urgently required across the industrialized world. Previous research has made forays into this field and has produced some valuable evidence and pioneering concepts, on which we readily draw throughout this book. Until now, the pieces of this jigsaw puzzle have not been systematically assembled. This book is our response to such a challenge.

The policy debate frequently starts with the assumption that learning is beneficial to all those involved: the individuals who receive it, the organizations they work for, and the economies of which they are a part. Numerous national government reports make this assumption. Furthermore, they often highlight the workplace as an important, if hitherto neglected, learning location (e.g. DfES, DTI, HM Treasury and DWP 2003; Strategy Unit 2002; PIU 2001). On this basis, learning at work has attracted much attention from policy-makers and also researchers concerned to challenge the notion that formal and informal learning are conceptually distinct (Marsick and Watkins 1990; Colley et al. 2003; Eraut 2004). The fact that 70 per cent of the UK workforce of 2020 are already in work has increased its saliency still further, since most are beyond the reach of schools and may be out of reach of further and higher education institutions (HM Treasury 2006, known as 'The Leitch Review of Skills'). Similarly, while the population of Europe grew by just over 6 per cent between 1975 and 1995, it is predicted to grow by roughly half that rate (3.7 per cent) from 1995 to 2025. One consequence is that the average age of the workforce is increasing. There are worries that significant shortages of skilled workers will start to appear, unless learning at, and before, work is enhanced to compensate for those who retire (Villosio et al. 2008). These trends are reflected in the continued concern about the changing relationship between individuals, the state and lifelong learning (Field 2005 and 2006).

Alongside the increased policy interest in workplace learning, researchers have also intensified their efforts to conceptualize the phenomenon and hence shed further light on its multi-faceted characteristics. In doing so, they have drawn on a rich tradition of intellectual inquiry which views learning as an essential human practice. In the case of workplace learning, many researchers work within what Beckett and Hager (2002) have called the 'emerging paradigm of learning'. Hager (2004: 246) argues that 'rather than being simply a change in the properties of the learner ... the main outcome of learning is the creation of a new set of relations in an environment. This is why learning is inherently contextual, since what it does is to continually alter the context in which it occurs'. This challenges the long-standing and still dominant 'standard paradigm of learning' (Beckett and Hager 2002) which asserts that 'the best learning consists of abstract ideas (concepts or propositions) that are context independent (universal) and transparent to thought'. Hence, he goes on to argue that in this paradigm 'non-transparent learning is either an aberration or a second-rate kind of learning' (Hager (2004: 244). This is important for studies of workplace learning because it takes us beyond the simplistic and restricted traditions of cognitivism and behaviourism and embraces the role of tacit knowledge. This is a feature of learning that the standard paradigm ignores because it is invisible and difficult to measure.

The contextual and social nature of learning was highlighted in the seminal studies of Lave and Wenger (1991) who, in stressing that learning is at its most meaningful when it is 'situated', showed how researchers should focus on the 'community of practice' rather than on the individual as the unit of analysis. In this book, while building on the work of a number of researchers working in the socio-anthropological-cultural tradition, we argue that much more attention needs to be paid to the meaning of context in relation to contemporary work organizations. In particular, our research shows that the relationship between context and learning is dynamic and symbiotic in that they both shape and are shaped by each other.

Similarly, Sfard (1998: 4) has used the notion of 'metaphors of learning'. The first metaphor – 'learning as acquisition' – views learning as a product with a visible, identifiable outcome, often accompanied by certification or proof of attendance. The second metaphor – 'learning as participation' – views learning as a process in which individuals learn as part of social engagement with other people and resources. Sfard (1998) emphasized that neither metaphor was adequate on its own. Researchers in the Cultural Historical Activity Theory (CHAT) tradition (see, *inter alia*, Engeström 2001) have extended the participation metaphor to emphasize the transformative potential of workplace learning by suggesting that that 'learning as (co-)construction' captures this dimension. The importance of this contribution is that it further highlights the dynamism of workplace contexts.

Viewed with these concepts in mind, it quickly becomes apparent that, despite the existence of other conceptualizations, the 'learning as acquisition' metaphor holds greatest sway over policy thinking. This can be seen most starkly in the continued use of qualifications as the proxy measure for skills, and in the number of surveys that depict learning related to the workplace *solely* in terms of formal episodes of 'training' that can be counted and costed (Stasz 2001; HM Treasury 2006). Once learning is viewed as a complex, contextualized process, the door is opened to additional insights into how knowledge and skills are developed, adapted, transformed and shared within the dynamic setting of the workplace. This is, of course, highly problematic in policy terms because the shift away from an over-reliance on a 'bean counting' approach demands a much greater willingness to accept a more holistic perspective on the development of skills strategies. It also demands a realization that employers need much more help if they are going to maximize the learning potential within their organizations. It is far easier to send people on formal training courses than to re-organize production processes or re-design jobs in order to expand opportunities for on-the-job and incidental learning.

Despite some exceptions – most notably workforce development schemes pioneered first in Norway, then in Finland and more recently in Wales (Payne and Keep 2005; Keep 2008) – governments have a fixation with initiatives to increase the supply of qualifications. These place little or no emphasis on helping employers reconfigure the way they organize work, but instead concentrate solely on the individual and the certification process. This, in turn, creates pressure on sectoral bodies who receive government funding, for they too are judged by qualification-led targets with the result that 'what is easy to count gets counted and what is not gets ignored' (Grugulis *et al.* 2004: 10).

Calls for increased learning are also based on the assumption that 'more is better', whatever the circumstances (TUC 2007). However, there is evidence to suggest that this does not universally apply and that the economic rationale for workplace learning varies in strength and, in some cases, does not exist at all. For example, according to a recent survey, around three-quarters of those who had not received some type of formal training in the previous year considered themselves to be in jobs where such training would be of little use. This was not because employers refused to provide formal training but because employees could not see how it would help them improve the way they carried out their work (Felstead 2007). Similarly, surveys of employers suggest that the absence of formal training sometimes is indicative that the business case for it is either weak or non-existent. For example, in 2007, nearly two-thirds of English employers who offered no formal training to their staff did so because the workforce was already fully proficient and the business would not benefit from such activity (Winterbotham *et al.* 2008: 133). The research implication, therefore, is that learning at work needs to be understood in the wider context of production. This means that for some jobs sending staff on training courses and enhancing their opportunities to learn may be inappropriate and even counterproductive – at least, on economic grounds and from the employers' perspective. In other words, the context in which learning takes place matters, and for employers there has to be a business case for improving learning.

It is for this reason that this book is entitled 'improving working as learning'. The title puts the emphasis on making changes, both inside and outside the workplace, in order to make increased learning activity economically worthwhile as well as an integral part of the conduct of work. Hence, the title of this book – as well as the evidence it reports – serve to underline the point that learning is a by-product of what workplaces are primarily about (Streeck 1989). In the private sector, profit is the ultimate driver of economic activity, while in the public sector meeting delivery targets – such as the number of patients treated or students taught – is the driving force. Learning is a 'third-order' issue. This puts it behind 'second-order' issues such as how work is organized and 'first-order' issues surrounding the nature of the product market served, the type of competition faced, and wider structures that impinge upon the ways in which products are made and services are delivered (Keep and Mayhew 1999; Keep *et al.* 2006). Exhortations to employers 'to change their ways' – and improve, enhance or increase workplace learning – without tackling these issues inevitably fall on deaf ears (Grimshaw *et al.* 2008). Many employers are locked into a set of relationships that makes responding to such laudable calls unthinkable without wholesale changes happening elsewhere in what we refer to in the chapters which follow as the 'productive system'.

Nevertheless, analytical progress has been made which illuminates some of the connections, especially those operating at the second-order level. Recent debates in human resource management and the sociology of work have begun to substantiate the suggestion that the quantity and quality of an employee's training and learning experience can, in part, be explained by the way in which work is organized. This is referred to using a variety of terms, such as 'high performance' or 'high involvement' work systems. These are based on four principles: employee involvement in decision-making about the completion of immediate work tasks; feedback on work performance and opportunities for development; rewarding performance and improving motivation; and sharing information and knowledge throughout the organization (Ashton and Sung 2002; Hughes 2008). Such principles are in stark contrast to Taylorist management techniques. Taylorism is exemplified by strict job demarcation, tight job descriptions, limited and firm-specific training, and minimal employee discretion exercised individually or as a team. A number of studies, based on survey evidence, suggest that 'high involvement' working and training are connected (*inter alia*, Frazis *et al.* 1995 and 2000; Osterman 1995; Lynch and Black 1995 and 1998; MacDuffie and Kochan 1995; Whitfield 2000; Felstead and Gallie 2004). The way work is organized has a powerful effect not only on the incidence and intensity of training but also on its quality and the usefulness of workplace learning in general (Felstead *et al.* 2008). Notwithstanding these findings, the evidence that 'high involvement working' is becoming more prevalent is far from unequivocal. The proportion of workplaces in Britain with team-working, multi-skilling and problem-solving groups rose from 22 per cent in 1998 to 29 per cent in 2004 (Kersley *et al.* 2006: 97). However, during this time, there was little change in the extent of individual discretion over the pace of work, its content, the methods used and quality standards (Green 2008). Moreover, the evidence suggests that while team-working became more prevalent between 1992 and 2006, the proportion of employees working in teams with decision-making powers over their work activities actually fell sharply (Gallie *et al.* 2009).

Focusing on job design has started to highlight the wider context in which workplace learning takes place. However, such an analytical focus remains rooted in the workplace and fails to extend beyond the factory gates or shop floor. It, therefore, stops short of examining, in detail, how the commodities made or services delivered are influenced by the overall sequence of production and the wider forces of regulation at work. In other words, first-order issues remain largely unexplored. This book sets out an ambitious attempt to research and connect these three 'orders' by examining workplace learning in a range of economic sectors. In so doing, we hope to equip other researchers with the conceptual and methodological tools with which to extend this approach to other sectors of the economy in the UK and beyond. The remainder of this chapter explains how we set about the research task, what tools and instruments we used, and how the remainder of the book unfolds.

Collecting the evidence

Previous research has tended to focus on particular parts of the economy and has therefore provided only a partial view of learning at work. For example, studies of how expertise is acquired in the workplace have typically focused on professional workers, such as engineers, accountants, nurses and teachers (Eraut *et al.* 1998; Hodkinson and Hodkinson 2004a). Similarly, studies of work organization have traditionally focused on the manufacturing sector to the exclusion of other sectors (e.g. MacDuffie and Kochan 1995; Appelbaum *et al.* 2000; Stroud and Fairbrother 2006). Nevertheless, some refocusing of the research efforts of both workplace learning scholars and those who study work organization has taken place in recent years. We now have, for example, studies of how non-professional workers learn in a variety of settings, such as those employed in the motor trade, sales, coal mining, the public sector and skilled occupations of various sorts (Barber 2003 and 2004; Kakavelakis *et al.* 2008; Fevre *et al.* 2001; Sawchuk 2006; Fuller and Unwin 2003). Similarly, the use and consequences of 'high involvement' work systems have increasingly been studied in sectors outside manufacturing, such as contact centres, care homes and the voluntary sector (Wood *et al.* 2006; Harley *et al.* 2007; Kalleberg *et al.* 2006).

This book – and the project on which it is based – follows this approach by casting its net widely to include sectors that have different histories, trajectories, product markets and driving forces. The sectors studied in the project were intentionally selected with this in mind, thereby generating data on learning in a range of contrasting contexts and involving different types of workers. They were as follows:

- back office staff and telephone operators and managers in a local authority contact centre;
- commission-based sales staff in the leisure industry;
- contract researchers in higher education;
- exercise to music instructors in health and fitness clubs;
- franchise chain operators, salon managers and hair stylists in hairdressing;
- health visitor teams in community healthcare;
- project managers in construction;
- research and development personnel in commercial sandwich manufacturing;
- service staff and managers in restaurant chains;
- shop floor workers and managers in automotive manufacturing;
- software engineers in 'hi-tech' industries;
- store staff and managers in supermarket retailing.

Given the constraints of space, the chapters that follow provide a detailed accounts of the obstacles, challenges, opportunities and circumstances for 'improving working as learning' in eight of these twelve sectors. However, in illustrating our arguments and developing our analysis, we also make occasional reference to our published work on the other four. The rich data collected in all the sectors will lead to more outputs in the future, thereby providing further empirical support for the research methods we have used and the conceptual framework we have developed.

Gaining research access is always a challenge for case study researchers, especially when the route into workplaces is through management. Very promising initial meetings with managers can often result in 'near misses' or 'blow outs' caused by managerial second thoughts or a change of personnel. We experienced both during the course of our research. On the other hand, researchers may be steered to study areas beyond the scope of their research brief. In these circumstances, researchers have to be resolute enough to walk away in the hope of securing access elsewhere and on terms that do not jeopardize the integrity of independent research. We experienced this in a mild form when we were mistakenly regarded as 'free' management consultants who could offer advice on best practice management techniques. Needless to say, we graciously made our exit at this point.

Negotiating access involves a delicate balancing act between, on the one hand, being pragmatic – gaining secure access without causing too much disruption to the business studied, hence avoiding becoming a nuisance – while, on the other hand, retaining the right to study issues of genuine research interest. To identify research sites meeting both of these criteria, we used what we termed the 'research shuttle'. This involved carrying out interviews at a range of sectoral and organization levels – macro, meso and micro – in order to provide insights into the first, second and third order issues identified above. More importantly, it involved shuttling back and forth to identify avenues where the research could have greatest impact (and therefore be of potential value to our respondents), secure introductions and gather important data. We also shuttled between refining our analytical framework and carrying out fieldwork, so that each influenced the development of the other as the research progressed.

Typically, we began the fieldwork by carrying out interviews with key stakeholders at the sector level. The aim of these interviews was to identify organizations of potential interest to comprise our long list of potential sites and collect macro-level evidence on the issues and challenges facing the sector. We carried out 26 such interviews. Interviewees were drawn from Sector Skills Councils, trade associations, industry training suppliers, trade unions, employers' associations and qualification awarding bodies. In several cases, the project's 15-member Advisory Group championed the project by providing leads, contacts and suggestions regarding whom we should approach. Organizational leads were also generated by following up those identified as adopting best practice with regard to employee involvement and/or organizational performance. These leads were sourced both from economy-wide organizations (such as the Involvement and Participation Association) and sector-specific bodies (such as Constructing Excellence). Their selection was informed by primary and secondary analysis of employer surveys, such as those carried out by the Chartered Institute of Personnel and Development (CIPD 2004).

This macro-level activity led to 80 interviews with organizational representatives (which we refer to as the 'meso' level in the 'research shuttle'). Many of these were facilitated by introductions from the sector gatekeepers identified above. In some cases, these discussions led to further leads at the macro-level, hence the 'shuttle' metaphor with interviews being carried out back and forth between these levels of enquiry. In addition, our meso-level contacts were sometimes in a position to provide introductions to other organizations located earlier or later in the sequence of production. These were often based upon their, rather than our, interpretation of the salient contextual features influencing workplace learning in the sector. Hence, research-based decisions were taken about which leads to follow up and which to ignore.

At the micro-level, our selection of workplaces was motivated by the desire to highlight points of contrast within the same organization and/or between organizations operating in the same product market. Hence, workplace level interviews with managers were conducted in contrasting sites within the same organization or in contrasting organizations operating in the same product market. In practice, this comparative approach took a number of forms. In some case studies we compared how the final market destination of a product – such as a pre-packaged sandwich – influenced how it was developed and the learning environments faced by those involved (see Chapter 7). In others, we compared how the reorganization of a work process – such as centralizing call handling into a single contact centre – altered the role of call operators and the opportunities they had to learn (see Chapter 3). In other sectors, the role played by everyday tools – such as stock controlling devices in supermarkets or competency portfolios in car part manufacture – were the focus of our research, identifying their various uses in and consequences for the nature of workers' learning and their progression (see Chapter 8). In yet other cases, we compared different segments of the 'knowledge economy', by identifying the pressures placed on software engineers and higher education researchers, and the consequences this had for their learning (see Chapter 6). Thus, comparison remained the unifying method-ological theme during the data collection phase of the project. This is reflected in the chapters that follow.

In total, 121 workplace level management interviews and 248 worker interviews were carried out. Around a fifth (48) of the latter were preceded by a period of work shadowing, ranging from just half an hour to over five days in one instance and almost two weeks in another. This involved one or more members of the research team in a wide range of activities. These included: working alongside interviewees on a sandwich making assembly line; participating in fitness classes run and organized by interviewees; monitoring how call operators complete questionnaires designed to reveal what they do; helping interviewees sell products from the back of a van; observing health visitors under-taking their work; taking part in training courses for newcomers to the organization; helping to produce a training video on how to ensure that car panels are produced to the client's specifications; and watching how managers recruit software engineers from university.

Micro-level data were also collected by a number of other means and sometimes mixed methods were used (see Felstead *et al.* 2009a). These included: the use of photographs taken by employees to elicit their experiences of working and learning; the completion of 'learning logs' through which employees record and reflect on their experiences of working and learning; the collection of learning artefacts (such as videos, manuals and portfolios) used by different organizations; administration and analysis of in-house surveys; and securing access to staff attitude surveys carried out by management. Where appro-priate, these additional data collection methods are discussed in the chapters that follow.

All respondents were given guarantees of anonymity, as were the organizations involved in the research. Accordingly, appropriate steps have been taken to protect the identity of respondents and the organizations involved. Pseudonyms have, therefore, been used throughout. Readers are provided with an indication of the source of quotations from interviews, and the position held by the respondent, but without compromising the identity of either. Unless indicated otherwise, all the quotations presented have been extracted from fully transcribed interviews carried out face-to-face with respondents.

The project also had, running alongside it, a quantitative data gathering strand that went beyond the collection of data at case study level. At the beginning of the project, we collaborated with the National Institute of Adult Continuing Education (NIACE) to produce a module of new questions on learning at work for insertion into the 2004 Survey on Adult Participation in Learning. The survey elicited responses from a representative sample of 1,943 employees in the UK. The questions aimed to reveal sources of learning associated with everyday work experience, identify the relative importance of different sources of learning and trace their workplace correlates. In particular, we operationalized and then tested the relative importance of the two metaphors of learning – 'learning by acquisition' and 'learning by participation' – referred to earlier (Felstead et al. 2005b). The key questions we developed were repeated by NIACE and now form a regular part of this important and influential data series.

We obtained agreement from NIACE to insert another batch of questions into its 2007 Survey on Adult Participation in Learning. These were designed to operationalize the concept of 'communities of practice', which was a theme that emerged as of potential relevance in some of our case studies (see Chapter 4; Wenger 1998; Hughes et al. 2007). From the resulting responses given by 1,899 employees, we have been able to trace the extent to which communities of practice are experienced by different types of workers (such as novices, experienced newcomers and old-timers); to map the extent to which they are associated with more helpful learning activities; and link them to the performance outcomes of the group and individuals (Aldridge et al. 2007; Felstead et al. 2007b). However, reporting the results of these two surveys is beyond the remit of this book, which is instead focused on the results of our sector case studies. These are presented not only as intrinsic contributions to the literature on workplace learning, but as demonstrations of the usefulness of our conceptual framework and as examples of what research techniques and tools can be used to enrich the field of enquiry.

Outline of the book

The book is designed for flexible use, so that individual chapters can be read in isolation. Thus, each chapter contains a short section outlining

the particular methods used to gather the data reported and a conclusion that summarizes its substantive empirical and conceptual
contribution. However, we strongly recommend that all readers begin
with the next chapter before reading any further since the analytical
tools it outlines are used throughout. Moreover, the chapters of the
book are presented in a particular order, with later chapters building
upon earlier themes. To aid further navigation of the book, we now
provide a succinct summary of each chapter and its focus.

Chapter 2, entitled 'Mapping the Working as Learning Framework',
sets out the key elements of the theoretical perspective that informs
all the chapters that follow. The Working as Learning Framework
(WALF) is built on three concepts: productive systems, work organization and learning environments. Our central argument is that in order
to understand whether learning at work is 'expansive' or 'restrictive'
(Fuller and Unwin 2003 and 2004), researchers need to examine how
work is organized and how, in turn, this is influenced by wider forces.
The model specifies the links between the broadest system of relationships that shape employment relations and the nature of workplace
learning. This approach enables us to explore how these broader
processes are played out in specific workplaces and in the narratives
of people's working lives. To illustrate the flexibility of WALF, each
of the subsequent chapters highlights and develops different elements.
Chapters 3 and 4, for example, emphasize the importance of understanding both the vertical and horizontal pressures placed upon
organizations and workplaces. Chapters 5 and 6, meanwhile, suggest
that, in certain circumstances, one of these dimensions may
predominate in explaining why some learning environments are more
expansive and others more restrictive. Similarly, WALF demonstrates
that the locus of control can vary in this two dimensional analytical
space – backwards or forwards on the horizontal; up or down on the
vertical. Chapter 7, for example, shows that large retailers can exercise
power backwards over those who produce goods for sale. However,
power can be exercised forwards by manufacturers over those who
interact directly with the final consumer, as demonstrated in Chapter
5. Furthermore, long-running debates, such as those surrounding the
utilization of artefacts, can also be examined afresh by adopting WALF.
This is illustrated in Chapter 8.

Chapter 3, entitled 'Processing calls', uses WALF to trace how
setting up of a contact centre in a public authority shifted the balance
of power between service departments, reconfigured job tasks and
led to the emergence of new, and largely unrecognized, kinds of

interactions for contact centre operators that called for distinctive knowledge and skills. These developments occurred because the contact centre was set up to occupy a central position and role within the local authority. This generated processes of standardization, systematization and codification of critical aspects of service delivery across the organization. The account we present demonstrates the analytical value of WALF in examining change by providing a 'before' and 'after' account of the discretion levels and the learning environments experienced by call operators.

Chapter 4, entitled 'Promoting health', discusses the attempts by a group of health visitors in a provincial English city to reform their working practices in order to work more collaboratively and, hence, create a more expansive learning environment. The chapter shows that their attempts to move in this direction were, in the end, thwarted by their relationships with a diverse and fragmented network of managers and fellow professionals. This analysis contextualizes the uncertain development of discretion and trust in the work organization of health visitors within the broader vertical and horizontal relationships of the productive system in which they were embedded. The chapter, therefore, argues that, while much was achieved and considerable learning took place, the group's vision was ultimately unsustainable due to the constraints placed upon them by the wider productive system.

Chapter 5, entitled 'Exercising to music', analyses how two different productive systems impinge upon the discretion levels enjoyed by, and learning experiences of, workers who lead group exercise to music classes, commonly referred to as aerobics. The chapter identifies two broad types of exercise to music classes currently on offer: 'freestyle' classes in which instructors own the product in terms of music selection, the moves made, combinations used, choreography and image conveyed; and 'pre-choreography' classes in which instructors deliver a pre-packaged product in which many of these decisions have been taken by those earlier in the horizontal sequencing of production. The chapter shows that while the former productive system places trust in instructors to deliver, and therefore allows them to expand their horizons and extend their abilities, the latter minimizes the uncertainty and variability of instruction by teaching instructors to follow scripts written by others, in whom more trust is placed. The chapter also shows how the individual biographies of instructors shape their response to these different learning environments.

Chapter 6, entitled 'Creating knowledge', focuses on two organizations many would unequivocally regard as part of the 'knowledge economy'. These are a research-led university and a cutting edge software engineering company. Although contract researchers and software engineers are in the business of creating knowledge, the learning environments in which they work differ quite markedly. These differences are explained by the different productive systems in which these organizations operate. In higher education, the demands on universities to widen access, diversify their funding base and increase research productivity have intensified. This expansion of activity, however, has been accompanied by little change in the way work, career structures and reward systems are organized for contract researchers. Furthermore, new legislation to give those on fixed-term contracts greater employment security has had minimal effect in counteracting these tendencies. By contrast, the vertical pressures under which the software company operated were much weaker. As a result, it organized the work of software engineers in a way that encouraged expansive learning. A high trust work environment was created, reinforced by management practices such as job rotation, team-working, employee share ownership, and the linking of pay to both individual and collective performance.

Chapter 7, entitled 'Making sandwiches', uses WALF to identify two contrasting productive systems in which pre-packaged sandwiches are made and distributed for sale. In one system, sandwiches leave the manufacturer's site as retailer branded products, while in the other they are sold under the manufacturer's label. The chapter discusses the consequences these two productive systems have for the discretion exercised, and the learning environment faced, by those whose responsibility it is to develop and launch new products. In a further development of the expansive–restrictive continuum outlined in Chapter 2, we argue that new product development does not have the same characteristics across these two productive systems, since neither can be placed at one or other extreme end of the continuum but are more appropriately positioned somewhere in between.

Chapter 8, entitled 'Utilizing artefacts', examines the role of artefacts and devices in the workplace in terms of their influence on both participation in and access to learning. The chapter argues that these everyday tools can provide the means through which those involved in particular stages and structures of the productive system can extend their reach. Hence, they have the potential to act as 'boundary objects' that facilitate learning between people in different parts of the productive system, including across and within work-places and job boundaries. However, this function can only be fully understood by situating inanimate objects in a network of active social relationships. The chapter draws on evidence from two contrasting sectors: automotive component manufacturing and retailing. In the automotive sector, national qualifications to accredit job competences became boundary crossing objects and stimulated a heightened interest in learning. In retailing, stock control devices were used by managers in supermarkets to both restrict and expand learning opportunities. Boundary objects, therefore, can offer another lens through which we can examine the nature of the productive system and the learning possibilities they provide.

Chapter 9, entitled 'Bringing working and learning together', concludes the book with a summary of our main methodological and theoretical contributions to the study of workplace learning. It also sets out a number of implications for policy-makers, practitioners and researchers as stakeholders across the world continue to seek meaningful ways of improving working as learning.

Chapter 2

Mapping the Working as Learning Framework

Introduction

The notion of 'the context of learning' has provided a persistent and powerful basis for the theoretical and empirical strategies underpinning the research that provides the foundation for this book (see, for example, Lee *et al.* 2004; Unwin *et al.* 2007; Fuller *et al.* 2006). It has also informed other important contributions to the field (e.g. Lave and Wenger 1991; Boreham 2002; Engeström 1994; Rainbird *et al.* 2004; Evans *et al.* 2006). In this chapter, however, we present a new articulation of the theoretical and conceptual meanings of 'context', which we refer to as the 'Working as Learning Framework' (WALF).

A focus on 'context' directs attention towards the ways in which a wide range of types of learning are shaped, distributed and evaluated within and through the multiple interconnected social relationships and processes that constitute the world of work. As a result of adopting this approach, our fieldwork yielded a rich harvest of case study materials. Indeed, the chapters which follow demonstrate the value of understanding learning in, through and as participation in a wide range of different contexts (Felstead *et al.* 2005b). However, this chapter goes beyond illustrating the utility of this approach in understanding particular cases and, instead, develops a general model of what is meant by 'context'. It places the focus on context in general, rather than contexts in particular. This chapter, then, systematizes and elaborates the idea of context within a broad conceptual framework.

In previous publications we have invoked a variety of metaphors in an attempt to elucidate the notion of the context of learning, and its associated research agenda. These have included notions such as 'Russian dolls' and 'worlds within worlds' (e.g. Unwin *et al.* 2007 and

2008b). This chapter builds on and develops that work by bringing together themes embedded in three different theoretical traditions in social science. From economic theory, we focus on the 'productive systems' model of economic activity; from the sociology of work, we incorporate concepts of 'discretion' and 'trust' that have been developed in the understanding of social processes in employment relations; and from the literature on workplace learning, we highlight the 'expansive–restrictive' characteristics of 'learning environments' and individual 'learning territories'.

Productive systems

The notion of 'productive systems' was developed by institutional economists dissatisfied with neoclassical theories that neglected to incorporate an understanding of the impact of social, political and cultural forces on economic life. To date, the concept has been applied to the analysis of the historical trajectories of major economies (Wilkinson 1983, 1998 and 2002; Burchell *et al.* 2003) and has informed some sector-based studies (Birecree *et al.* 1997; Konzelmann *et al.* 2006). However, it remains a relatively underdeveloped idea and, moreover, until now has not figured in the workplace learning literature at all.

Productive systems comprise the *totality* of social relationships entailed in processes of commodity production. They are constituted by the multiple, interlinked social networks through which economic activity is organized, and commodities are produced and consumed, within capitalist societies. Productive systems, then, are networks of networks, 'worlds within worlds' (cf. Jewson 2007; Unwin *et al.* 2008b). As employed here, the concept does not simply refer to the conventional categories of political economy (the interconnections of state and markets). Rather, it traces the overall configuration of social relationships within economic systems, stretching from individuals and small work groups through to global financial and political systems.

We argue that the understanding of workplace learning in its fullest sense requires the analytical reach offered by the productive system perspective. It allows us to investigate where effective control over the whole productive system is located and how this impacts on learning within any particular workplace. It highlights the importance of establishing the locus of power within the productive system as a whole. It requires us to consider how the meaning, impact and outcomes of learning processes within workplaces are, in part, shaped by a wide range of relationships that exist beyond and outside the employing establishment or organization. Furthermore, the productive systems perspective offers analytical purchase across the economy, including the public and private sectors, manufacturing and services, and in voluntary and paid work. This scope is reflected in the span of the case studies in the chapters that follow.

Productive systems may be analysed in terms of two axes: vertical interconnections of scale, which we designate 'structures of production' (see Figure 2.1); and horizontal interconnections of transformation,

Figure 2.1 Structures of production

which we refer to as 'stages of production' (see Figure 2.2). Each axis is composed of constituent parts, which themselves take the form of networks of social relations.

Vertical interconnections of scale consist of hierarchies of regulation and control between the constituent networks of productive systems, defined by the extent and forms of their reach through time and space (see Figure 2.1). The relatively autonomous spheres of social activity that constitute the structures of productive systems may be analytically arranged along a continuum from micro to meso to macro sets of relationships. Macro sets of relationships (e.g. international regulations and national legal systems concerned with health and safety) exert a greater reach in time and space than, and set constraints upon the operations of, micro relationships (e.g. procedures for operating machinery within a particular plant). Macro relationships, then, regulate the scope, functions and outcomes of relationships at the meso and micro-levels, but without necessarily completely subsuming them. The latter may retain a degree of relative autonomy, potentially blocking or disrupting the regulatory impact of macro influences. The extent of the relative autonomy of nested regulatory networks in any particular productive system is an empirical question to be investigated in each case. For example, a team of workers may be subject to supervision, monitoring and control from managers employed in the same workplace, while retaining some degree of discretion or resistance. The autonomy of workplace managers may, in turn, be curtailed by the requirements of regional or senior management. The operations of the organization as a whole may be regulated by still 'higher level' sources of control, such as legal statutes, government policies, accreditation agencies, shareholder meetings, auditor reports, banking procedures, and so on.

For the purposes of analysis, the structures of productive systems can be divided into a series of sub-systems (see Figure 2.1). These may include: supra-national political organizations; national government and state institutions; sector-wide regulatory bodies; forms of organizational ownership of economic enterprises; board level corporate controls and senior management; intermediate management

Figure 2.2 Stages of production

at regional or division level; supervision at firm, shop floor or work group level. It should be emphasized, however, that these categories are offered as a pragmatic basis for investigation, not as a definitive and comprehensive list. In any particular productive system some structures are likely to be more or less salient than others and some may be absent altogether. Each may include a range of possible alternative arrangements; for example, forms of ownership of economic enterprises may potentially encompass private equity funds, sovereign wealth funds, private shareholders, family ownership, management buyouts, insurance companies, nationalized industry boards, and so on. There may, then, be critical divisions or stratifications within each of these groupings that shape the overall functioning of the productive system.

Horizontal interconnections within productive systems focus on the sequences through which raw materials are transformed into goods and services that are consumed by end-users (see Figure 2.2). Analysis of this axis involves examination of the relationships between the steps or stages that constitute production and consumption, highlighting the temporal inter-relationships of the transformative processes involved (Birecree *et al.* 1997: 4). The principal stages of productive systems commonly include: sourcing raw materials; transformation of raw materials through manufacturing processes; wholesale purchase of manufactured commodities; distribution of products to retail outlets; retail sales; and consumption by end-users. However, as with the structures, these stages of productive systems are suggestive rather than definitive; precise relationships must be established in each case. Some stages may be absent, truncated or compressed, while others may be elaborated or differentiated into lengthy sequences. These patterns can only be revealed by empirical investigation.

Analysis of the vertical and horizontal dimensions of productive systems leads us to consider how the articulation of the structures and stages of productive systems *together* shape and influence learning at work. The concept of 'articulation' refers to ways in which networks of social relations are linked or connected vertically and horizontally within a productive system to constitute the generative activities that make up production. In the case studies reported in this book, the issue of how the structures and stages of the productive system articulate with one another, and the impact this has on overall power relations within the productive system, is a recurring theme. For example, our research in sandwich manufacturing highlights the crucial role of food hygiene regulations and the lengths to which major supermarkets go to ensure that suppliers, manufacturers and distributors conform to these standards (see Chapter 7). Elsewhere, sector bodies may support and encourage best practice through self-regulation. For example, some of the largest health and fitness clubs have collaborated to establish a registration scheme to ensure that employed fitness instructors are qualified to a specified level (see Chapter 5). Tools and artefacts can also be sources of regulation. Devices such as the 'symbol gun', used in supermarkets to control and monitor stock levels, connects local stores with head office, facilitating regulation and co-ordination of the activities of workers at a variety of positions in the structures and stages of the productive systems (see Chapter 8).

Productive systems differ with respect to the location of the principal levers of overall control within and between their structures and stages. Thus, one or more of the structures of the productive system may be salient, exercising powers that constrain the activities of other parts. For example, productive systems comprising national-ized economic enterprises, funded and regulated by state agencies, are likely to be subject to a significant degree of political control and direction. In contrast, where productive systems are dominated by trans-national and multi-national corporations, funded via inter-national stock exchanges and money markets, the capacity of national political institutions to determine decision-making may be eclipsed by the power of shareholders and boards of directors. Similarly, a focus on the stages of productive systems highlights the way in which power relations are shaped by the temporal organization of the overall sequences of production. For example, all those engaged in earlier stages of a productive system may be subject, *de facto* or *de jure*, to regulation by those who control key later stages, such as access to consumers. A case in point is the influence that major infrastructural clients, such as airport authorities and highway agencies, have on the construction supply chain. By setting the terms of the contracting regime, they have a major influence on the way in which building work is carried out at each stage of the construction process (Bishop *et al.* 2008). In contrast, within other productive systems the locus of effective control may lie earlier rather than later in the sequence of productive transformations; for example, control over the supply of raw materials may determine the overall pattern of the productive system. Thus, as shown in Chapter 5, designers of some types of aerobics class have been so successful in marketing the brand that they are able to extend control over venues and the instructors who teach these classes from a much earlier vantage point in the productive system.

More generally, our focus on the structures and stages of productive systems highlights the crucial importance of investigating and specifying the particular forms of power balances between sub-systems within productive systems. These might take the form of bureaucratic regulations, partnership agreements, financial contracts, normative codes, ideological commitments, and so on. These, we argue, have a direct effect on the forms and outcomes of learning at work. For example, in the construction industry, referred to above, a partnership rather than adversarial approach to build completion ensures that 'knots' of workers are able and willing to work closely together, and thereby share good practice (see Bishop *et al.* 2008).

Mapping an entire productive system for even just one commodity can be a very substantial and daunting task (cf. Harvey *et al.* 2002). However, in practice the utility of the concept of productive systems in understanding workplace learning lies in its capacity to position a particular work group or organization within a network of wider influences, constraints and opportunities. Rather than seeking to identify all the dimensions of a variety of different productive systems, therefore, in this book we have utilized the concept to explore and understand specific research sites. This approach leads us to ask how the horizontal axis of the stages of production articulates with the vertical axis of the structures of production *within any specific work situation*. Thus, particular groups of workers may be viewed as a distinctive intersection of horizontal and vertical relationships within a productive system. Their activities, interactions and learning processes may be analysed as a specific point of articulation within a productive system. Their position within the productive system as a whole concerns their relationship to other workers who are 'earlier' or 'later' in the sequence of commodity production, as well as other networks of relationships that are 'above' and 'below' in hierarchies of regulation and control. From this perspective, the way in which work is organized can be conceived as the articulation of broader horizontal and vertical relationships within a productive system. For example, in Chapter 3, we examine the ways in which the advent of a contract centre within a local authority, dealing with enquiries and queries from the public, resulted in fundamental shifts of power, authority and control within and between all departments within the organization.

The productive system perspective highlights, organizes and prioritizes complex causal relationships. It sets out an agenda for multidisciplinary investigation that may be addressed by theorists and empirical researchers. It is, thus, quite in order for case studies to illuminate limited and selected parts of the totality of the processes that constitute learning within productive systems. Indeed, the model enables researchers to be systematic and strategic in identifying those parts of the overall picture that it is appropriate to explore in particular projects.

Work organization

The focal point of our analysis now shifts from productive systems to the second theme of our conceptual framework, the organization of work. The literature on the organization of work is enormous and contains numerous theoretical approaches. From this huge array, we have selected 'discretion' as a key concept of relevance to the understanding of learning at work.

Discretion refers to the degree of autonomy and responsibility exercised by workers in the labour processes in which they are engaged. Discretion should be conceived as a continuum exercised by individuals and/or groups. Moreover, there are a number of different forms or dimensions of discretion, which entail exercising qualitatively different types of autonomy. These include:

- *Discretion in the conception of work* involves the extent to which employees have control over the aims and objectives of their work process.
- *Discretion in work execution* involves control over the way in which given objectives are attained and tasks are executed.
- *Discretion in the evaluation of work outcomes* involves taking responsibility for monitoring work outcomes.

The exercise of discretion, in all its forms, introduces potential uncertainty, indeterminacy and risk into the work process. Managers seek assurance that workers will make use of the autonomy that discretion brings in ways which enhance productivity. Workers wish to be reassured that the exercise of discretion in good faith will not be penalized or rescinded. Such uncertainties may be contained and defused within relationships of 'trust' (Fox 1974) between managers and workers that legitimize and specify the exercise of discretion.

Trust bridges the gap between the known and the unknown, the predictable and the unpredictable. Where everything is certain, trust is irrelevant (cf. Luhmann 1993). Furthermore, trust reaches beyond the instrumental calculation of interests or risk assessment. Trust involves good faith and good will – a shared belief that all parties are genuinely working towards some agreed purpose or objective. Three modes of trust are particularly important:

- *Habitual trust*, in which the granting and exercise of discretion is legitimized and validated by a (real or imaginary) long-term history of tradition, reliability and solidity.
- *Symbolic trust*, in which the indeterminacy surrounding discretion is validated by symbols of moral and ethical values.
- *Communal trust*, in which the parties identify with one another and share in some sense of communal bond that is highly emotionally charged.

Employment mediated by capitalist labour markets involves contractual, calculated, instrumental exchange; that is, the exchange of wages for time spent in the workplace. This remains the bedrock of employment relations, even when they are overlaid with other aspects of trust. Moreover, the mobilization of the productive potential of workforces is typically unlocked by managerial decisions that involve the division and co-ordination of labour. This, too, is integral to work situations and involves the exercise of authority and power. High trust and high discretion modes of work organization represent only one response to these challenges. The potentiality for a spiral of distrust always remains. Distrust refers to a situation where parties in a relationship have ingrained suspicions about the motives, objectives and predictability of the other(s). It entails an absence of belief in the authenticity, good faith and good will of others in the relationship. Distrust may be mutual or unilateral. A typical response in these circumstances is to eliminate, as far as possible, scope for discretion in the reactions and behaviour of others. In construction, for example, this is referred to as 'adversarial' contracting (see Bishop *et al.* 2008). Trust can also be eroded by pressures in the productive system. This is exemplified by the history of the health visitor teams discussed in Chapter 4, whose attempts to introduce innovative new ways of working gradually eroded their trust in management, colleagues and other healthcare professionals.

The relationship between discretion and trust, then, is a complex one. Each influences and shapes the other, although it should not be assumed that low discretion work organization is always a product of low trust between management and workers. In our restaurant chain case study, for example, employees exercised very little discretion in their daily work activities but management–worker relationships were based on high levels of communal trust (Kakavelakis 2008). Low discretion may be a product of particular technologies that are adopted because they yield high productivity or consistent outcomes. In these circumstances opportunities for trust to grow within the employment relationship may be constrained by the pressures of discipline and surveillance that typically accompany such work processes. In these circumstances, there is a tendency for management to view labour as consisting of equivalent, substitutable and interchangeable units. Such perceptions are likely to shape learning policies and strategies within the workplace.

Relationships of trust and discretion may be traced not only within workplaces but also along the vertical and horizontal dimensions of productive systems. Furthermore, the propensity for high trust and high discretion relationships to develop within specific workplaces is conditioned by the presence or absence of trust and discretion within the structures and stages of productive systems as a whole. For example, the foreign owners of the car parts manufacturer, discussed in Chapter 8, required the company 'to prove' that shop-floor workers were competent to meet specified quality standards. In this case, trust alone was not enough to bind the productive system together.

As a result of the complexity and indeterminacy of productive systems, relations of trust in the workplace and the exercise of discretion by employees all generate (greater or lesser) levels of uncertainty and unpredictability for managers. Managers respond with strategies and tactics that are a mixture of deliberate, purposive plans and unexamined assumptions and practices. Management strategies typically encompass three elements: organization of the division of labour; regulation of recruitment processes and the allocation of personnel to places in the division of labour; and regulation of processes of learning by members of the workforce.

As a broad generalization, management strategies may attempt to cope with uncertainty by either seeking to eliminate uncertainty and indeterminacy wherever possible or by seeking to harness indeterminacy to organizational goals, including enhancing worker discretion. An example of the latter is the use of so-called 'high performance management' techniques, which seek to maximize employee discretion, albeit within prescribed boundaries (Butler *et al.* 2004; Hughes 2008). Managers may, of course, apply contrasting strategies to different parts of the workforce. Hence, high levels of trust and discretion enjoyed by some sections of the workforce by no means precludes low levels for others in the same workplace.

Workplace learning

In this section we shift the analytical emphasis once more, this time to a consideration of our third theme, workplace learning. We take two key concepts from a growing body of research: 'learning environments' and 'learning territories'.

Learning environments are bounded networks of social relationships in which people interact with artefacts and devices that are intrinsic to the performance of their work tasks and roles. Such artefacts and devices contribute to the exercise of power and control over other people and things through time and space. The role of the stock control device – known as the 'symbol gun' – in exercising surveillance and discipline within a supermarket has already been noted. This is discussed in more detail in Chapter 8. Similarly, in Chapter 4 we show that baby weighing scales were perceived by a group of health visitors as devices that limited their opportunities to develop new ways of working and tied them into managerial relationships that restricted opportunities to share their learning with one another.

It is now widely acknowledged that the teaching and learning of concepts, skills and practices take place in a variety of ways that, together, constitute a learning environment. Our analysis draws on the concepts of participation in 'expansive' and 'restrictive' learning environments, as developed by Fuller and Unwin (2003 and 2004). This approach highlights three aspects of participation in workplace learning environments:

- engagement in multiple and overlapping communities of practice at and beyond the workplace;
- access to multidimensional approaches to the acquisition of expertise work through the organization of work and job design;
- opportunities to pursue knowledge-based courses and qualifications relating to work.

'Expansive learning environments' are defined as ones in which these aspects of participation are extensively and fully realized, whereas 'restrictive learning environments' limit these opportunities. The distinction should, however, be conceived as a continuum.

Management initiatives with respect to workplace learning may also be arranged along a continuum stretching between expansive and restrictive approaches. Hence, 'organizations, departments, or targeted groups within organizations, can be analysed in terms of their expansive and restrictive features' (Fuller and Unwin 2004: 127). Expansive approaches to workforce development facilitate boundary crossing of many different kinds, such as participation in multiple communities of practice, cross-company experiences, off-the-job education and training, multi-skilling and multi-tasking. Thus, 'an expansive view of expertise entails the creation of environments which allow for substantial horizontal, cross-boundary activity, dialogue and problem-solving' (Fuller and Unwin 2004: 136).

The development of the characteristic features of learning environments is closely linked to the nature of productive systems. For example, where strategies to enhance shareholder value are achieved by means of job intensification, asset stripping and financial engineering, investment in long-term, sustainable learning environments for employees is likely to be a low priority (Froud *et al.* 2000a and 2000b). This, in turn, is likely to shape the distribution of skills and knowledge within the organization as well as perceptions of the relevance and value of training. In these circumstances, expansive learning environments may well be regarded by key decision-makers as unnecessary and irrelevant to business activity. Training and other forms of workplace learning by employees may be confined to activities that are perceived to yield immediate financial returns to owners and shareholders.

The organization of productive systems may also shape learning environments by influencing the distribution of knowledge and skills. Variations in the locus of control between and within the structures and stages of productive systems, discussed above, may be of significance here. Institutions and groups that exercise high levels of overall control within the structures and stages of productive systems may seek to monopolize or contain key skills and forms of knowledge. As a result, critical organizational competences may be highly concentrated within particular parts of the productive system. Skills and knowledge that remain widely dispersed may be those which senior decision-makers regard as relatively easily reproduced, substituted or replaced. Furthermore, where control lies in the earlier stages of production – for example, with suppliers of raw materials or manufacturers – access to training and other learning opportunities may be diminished for employees engaged in economic activities that come later. In contrast, a retailer who is the sole purchaser of a product may be able to exercise considerable leverage over patterns of learning of manufacturers and suppliers located further back in the productive system. 'Pre-choreographed' aerobics classes, discussed in Chapter 5, and 'retailer label' sandwich manufacture, discussed in Chapter 7, provide good illustrations of patterns of control located respectively earlier and later within productive systems.

Learning environments also reflect the organization of work tasks. High trust and high discretion workplaces are more conducive to the creation and maintenance of expansive learning environments than those characterized by low trust and low discretion. The existence of managerial strategies that cultivate high trust and high discretion relationships in the workplace is, in turn, linked to the extent of the devolution or concentration of power within productive systems. This was most evident in our software engineering company, discussed in Chapter 6, which devolved decision-making to project teams and tied employee rewards to company performance.

It is, of course, quite possible for expansive and restrictive learning environments to exist alongside one another for different groups of employees within an organization, as well as within different struc-tures and stages of productive systems. Indeed, the connections between restrictive and expansive learning environments, at the work-place and within productive systems more generally, is an important line of enquiry that is highlighted by the Working as Learning Framework. It is typical of productive systems, work organizations and managerial strategies that they generate unequal opportunities for employees to participate in expansive learning environments. So, for example, those working on sandwich-making assembly lines occupy restrictive learning environments that allow very limited, if any, access to on-the-job learning, participation in multiple commun-ities of practice, multi-skilling or multi-tasking. Even the effect of job rotation is restrictive, since it entails very similar assembly line tasks. Those involved in designing and developing new types of sandwiches, however, have much greater exposure to new knowledge, skills and practices (see Chapter 7).

In order to understand the relationship between work and learning it is necessary to examine the ways in which specific individuals perceive, experience and make sense of their learning environments. Their interpretations of the learning constraints and opportunities that confront them, both formally and informally, shape their responses and reactions to potential learning contexts. These, in turn, influence the ways in which employees engage with and perform work tasks and roles. Thus, while the concept of learning environments draws attention to the networks of relationships within which learning takes place, the concept of learning territories highlights the personal learning histories of individual employees. It focuses on the trajectories of the learning biographies of individual workers, before and during their current employment, within and outside the workplace. The concept of learning territory, therefore, draws attention to the idiosyncratic, unfolding, personal learning experiences, perceptions and memories of specific individuals. Thus, learning environments are populated by individuals each of whom 'has, and has had, access to a (unique) range of learning opportunities which make up their learning territory' (Fuller and Unwin 2004: 133).

The concept of learning territory, then, acknowledges that each person has a distinctive history of engagement in learning environments. This opens up the possibility of analyzing the differences between the dispositions of individuals in a way which is thoroughly social and relational. The concept of learning territories thus has a strong processual or historical character; it refers to the accumulated experience of learning over a lifetime. The concept also provides a framework for considering the significance of learning environments outside the workplace for approaches to learning within employment contexts. Thus, learning territories refer to the totality of past and present learning experiences of employees, and the ways in which these shape their dispositions to pursue learning in the workplace in the here and now (Hodkinson and Hodkinson 2004b).

The character and scope of individuals' learning territories influences how they perceive and respond to opportunities and barriers institutionalized in the various learning environments they encounter at the workplace. In some cases, the form of the learning environment afforded by the organization of work corresponds to the form of the learning territories characteristic of employees; there is a match between the learning expectations of workers and management. Some organizations will deliberately cultivate such correspondence. However, another possibility is that the form of learning environments available within the organization of work fails to correspond with the pattern of personal learning territories characteristic of most employees; there is a mismatch between learning environments and learning territories. Frustration and anomie may be generated either when workers with expansive learning territories find themselves confronted by restrictive learning environments or when expansive learning environments are presented to employees with restrictive learning territories. In Chapter 4, the senior health visitors who were the driving force behind new ways of working are examples of the former, whereas their reluctant colleagues located elsewhere in the area illustrate the latter. Chapter 5 demonstrates that aerobics instructors with many years experience often resent having to follow a pre-prepared class format, which strips them of their role as 'recipe writers' and treats them as 'recipe followers'. Such mismatches may be the product of chance but they may also be generated by structural processes within productive systems. For example, recruitment procedures may be skewed in ways that deselect individuals at odds with the learning environments embedded in the particular parts of the organization to which they are deployed. Shifts in managerial strategies may reorganize the workplace in ways that make new and unwelcome demands on the learning careers of staff. Thus, changes in ownership patterns and fashions in managerial rhetoric may thrust expansive learning environments upon an unprepared and unaware workforce that is wedded to restrictive learning territories.

Power and indeterminacy

The analysis of power relations plays a central part in our approach. However, it is important to record that we conceive power relationships as a (usually unequal) balance of forces, rather than a one-way pattern of subordination. We take it as axiomatic that power is not a 'thing' that is possessed by one party to a relationship and denied to another. Rather, power is a two-way attribute of social relationships. Power relations comprise a dynamic interchange between stronger and weaker parties, rather than a zero-sum game (Elias 1978; Mennel and Goudsblom 1998). Even when the balance of power is weighted heavily in one direction, subordinates are always able to exercise some influence in return. This conceptualization applies to relationships between individuals, groups, institutions and still larger social networks. Outcomes of power relations are, then, typically unintended, in as much as they are a synthesis of the aims and actions of different participants pursuing more or less contrasting agendas.

Thus, for example, structures of the productive system lower down the axis displayed in Figure 2.1 are not simply subordinate to those higher up the axis. Shareholders may exert pressure on boards and head offices to increase dividends and shareholder value; such market constraints may be transmitted to, and shape the practices of, lower order sections of management and the workforce through a variety of channels (e.g. Froud *et al.* 2000a and 2000b). However, managers and workers directly involved in production may themselves exert countervailing influences on senior management and shareholders. These may take the form of (active or passive) resistance; they may, however, also take the form of more co-operative and collaborative relationships that seek to advance productivity. Strategies of management control can have a major mediating influence on the balance and trajectory of power relations within productive systems; for example, 'high performance management' techniques may, under certain circumstances, facilitate both co-operative workplace relations and enhanced output, although the relationship is far from certain or straightforward (Butler *et al.* 2004; Hughes 2008). However, the dynamic nature of power relations means that outcomes of managerial initiatives may well be unexpected or unintended by all parties.

Discussion of power balances leads into examination of the nature of social interdependencies more generally. Productive systems, managerial strategies and learning environments may all be conceived as networks of human and non-human elements that shape the constraints and opportunities of their members. Power is an emergent effect of the organization of such networks; it is an aspect of network relationships. The organization of networks is an active process that ensures that their disparate elements, which frequently have many reasons to fly apart, are mobilized and held together around specific identities, discourses and objectives. The concept of 'translation', developed in Actor–Network Theory (ANT), refers to the process whereby the makers and builders of networks draw others into a web of commitments and influences, thereby increasing their reach through time and space (cf. Callon 1986; Law 1986). By maintaining network organization, power effects are achieved and networks gain in purchase and membership. Learning processes are central to these endeavours, since one of the main ways in which translation is achieved is through the dissemination of knowledge, skills and practices. However, networks may also unravel, be invaded or colonized. Networks are not, therefore, self-perpetuating systems but have continuously to be reproduced through enacted performances of key members. They are always unfinished projects. Nor are networks necessarily internally coherent; there may be tensions, misalliances and even contradictions between the parts.

The translation processes of network formation incorporate not only people but also non-human elements, such as animals, tools, books, communications devices, transport systems, and so on. Indeed, human relationships of all kinds are always mediated by non-human objects. However, artefacts gain meaning and value from their context within networks, such as productive systems, managerial strategies and learning environments. Thus, for example, in the bathroom of a private citizen, weighing scales and hair brushes are items for personal grooming; but in a health visitor's professional kit bag, or a hair stylist's salon, they become tools of production within particular structures and stages of productive systems. It also follows that qualities of individual people are also network effects. Thus, the agency of individuals is actually a function of their network participation.

Enough has been said in this and previous sections to indicate that our conceptual framework acknowledges a high degree of complexity and indeterminacy in the contexts of workplace learning. More recently, Complexity Theory has drawn attention to the non-linear, indeterminate character of many systems in the natural and social worlds that are subject to unpredictable, unquantifiable and extraneous influences (Anderson 1999; Byrne 1999). Such systems continually import new and variable influences and energies, at the same time as exporting other energies to the wider environment. Their dynamic relationships mean that they are constantly evolving and shifting. Small additional inputs can have large subsequent effects when applied at critical points in the overall system. Detailed deterministic outcomes of complex systems of this kind can rarely, if ever, be calculated or predicted with certainty or precision. However, their general trajectories or phases of development can be mapped over time. Studies of a wide range of complex systems have identified a number of typical trajectories, such as equilibrium, oscillation, cycle and chaos. Dialectical struggle generated by sources of internal contradictions, and ultimate revolutionary transformation, is yet another possibility within non-linear systems.

Researchers working in the tradition of Cultural Historical Activity Theory (CHAT) position these contradictions as the fundamental explanation for why and how learning occurs in the workplace. In this respect, our position differs from that of activity theorists as we see contradiction as but one of a number of potential triggers for learning. As the following chapters in this book will show, learning occurs as part of everyday work activity involving the need to solve practical problems and find innovative solutions related to the production of goods and services. Some of this activity may arise from contradictions inherent in the work/labour process, but much will not. In the course of any day, the dynamic of the social practice of work itself stimulates learning. In order to excavate and understand this process, therefore, we are not privileging one activity/form of learning over another. Our conceptual framework has arisen from, as opposed to having preceded, the analysis of our wide-ranging empirical data. In addition, we contend that our approach is more effective in specifying the connections between the multiple networks of social relations within which learning occurs.

Diverse and complex systems such as these have emergent properties. There is constant interaction between changing variables. The system is not a transcendent entity that dictates the behaviour of its parts; it is an immanent entity that generates and transforms itself. The multiplicity of interconnected processes entailed in productive systems inevitably generate unintended consequences and risks, which impact directly on workplace relationships and the learning opportunities they entail. This creates systemic uncertainties within particular workplaces, creating challenges for workers and managers at all levels. Learning processes are one of the ways in which those challenges may be confronted, interpreted and surmounted.

Our application and use of the Working as Learning Framework, thus, avoids over-determinism. It does not subscribe to a view of productive systems as over-arching reified 'structures' that determine every aspect of the behaviour of individuals ('agents') at work. Some researchers have suggested that individual employees can exert agency by the way they engage with and create opportunities for learning (see Billett 2002; Hodkinson and Hodkinson 2004a and 2004b). Each individual's behaviour reflects their life history and their different dispositions to learning developed over time. While these insights are important, we would argue that to fully understand the ways in which learning occurs in the workplace, we need to integrate individual and structural perspectives. Crucially, as this chapter has shown, giving particular prominence to individuals as agents who are in control of their learning is highly problematic as this separates them from the way work is organized and the wider institutional and political features which also constitute the workplace as a learning environment.

Conclusion

In this chapter, we have outlined the Working as Learning Framework (WALF). Our interpretation of the contexts of workplace learning avoids, on the one hand, over-determinism and reification, and, on the other, voluntaristic individualism. It is built around the following concepts: productive systems; work organization; learning environments and learning territories.

Our key contention is that in order to understand learning at work, researchers need to examine how work is organized and how, in turn, this is influenced by wider forces. The concept of 'productive systems' provides the broadest perspective since it offers a holistic, relational model of economic activity that identifies interlocking levels of institutional practices and controls. This takes us beyond a workplace or even an organizational level focus – typical of concepts such as 'high performance work systems' (Appelbaum *et al.* 2000). Instead, the notion of productive systems encompasses a multitude of stakeholders: customers, suppliers, sector bodies, as well as the employing organization. It refers to the totality of social relationships entailed in processes of commodity production, which have horizontal and vertical dimensions.

Although we have not placed theories of 'high performance work systems' at the centre of our conceptualization, we readily concede that the concepts of discretion and trust do have relevance to the understanding of learning in the workplace. We therefore use the concept of discretion to capture the degree of autonomy and responsibility exercised by workers in the labour processes in which they are engaged. The nature of the productive system may, of course, influence the latitude they are given as well as the level and nature of trust in the employment relationship. Managerial strategies may respond to the uncertainties inherent in complex productive systems either by enhancing or by minimizing discretion and trust in the workplace.

Our prime focus is on learning environments; that is, the networks of relationships within which learning takes place. Our analysis here draws on the concepts of expansive and restrictive learning environments (Fuller and Unwin 2003). It offers a generative, transformative, processual conception of learning. Moreover, the notions of expansive and restrictive extend to include the learning territories of individuals. Thus, the expansive–restrictive model links the organization of work (in its broadest sense) and learning processes of individuals. Integrating the expansive–restrictive model with the productive systems perspective creates a conceptual framework for understanding learning at work. This framework addresses systemic issues at the same time as illuminating the experiences of specific individuals.

Moreover, it takes a dynamic view of these linkages. There is an emphasis on process, change and development – the trajectories of learning.

Our aim in incorporating the concepts of productive system, workplace organization and managerial strategies in our conceptualization of workplace learning is systematically to *specify* the contexts of learning. The Working as Learning Framework not only highlights the links between the broadest system relationships that shape employment relations but also, as the chapters that follow reveal, enables us to explore how these broader processes are played out in specific workplaces and in the narratives of people's working lives.

Chapter 3

Processing calls

Introduction

This chapter analyses the ways in which the introduction of a contact centre (County Talk) into the productive system of a local authority (Shire County) shaped the form and location of knowledge and skills, patterns of organizational control and the character of service encounters. It focuses on the learning environments of contact centre operators, but locates these within the web of competing pressures generated by their position within the overall productive system. The chapter has three aims. First, to demonstrate the utility of the Working as Learning Framework (WALF) outlined in Chapter 2 and, in particular, its usefulness in revealing how changes in the productive system impact on the level of discretion exercised by workers and the learning environments they consequently face. Second, to illustrate how strategically located groups of workers may experience diverse and cross-cutting demands in their work tasks and learning environments as a result of their position within the productive system. Third, to explore how systemic breakdowns and malfunctions within productive systems may impact on learning environments within organizations.

Contact centres have attracted much attention from social scientists since the 1990s, prompting one observer to comment that they have become 'one of the most researched' workplaces (Glucksmann 2004: 795). Despite only having taken root in the UK in 1989, contact centres have grown exponentially (Marshall and Richardson 1996; CM Insight 2004). By the end of the first decade of the twenty-first century, they accounted for some 650,000 agent positions and directly employed over a million people. Much academic work has focused on what happens inside contact centres as self-standing workplaces.

This includes studies of: the varied nature of the contact centre labour process (Batt 1999 and 2000; Frenkel *et al.* 1998 and 1999; Knights and McCabe 1998; Taylor and Bain 1999); the mechanisms of workplace surveillance and controls over employee subjectivity (Fernie and Metcalf 1998; Knights and McCabe 2003); worker resistance either collectively or individually (Bain and Taylor 2000); and the selection, recruitment and training of front-line staff (Belt 2000; Callaghan and Thompson 2002; Wallace and Eagleson 2000). However, the focus of this chapter is on how contact centres fit into the overall structure of organizations and, in particular, how they mesh with other stages in the horizontal axis of the productive system, which link consumers with services and products. It explores the role of contact centres as intermediaries, within the backward and forward linkages that comprise the horizontal axes of productive systems, and the implications for workplace learning by their staff (Glucksmann 2004; Taylor and Bain 2006 and 2007). In our case study, this analytical perspective highlights the processes through which aspects of the knowledge and skills of a diverse range of specialist 'back office' functions were transformed and transferred to generalist contact centre operators, who thereby became a unitary 'front office' for a variety of service providers and users. This entailed a reconfiguration of the overall productive system, moving the locus of control over key aspects of service encounters (e.g. social services, education, housing and transport) within the organization. The effect was to move control away from semi-autonomous departments towards a central unit – the contact centre – and, thereby, shift the balance of power within Shire County towards strategic corporate groups. Thus, the reorganization of the horizontal axis of the productive system of the local authority was a function of shifts in power balances within the vertical axis.

Our analysis also demonstrates that productive systems and learning environments may embody a range of different and contrasting learning affordances, opportunities and demands (Billett 2004). A high proportion of the work of contact centre operators in County Talk involved routine, predictable and closed encounters with callers. Indeed, the introduction of the contact centre was intended to replace haphazard and idiosyncratic responses to public enquiries with a more reliable and consistent public face of the organization. Although requiring continuous updating and amending of their wide-ranging knowledge base, the learning processes associated with this aspect of operators' work were characterized by detailed didactic instruction rather than critical reflexivity. However, the positioning of County Talk within the productive system of Shire County generated additional tasks that were woven in and through more mundane functions. These called for skills in customer care, customer advocacy and colleague relationships that required contact centre operators to develop a more open-ended and autonomous approach to their jobs. They facilitated the growth of skills in emotional labour, problem solving and inter-personal negotiation. These, in turn, were also reflected in the learning environments of operators, albeit often in unofficial and non-formal ways. This chapter, then, not only indicates how learning environments are shaped by productive systems, it also explores the ways in which competing demands within productive systems may generate a range of different types of skill requirements, and learning affordances, within any particular occupational role. What appear to be relatively routine jobs may incorporate elements that call for the exercise of discretion and facilitate a degree of expansive learning (Fuller *et al.* 2007). This chapter also shows that job tasks and learning at work can be shaped not only by the smooth operation of productive systems but also by the malfunctions and systemic blockages within the overall network of relationships.

The chapter proceeds as follows. The next section describes how we collected our research evidence. This is followed by an overview of shifts in the structure of the productive system of Shire County, initiated by the introduction of County Talk. The chapter goes on to identify the groups within the local authority that drove forward the reconfiguration of the productive system, and the implications for power balances within the organization. Attention then turns to an examination of the pressures within the reconfigured productive system that generated the rationalization of work tasks in the contact centre and the routinization of the learning environments of operatives. The chapter then discusses countervailing influences within the productive system that enhanced the discretion and initiative exercised by contact centre operatives, with corresponding implications for their learning affordances. The chapter ends with a brief conclusion.

Collecting the evidence

We investigated the introduction and functioning of County Talk at a variety of points in the productive system. These included the political leadership of the council, management at different levels (corporate, service department and contact centre) and contact centre operators. The early interviews gave us insights into the establishment and evolution of the contact centre. However, all of them were arranged by a corporate management contact. This meant we were steered to the service departments whose first point of access calls had been successfully transferred into County Talk rather than those where resistance was strongest. Nevertheless, we heard about the concerns of staff within 'difficult' departments, albeit indirectly. Among them was the worry that their skills were being diluted by the call guides and on-screen menus used by contact centre operators in handling calls from the public that previously would have been dealt with directly by departments. In addition, there was concern that, ultimately, service department jobs would be lost as departments no longer acted as the first point of contact for service enquiries.

Our early interviews also revealed that while some data gathering potential was built into the software used to log calls (such as call times, wrap-up times, call volumes and waiting times), far less was known about the nature of each call. Several management interviewees lamented the absence of such data. We therefore made a pitch to our gatekeeper that we would be happy to conduct a short survey of all the calls received by operators over a two-week period, input the data into a statistical package and present the results in a report for circulation. We also suggested that being in the contact centre to administer the questionnaire would give us a chance to observe and become better acquainted with the work activities of call operators and managers.

Setting up and agreeing the questionnaire necessitated an additional series of interviews and the gathering of further data. This meant that during the course of the research we carried out interviews in both Shire County and County Talk. The former included two corporate managers, two service managers and two political leaders; while the latter comprised four managers, six team leaders, two supervisors and four call operators.

The survey required call operators to complete a two-sided sheet of ten 'tick box' style questions after dealing with each call and placing them in collection containers. To maximize response rates, we trailed the survey, its purpose and our credentials in several ways. First, at our request, County Talk management emailed operators outlining the aims of the survey, the research team and announcing that extra 'wrap-up' time – that is, the time between calls – would be built into the system for the duration of the survey. A total of ten seconds was added to the time between calls while the survey was carried out.

The same information was displayed on a series of exhibition boards we set up in the entrance of the contact centre. It was also made clear that, in addition to administering the questionnaire, the research team would be present in the contact centre to observe the day-to-day tasks and practices of contact centre operators. Second, in the week before the survey began, two members of the research team briefed all the operators in small groups of between two and four. This entailed two separate trips to the contact centre, with the briefings taking place at different times of day and night. On each day, a ticker-tape message was sent across call operators' screens announcing our presence and the day's timetable of briefing groups was pinned up on the daily activities notice board for all to see. In these sessions, we presented the overall aims of the project, the mechanics of the survey and discussed each of the ten questions one by one. Operators also introduced themselves to us and we quickly got to know their names. The sessions lasted for approximately 30 minutes and generated a lot of qualitative evidence that was collected in field note diaries kept by the researchers.

For the first three days of the two-week survey, three of the research team were on site to answer any questions that arose as the survey went 'live'; thereafter at least one researcher, or more often two, were on site. Unlike our earlier interviews in County Talk, we were stationed inside the contact centre on a vacant circular pod of six desks, visible to all. The survey was produced in pads of 50 so that operators could complete a form, tear it off and place it in collection boxes that were placed on a small circular bookshelf accessible to all those sitting at that pod. The mechanics of carrying out the survey placed us in a unique position. We were neither participant observers, in the sense that we were not doing the same work as call operators, nor non-participant observers, since we were not overtly observing call operators at work but doing work of our own. Rather we were in the position of 'legitimate peripheral participants' in that we were not centrally involved in the contact centre's activities but were, nonetheless, engaged in legitimate work tasks (see Felstead et al. 2009a for a more detailed discussion). We collected and processed 8,874 survey returns over a two-week period. These were all numbered, dated and time stamped. The data were then input into a statistical software package using a laptop. After being processed, the paper returns were tied up in bundles and boxed up for carriage. As a result, we were on site before the morning shift began and were there well after most had left work. This gave us legitimacy to circulate around the contact centre, picking up survey returns and chatting to operators during slack times and in their tea breaks. We were also able to hear the dialogue they had with callers, the interaction they had with one another while the caller was 'on hold' and the work discussions they had among themselves on the rare occasions they were waiting for calls (for example, on Saturdays when call volumes were much lower). We were even invited to listen in to phone calls using auxiliary headsets, an opportunity which exemplified the recognition that our interest in the challenges faced by call operators was genuine. Towards the end of the two-week period, we carried out a series of debriefing sessions with operators. This was opportunistic, since not all operators were on shift at the time. Nevertheless, we talked to a third of operators; sometimes on a one-to-one basis, sometimes in groups of two. This chapter is therefore based on interview data and observations collected before, during and after the survey was completed as well as some of the quantitative findings that emerged.

Productive system in a local authority

In 2001, Shire County's switchboard was replaced by a contact centre providing a single point of access for users of a growing range of council services, via a widely advertised telephone number charged at local rates. Prior to the advent of County Talk, the job of switchboard operators had been to pass callers on, as quickly as possible, to service departments, where specialist reception staff received enquiries from the public and initiated responses. Each service department, then, maintained its own front office. From the outset of County Talk, however, operators were expected to be proactive agents dealing with the needs of all callers, rather than simply passive conduits of messages to service departments. Multiple front offices, located in service departments, were replaced by a single front office, located in the contact centre. Henceforth, most service requests (78 per cent in our survey) were dealt with by contact centre operators over the telephone without reference to service departments; either by offering information or by undertaking simple service tasks, such as renewing library books via their computer terminals. Some calls (26 per cent in our survey) generated electronic service orders that operators transmitted to specialist departments, at which point back office staff became responsible for service delivery. However, if for any reason an appropriate response was not forthcoming from the service department, the contact centre remained the point of contact for the member of the public and County Talk operators were required to keep callers informed about the progress of enquiries and complaints.

County Talk was popular with the citizens of Shire County. By 2006, 34 full-time equivalent staff were answering on average over 4,000 calls per week, dealing with half of the main types of enquires the council received (an estimated 151 out of 360 'events'). Furthermore, additional functions were continually being imported to the contact centre. In 2004, County Talk became a 24-hour operation with the addition of night time social services and social care calls. In 2006, it also started to take day time social care calls for part of the county, with plans to extend the service at a later date.

Before the advent of County Talk, the productive system of the council comprised a series of semi-autonomous departments, each surrounded by heavily defended boundaries (see Figure 3.1). Moreover, some departments were further subdivided into sections,

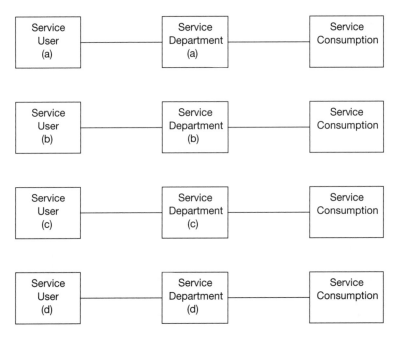

Figure 3.1 Stages of production in Shire County prior to the advent of County Talk

functions and geographical areas – silos within silos. Over the years, these bounded operational units had developed distinctive practices, shaping service provision, recruitment/selection procedures and customer access. Service users were faced with navigating their way through multiple offices, personnel, telephone numbers, access points and eligibility criteria. The horizontal axis of the productive system of the local authority at this juncture, then, can be represented, in simplified form, by Figure 3.1; that is, as a series of semi-autonomous and self-referencing service streams, each maintaining its own access points. Multiple front offices served multiple back offices.

The introduction of County Talk represented far more than just a new access point bolted onto existing service provision. Rather, its mission was to become the single point of access to all the departmental services offered by the council (see Figure 3.2). The contact centre became the front office of Shire County as a whole; the separate and divergent service departments became a suite of back offices. The newly emerging horizontal axis of the productive system is illustrated in Figure 3.2. Contact centre operatives were charged with the delivery of a growing number of the more routine and predictable services offered by the council, relieving service departments of these

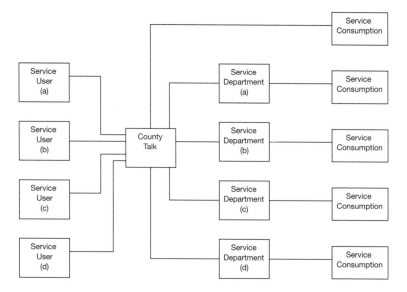

Figure 3.2 Stages of production in Shire County after the advent of County Talk

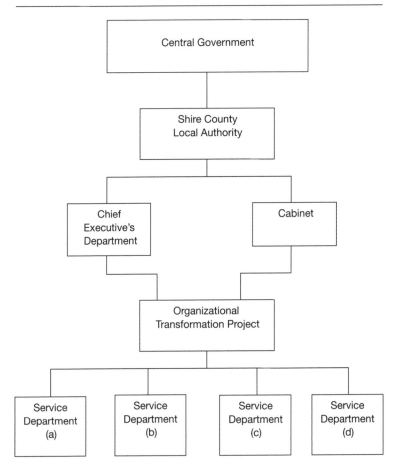

Figure 3.3 Structures of production in Shire County

tasks altogether. Those calls that were too complex or serious for operatives to deal with, they referred to appropriate back offices. In these cases, the function of County Talk within the productive system became that of translating the incoming needs, problems, comments, complaints and desires of potential service users into the language and formats of service departments. The messy, irregular demands of the outside world were processed, ordered and arranged into the smooth and laundered formats required by the internal world of local authority institutions and organizations. This work of 'translation'

(Callon 1991 and 1994) entailed identifying, classifying and prioritizing. The contact centre thus became responsible for organizing consumption, mediating between service providers and users, and mundane service provision. It became the bridge in the horizontal axis of the productive system that connected service consumers and service providers.

Three aspects of the vertical axis of the productive system of Shire County were of particular importance in driving forward the advent of County Talk and the reconfiguration of the productive system (see Figure 3.3). These represented major shifts in power balances within the organization, with direct repercussions for the work of contact centre operators. They included: a bid by strategically-located units within the organization to recapture control from semi-autonomous departments; pressures on council officers and politicians (referred to as elected 'members') from central government to cut operational costs and achieve productivity gains; and pressures on elected members from the ballot box.

These processes all found expression in the Organizational Transformation Project (OTP). From 2000 onwards, a series of major changes in the operations of the local authority were introduced under the auspices of the OTP, run by a tightly-knit team located in the Chief Executive's office. This project was strongly supported by Shire County's Cabinet, which itself had only come into existence in 2001, and the Chief Executive. Departmental heads and other elected members were linked into the programme but it was very much the initiative of strategically-located elites among officers and politicians. The OTP encompassed a variety of ventures, many of which were IT-based. However, the objective was not simply that of replacing old technology with new. The process of 'service redesign', critical to the development of County Talk, was at the heart of the initiative.

'Service redesign' involved OTP officers and departmental staff working together in a three-stage process, initiated by the former and often far from welcomed by the latter. First, localized practices and procedures across geographically-dispersed offices within a service department were standardized. Second, agreed standardized procedures were codified into forms and guides that could be embedded in electronic systems and utilized by non-specialist call operators. Third, standardized and codified tasks were transferred from the service department to the contact centre, particularly those involving initial service requests and simple service operations. In the process, the tacit knowledge of departmental specialists was made explicit, old skills were rendered redundant and access to skills and practices were opened up to County Talk operators. Operators acquired a basic understanding of a wide range of different topics, spanning council business; 'fast knowledge' was extracted from the back office and locked into systems and procedures (Besley and Peters 2005). Budgets, including funding for posts, followed the relocated work tasks. Thus, service redesign represented a powerful means to review, reform and reposition back office practices, as the following comments show:

> The service redesign representatives, which have been in all departments, have literally gone in and done an 'as is' process map [on] the work that's current. And then they've gone away as a group and looked at potential for improvement and come up with redesigned process maps. And in some cases, as a recommendation from that, they've highlighted services that really are perfect for the contact centre.
>
> (Amanda, County Talk, Manager)

> It [service redesign] actually gave us the opportunity to standard-ize all the processes ... The localized interpretation of the rules has gone, because what we're actually working to is a standard.
>
> (Harry, Shire County, Head of Organizational
> Transformation Project)

County Talk was located in the Chief Executive's Department and lines of managerial control went straight to the Chief Executive. The OTP and Cabinet were also, of course, closely tied to the Chief Executive's Department. The restructuring of the productive system of Shire County, focused around service redesign and the contact centre as front office, thus facilitated a new balance of power within the organization as a whole. It shifted the locus of control away from multiple insulated departments towards a central hub within the horizontal axis of the productive system that was directly responsible to centralizing elites within the organization. The reorganization of the horizontal axis of the productive system was a function of shifts in power balances within the vertical axis.

> Because what we're really doing is taking control off a department and putting it back in the organization ... We were very much silo based. We were a huge silo based organization ... And that's been part of the role as well. To basically put this corporate

framework together, to make sure that everything does go in the same direction.

(Harry, Shire County, Head of Transformation Project)

This is [Shire County]. It's not [Shire] education and [Shire] social services . . . People are now looking at it more corporately. We're all part of the same job, this council.

(Arthur, Shire County, Political Leader)

Not surprisingly, some service department personnel argued that the complexity and/or confidentiality of their work prohibited service redesign. The incorporation of night time social services calls into County Talk played a key role in overcoming these objections. The OTP team deliberately launched this innovation early in the life of the contact centre. By standardizing, codifying and transferring some of the most challenging and potentially risky tasks undertaken by staff within the local authority, the OTP faced down the claims of specialist departments to be the sole locus of safety and expertise.

Shifts in power balances within the organization were reinforced by two further processes: increasing central government surveillance and the politics of the ballot box. Shire County, like other authorities, was under pressure from central government to cut costs and enhance productivity. These constraints were channelled through the setting of local authority grants, controls over local taxation, evaluations of council performance, demands for efficiency programmes and targets for greater accessibility to services. Most notably, the Gershon Review, driven by central government, recommended efficiency savings across the public sector, pinpointing economies to be made by streamlining back office functions and conducting service encounters online or through contact centres (HM Treasury 2004; Coats 2004). County Talk was one of the major responses by Shire County to this climate. It was highlighted in performance reports as generating both 'cashable' and 'non-cashable' savings (Carey 2003; Kirkpatrick and Hoque 2006; Kessler *et al.* 2006). Strong as these pressures undoubtedly were, they dovetailed neatly with the objectives of those senior officers and politicians who sought a rationale for engineering a shift in organizational power structures.

I'd get slaughtered if I said: 'I think Gershon's great!'. But it's great for me because it gives me a lever to make the improvements.

(Harry, Shire County, Head of Organizational Transformation Project)

The contact centre also played a part in mediating relationships between elected politicians and the citizens of Shire County. Elected members were acutely conscious that popular perceptions of council services, which had not always been positive in the past, fed through to the ballot box. Thus, both officers and elected members sought organizational transformations that impacted on public attitudes towards the council. Their aim was not only to make services better but also to be seen to deliver improvements. County Talk was central to this agenda because of its high visibility. From the outset, the contact centre had been conceived as integral to a rebranding of Shire County's image, demonstrating the corporate presence of the local authority in the community. The widely advertised County Talk telephone number was intended to represent the council to voters as accessible, friendly, reliable and effective. County Talk projected the message that the council cared about the welfare of citizens and service users.

> They [contact centre operatives] are, if you like, the face of [Shire County]; the ambassadors for it.
>> (Ben, Shire County, Corporate Manager)

> So it made the people of [Shire County] feel as if they were getting a decent service at the end of the day.
>> (Arthur, Shire County, Political Leader)

The creation of County Talk, then, was at the heart of power struggles within Shire County. Reconfiguration of the horizontal axis of the productive system shifted into the contact centre operations previously undertaken by service departments. As a result, and to varying degrees, control over a growing number of skills, practices and bodies of knowledge were also transferred from back office specialists to front office generalists. This reflected shifting power balances within the vertical axis.

Rationalization of work tasks

The tasks undertaken by contact centre operators had, therefore, been consciously designed in as rational and simplified a way as possible. They had been broken down into discrete activities, integrated into 'trees' within flow charts, and embedded within electronic web pages and guides that prompted appropriate responses. They were specifically designed to be operated by personnel who did not have in-depth knowledge of the technicalities and culture of service departments. Electronic portals swiftly led to relevant information, service forms and procedural guides which framed encounters with callers. Frequently, electronic systems allowed little discretion to operators (e.g. library book renewals and literature requests). In nine out of ten calls, operators immediately identified the service the caller required without further questioning (94 per cent in our survey).

> It's almost like multiple choice questions ... ways in which to proceed. So, it sort of routes you through ... a bit like telling you how to tie your shoes.
>
> (Ben, Shire County, Corporate Manager)

County Talk, then, constituted a powerful vehicle for the rationalization of the productive system of the local authority. The previously somewhat ramshackle procedures of Shire County, generated by the autonomous functioning of service departments, underwent major reform and standardization. For example, a plethora of different departmental house styles were replaced by a single authority-wide design for letterheads, logos, adverts, welcome messages, websites and electronic formats. For the first time, callers from different locations in Shire County received the same pattern and quality of service, irrespective of their geographical location. Job application processes were centralized and standardized, resulting in dramatic reductions in wastage and increases in transparency.

The implication for contact centre operators was that much of their work was predictable and standardized; for example, one third of all calls (33 per cent in our survey) were for library book renewals, completed on-screen in seconds. Learning opportunities organized by management for operators were focused either on the introduction of new events or on updating procedures with respect to existing ones. Operators were mostly trained in handling new events through short courses within the contact centre. Updates on existing events were achieved by short briefings at the beginning and end of shifts and through emails, revised intranet pages, and notice boards.

There was little doubt that contact centre operators had considerable breadth of knowledge, covering legal provisions, service eligibility, service delivery, citizens' rights and duties, the organization of the council, council departmental functions and council personnel. There were few aspects of council services with which they were not familiar or called upon to render advice. Our survey revealed a huge range of issues raised by callers, some of which were way beyond the official remit of operators. Even managers in the contact centre admitted that they found it very difficult to go onto the phones themselves because they were not up to speed with all the material that operators had absorbed. New recruits to the contact centre struggled with gaining command over the sheer volume of information that 'old timers' had gradually built up over the years. However, notwithstanding their breadth of knowledge, there were reasons to believe that the bulk of the work of contact centre operators did not afford highly expansive learning opportunities. First, the knowledge of call operators was wide but not deep. As a County Talk manager remarked: 'They know a little about a lot.' However, it was noticeable that particular individuals acquired, or brought to the job, considerable understanding of and insight into specific services in which they had a personal interest. In the terminology used later in this book (see sandwich making discussed in Chapter 7), contact centre operators had recourse to many different bodies of knowledge but their acquaintance with each was relatively superficial, or 'thin'. This limited the extent to which they could engage in expansive learning. Second, the updating and amendment of their knowledge predominantly took the form of didactic instructions. There were few opportunities to reflect or engage in critical dialogue, with one another or management, other than to seek clarification. The nature of the information they were expected to impart, and the procedures that they were expected to operate, yielded discrete 'right or wrong' answers.

For their part, contact centre managers and OTP leaders were keen to emphasize the routine, straightforward character of the work done by operatives. This perception suited their aim of ever greater expansion of the remit of County Talk across and into the activities of service departments. They had an interest in presenting the roles of call operatives as unproblematic and their learning processes as routine. Our research confirmed that this was an accurate portrayal of the bulk of their work. Nevertheless, our research also suggested that, in a number of respects, the work of contact centre operatives entailed skills, and generated learning opportunities, that were not wholly recognized in the account of senior managers. These activities were in addition to the more rationalized and standardized tasks described above. They were a function of the location of the contact centre within the work flows of the horizontal axis, and its position within the politics of the vertical axis, of the productive system. These

less routinized roles can be summarized as, on the one hand, a requirement to enhance customer care and, on the other, a need to engage
in negotiations with colleagues in service departments.

Enhancing the experiences of service users

As we have seen, County Talk was intended to enhance the perceived
quality of customer care experienced by citizens who contacted their
local council. From the outset, it had been made explicit that County
Talk was not simply a device for passing callers on to a 'merry-go-
round' of contacts within departments. The intention was that as many
enquiries as possible would be handled within the contact centre.
If the request could not be dealt with there and then, the operator
would seek out further information and get back to the caller as soon
as possible. In these circumstances, operators were expected to stick
with an enquiry until it had been resolved, acting as advocates or
agents of callers and keeping them fully informed.

> The accent here isn't on cracking through the calls as quickly as
> possible. The accent is keeping the caller until you've satisfied
> as much as you can their every need.
> (Ben, Shire County, Corporate Manager)

Contact centre managers argued that, even when it was necessary
to refuse a caller's request, it was always possible to make callers
feel that they had been treated in a friendly, polite and respectful
manner.

> Very often they're not ringing us about positive things, but we're
> trying to make a positive experience out of it.
> (Nick, Shire County, Social Services Manager)

The emphasis on customer care, which was fully understood by
contact centre staff, was reflected in a number of aspects of the work
and learning of operators, both formally and informally. Drawing on
knowledge generated by their distinctive location within the productive system, operators helped callers to navigate through the council
bureaucracy to find the services they required. In general, contact
centre operators had a much better understanding of the complexities
of local authority administration than callers. Some service departments had titles that did not make their functions clear to the general

public; in others, the division of tasks between sections, departments and other councils were difficult to fathom, even downright bizarre.

> Everybody got that frustrated that you'd ring an authority up, a local authority, probably not knowing the basics of the authority ... And you might have to have three or four different phone calls before you eventually got there. So we wanted one port of call where somebody could answer a question. They got a name behind the person who was answering the question and they got an answer or got a response immediately on it.
>
> (Arthur, Shire County, Political Leader)

> Local government has this awful reputation of, you know previously, of being a waste of time if you like. People think they phone through and, you know, it's never my job and you need to speak to so and so ... I feel that it's very important for the people here to try and get through to the customer that we are actually going to deal with it. We are taking you seriously and something will happen.
>
> (Eleanor, County Talk, Team Leader)

Much of the time, pointing callers in the right direction was relatively straightforward. However, where callers required a number of different services, or their needs were unusual and multiple, the task could become more complex and challenging. Our survey suggested that about one in twenty calls (i.e. some 60 or 70 coming into County Talk each day) were of this kind and we observed that these encounters could go on for extended periods. In these circumstances, operators found themselves devising tailor-made solutions to one-off problems, linking together different service options and information sources. They were engaged in a type of negotiated knot working (Engeström et al. 1999; Engeström 2004). Furthermore, the success of County Talk generated an increasing volume of non-routine calls. It was widely perceived by the public as an all purpose help or information line. As a result, operators found themselves fielding a proportion of calls that went well beyond the scaffolding provided by call guides and, indeed, in some cases well beyond the remit of the council.

Urgent calls, demanding swift interventions and requiring detailed data collection before service departments could respond, also generated proactive and non-routine responses from operators. For example, around one in twelve calls (8 per cent in our survey) concerned highway hazards, with callers frequently calling for prompt action. Often members of the public did not know or understand the information that operators required. Operators not only had to collect the relevant facts but also to summarize them precisely in designated formats on electronic service forms that were passed back to service departments. In addition, operators themselves were required to decide upon the urgency with which service departments should respond to these calls. These service encounters, then, drew on operators' skills in questioning callers, capturing and summarizing detailed data, presenting information in a form sufficiently comprehensive and relevant for service departments, and prioritizing competing service requests.

However, even routine calls provided scope to enhance customer care. In all their interactions with the public, operators were required to use an expressive and friendly tone of voice and to keep talk jargon-free and informal. With the exception of a standard initial greeting, operators were not confined to the use of specific formulations, scripts, words or terms within even the most routine of service encounters. They were allowed, indeed encouraged, to develop their own distinctive way of conducting service encounters, reflecting their individual personalities. Furthermore, operators would on occasion make time for small talk and chatting with callers. Authenticity and freshness of response were, thus, conveyed through the personal demeanour developed by each operator.

> We're not chickens. I think that's good. We're allowed to do it our own way.
>
> (Dennis, County Talk, Operator)

Operators frequently helped callers through the completion of online forms, volunteering interpretations of obscure questions, suggesting suitable answers and, in some instances, skipping questions that might seem irrelevant or intrusive. Largely unknown to callers, operators used 'work arounds' to navigate service forms in ways that minimized the frustration or disappointment of members of the public (Hennessy and Sawchuk 2003). Operators also frequently offered callers the benefit of their considerable knowledge about the practical realities of service eligibility criteria. They might, in effect, coach callers in how to pitch their service requests to gatekeepers in ways that maximized chances of success. In addition, operators sought to probe the underlying needs of callers in order to draw their attention to services and benefits of which they were previously unaware. Even simple requests for verbal or written information could turn into an investigative process; for example, a request for job details might prompt the operative to undertake a search for other similar vacancies. All these activities drew on the proactive questioning skills of operatives and their capacity to make empathetic relationships with callers. They also entailed a degree of judgement by operatives about how and when to deploy their expertise.

A further aspect of customer care, calling for tact and diplomacy on the part of operators, concerned the handling of complaints about previously requested services (6 per cent of calls in our survey). Where calls resulted in service forms being passed to back office departments, the contact centre remained the point of reference and remedy if something went wrong. The role of the contact centre, thus, included making apologies to irate citizens who felt that they had not been dealt with appropriately by service departments, even though the fault was rarely the direct responsibility of operators themselves. Operators also conveyed complaints back to departments and could choose to initiate procedures that required relevant service department staff to make immediate and direct contact with dissatisfied consumers. Furthermore, where errors had occurred (e.g. the non-appearance of requested job details), contact centre operators were empowered to negotiate with the service department on behalf of the caller to obtain recompense (e.g. an extended deadline).

Enhanced customer care was facilitated by the structural position of the contact centre within the horizontal axis of the productive system of the local authority. From their hub within the productive system, County Talk operators were able to offer multiple services in response to a single call, direct callers to a variety of appropriate service points within diverse back offices, and turn around bad experiences of service users by taking complaints back to those who they knew to be responsible. Although their knowledge of the productive system was shallow, it did have breadth; operators had a form of 'work process knowledge' (Boreham *et al.* 2002). Customer care roles, then, were central to the mission of contact centre operators, highlighting skills in emotional labour, customer advocacy, customer support and insider advice. These skills and practices were discussed within formal training situations arranged by management but they remained embedded within the personal character of each operator. Natural, fresh engagement of operators with callers was valued over the delivery of standardized responses or measured wrap-up times. Consequently, each operator approached their work in a different way, reflected in their tone, mannerisms, chattiness and provision of specialist expertise. Here, then, there was scope for operators to develop a more expansive approach to learning, drawing on their previous learning environments and personal learning territories. Moreover, it was one in which they developed their individual style of engagement with their work.

Negotiating with service providers

Contact centre operators were also called upon to exercise skills in handling negotiations with personnel in service departments. We have already touched upon the requirement for operators to take complaints by callers, about service quality and personnel, back to departments. However, this task was part of a bigger emerging process of surveillance exercised by the front office over back offices, which met with resistance from service departments. Moreover, resistance was facilitated by lacunae and malfunctions within the communication channels of the productive system. As a result, in responding to a small minority of calls, contact centre operators attempted to develop strategies that compensated for these difficulties.

In becoming the main point of initial public access to the local authority, County Talk exerted ever greater influence over the delivery and conduct of those service operations that remained in the hands of back office departments. Because of their position within the horizontal axis of the productive system, operators were responsible for receiving, organizing, prioritizing and distributing the flow and format of service requests, thereby systematizing procedures, co-ordinating practices and monitoring complaints. As a result, the activities of back office departments became subjected to new forms of monitoring, exercised from the contact centre. Contact centre operators and managers knew, and could compare, the operational criteria employed by different departments and units within departments. They were aware if service providers departed from agreed schedules and protocols. They received, and monitored, the complaints of members of the public when services were not delivered in a satisfactory manner. They conveyed these grievances back to departments, eliciting the information necessary to placate disgruntled callers, connecting them to relevant managers within service departments and initiating immediate responses from service providers. Thus, County Talk became a conduit of feedback on performance that impinged directly on back office operations. Moreover, the position of County Talk within the vertical axis of the productive system meant that all this data was available to the Chief Executive, Cabinet and OTP.

These emerging relationships of surveillance exercised from within County Talk triggered resentment and resistance from some service department personnel. We were repeatedly told that, initially at least, service department staff had perceived County Talk to be a direct threat to their jobs. Much of the most vehement opposition had attenuated by the time of our research but there remained a residual distrust. This was fed by the continuous importing of new services into the contact centre, resulting in the elimination of functions and posts elsewhere. Council leaders were committed to avoiding redundancies but the disappearance of posts, redesign of jobs and breakdown of bureaucratic silos generated insecurity. Furthermore, the role of County Talk as a channel of complaints to, and monitor of correct procedures by, service departments also fuelled resistance to close co-operation and even a desire to undermine County Talk's effectiveness.

Those within service departments who sought to resist perceived encroachments of the contact centre found that they could exploit weaknesses in channels of communication within the horizontal axis of the productive system, between the front office and multiple back offices. Connections between County Talk and service departments were subject to blockages and breakdowns that offered opportunities for opponents of change. Thus, for example, contact centre operators dealing with complaints or complex cases often needed to speak to back office staff in person. In these circumstances, operators we interviewed said that some back office staff were difficult to contact, obstreperous, or passed them around from one unhelpful person to another. Operators found themselves negotiating with back office personnel in order to get the help they needed, regarding a positive response as a personal favour rather than as a professional obligation. In response, operators tended to steer enquiries towards contacts in service departments who they knew to be co-operative. This distorted the flow of work from front to back offices, with some service department personnel taking on work loads and responsibilities well in excess of their pay grade.

Difficulties in maintaining effective channels of communication throughout the productive system in part reflected the way in which knowledge and skills had been repositioned during the process of service redesign. In some instances, substantial portions of service delivery had been wholly located in the contact centre. In others, operators had only a limited knowledge of, or skills in relation to, service requests. Where the reach of County Talk into back offices was not extensive, operators were more likely to refer callers to service departments at an early stage in the encounter. In these circumstances, operators were vulnerable to negative feedback from departmental staff. Operators could be accused of being ill-informed, referring inappropriate cases, or presenting information in a way that was badly translated into the language and networks of service departments. This could be represented as evidence of failure on the part of individual operators but also of the contact centre in general.

Another tactic adopted by some service department personnel who sought to exert passive resistance to the advancement of the contact centre was that of failing to update County Talk on changes in back office personnel and functions. Service departments were not required to download the names and telephone numbers of new staff or to keep County Talk operators informed of organizational changes. A web link existed for this purpose but sometimes service departments (in the words of a contact centre operator) 'forget' to use it. As a result, when operators had to contact back offices directly, they might get in touch with the wrong person or section, appearing incompetent or inept. Some operators sought to remedy this situation by, on their own initiative, periodically calling up departments in order to find out about the latest moves of people and posts. The result of these competing pressures was that, on occasion, operators were unable to gain the information they needed to advise potential service users or could not put members of the public through to departments. Sometimes operators themselves gave advice that they believed should have come from service departments because they were reluctant to send the caller away empty handed.

The involvement of operators in negotiations with service department personnel thus spanned both formal and informal channels of communication within the horizontal axis of the productive system. Although only a small part of their work loads, these cases figured prominently in operators' perceived sense of the demands and skills of their job. They called for initiative and diplomacy in balancing the needs of service users and service providers. Thus, only a small proportion of calls were said by operators to make 'medium' (5 per cent in our survey) or 'high' (1 per cent in our survey) emotional demands upon them. However, the greatest proportion of these more stressful calls entailed a fault in, or failure to deliver, a previous service request (19 per cent in our survey), a comment or complaint about a service or person (25 per cent), or referral to a department or specialist officer for immediate follow up and action (16 per cent). Furthermore, it was clear that certain service departments figured more prominently in the pattern of stressful encounters than others.

In summary, then, interaction with back office service departments was integral to the work of County Talk. Occasionally, these contacts entailed the management of complaints about service delivery; more generally, the position of the contact centre as a hub within the horizontal axis of the productive system placed operators, and their managers, in a position to monitor and evaluate the work of service departments. The form and contents of struggles over the execution of both these roles were shaped by the organization of the productive system. Contact centre operators sought to maintain their customer service roles by finding ways to counter the obstructions they encountered from some back office personnel.

Conclusion

The introduction of a contact centre, County Talk, heralded the reconfiguration of the horizontal and vertical axes of the productive system of Shire County. A series of pressures propelled this change, including internal struggles for control over of the organization, external demands for cost cutting and efficiency gains, and the desire of officers and politicians to be seen to be improving services. The advent of County Talk resulted in the transformation and transfer of knowledge, skills and practices that had been the preserve of specialist service departments to generalist contact centre operators. The position of the contact centre within the horizontal axis of the productive system enabled operators to offer enhanced customer care to callers, facilitating their role as 'advocates' or 'agents' for members of the public. At the same time, countervailing pressures were exerted by those in service departments whose interests led them to resist change. They were able to exploit structural lacunae and blockages in the horizontal axis of the productive system in an attempt to reassert their autonomy from centralized regulation and surveillance exercised through the vertical axis of the productive system. The cross-cutting demands generated by the position of contact centre operators within the horizontal axis of the productive system generated a range of different kinds of work roles and learning environments. Most of their tasks were routinized and their corresponding learning environments afforded few opportunities to be critical, reflexive or innovative. The 'job redesign' process had introduced rationalization, standardization and codification. However, the injunction to enhance customer care, and the need to negotiate sometimes stressful relationships with back office personnel, meant that at least some of their encounters in the workplace prioritized proactive interventions and work process knowledge.

This case study develops and elaborates the Working as Learning Framework (WALF) in several ways. First, it provides further evidence in support of the argument that the overall configuration of the productive system has a major influence on patterns of discretion in the workplace and the learning environments of employees. The transformation of the organization of the productive system of Shire County prompted by the advent of County Talk offers a particularly sharp illustration of this thesis. The distribution, form and contents of job-related knowledge across the organization were profoundly influenced by the introduction of centralized and rationalized procedures, made possible by the contact centre. A shift in the organization of the horizontal axis of the productive system repositioned control over and revised the definition of knowledge, skills and practices (cf. Figures 3.1 and 3.2).

Second, this case study illustrates the contradictory and competing demands that productive systems sometimes place on strategic groups of workers. The emergence of the contact centre was associated with the standardization, rationalization and simplification of many, if not most, tasks undertaken by staff whose job it was to receive initial calls from members of the public enquiring about council services. A great deal of the work of contact centre operators was routine and predictable. As such, their learning environments involved a good deal of didactic transmission of procedures and information. These characteristics of their workplace learning reflected their position within the reconfigured productive system. However, the productive system also charged them, formally and informally, with other tasks that called for different skills, such as customer enchantment, emotional labour, customer advocacy and negotiation with back office (i.e. service department) staff. These roles called for more proactive and engaged relationships with callers and colleagues, requiring a degree of initiative in solving problems and emotional labour in managing encounters. Although these skills only came to the fore in handling a small minority of calls, they figured in the call operators' perception of the nature of their jobs and their sense of occupational identity. Moreover, this aspect of their work was associated with broader and more expansive patterns of learning. Thus, the underlying demands of the learning environments of contact centre operators pulled in different directions: on the one hand, mostly towards the compliant absorption and disciplined reproduction of procedures and, on the other, occasionally towards the exercise of initiative and proactive judgement.

Third, this case study illustrates the significance of shifting power balances within productive systems in determining the form and evolution of learning environments of different groups of workers. Changes in the power relations in the vertical axis of the productive system of Shire County had profound implications for the development and operation of the sequences or stages of the horizontal axis of the productive system. The reconfiguration of relationships between service departments, the contact centre and members of the public within the horizontal axis of the productive system (illustrated in Figures 3.1 and 3.2) reflected attempts by strategically placed power holders within the local authority (cf. Figure 3.3) to reassert central control over sections of the organization that had become semi-autonomous. These developments gave rise to the range of different, and sometimes divergent, learning processes experienced by call operatives. They also generated perceptions among some staff in service departments that their skills were being diluted and their learning environments were being made obsolete.

Fourth, this case study demonstrates that learning environments are not simply a product of the smooth operations of productive systems. Rather, dysfunctions and systemic blockages within productive systems also shape patterns of learning at work. In this case, the learning environments of contact centre operators were influenced by opportunities that the productive system gave for service department personnel to offer resistance to the surveillance exercised from County Talk. This underlines the point made in Chapter 2 that the vertical and horizontal axes in the productive system lead to indeterminate outcomes that can vary over time and can be subject to breakdown.

Chapter 4

Promoting health

Introduction

This chapter utilizes the Working as Learning Framework (WALF), outlined in Chapter 2, in examining attempts by a group of health visitors in an English city (Mid City) to enhance their professional practice and, in particular, to forge an expansive learning environment. Our study followed the ups and downs of their project over a two-year period. The chapter analyses the sources of their commitment to innovation, the obstacles they encountered and the forces that ultimately thwarted their objectives. The fate of their project was a function of their distinctive location within the productive system of community healthcare within Mid City. Aspects of the horizontal axis facilitated their efforts; in particular, their professional training, the character of the care they offered to clients, and their multiple relationships with other health and social care occupations. However, pressures in the vertical axis contributed to the breakdown of trust between the health visitors and their managers. As a result, their attempts to generate an expansive learning environment were gradually undermined by a lack of appropriate institutional and organizational supports.

The health visitor teams who are the focus of this chapter consciously referred to themselves as 'the community of practice', echoing the work of Lave and Wenger (1991) and Wenger (1998). However, they did not slavishly follow their model (cf. Hughes *et al.* 2007; Fuller *et al.* 2005). Rather, the phrase captured their intuitive feelings about how they hoped to develop their work; that is, as a self-directed professional community, reshaping practice for themselves. Since it had no formal organizational standing or title, we too refer to the group by the name it gave itself; that is, the 'community of practice'.

The next section of the chapter describes the data collection process. This is followed by an examination of the roles and status of health visitors as an occupational group in the UK. The chapter then analyses the productive system of health visiting through the lens of the Working as Learning Framework outlined in Chapter 2. The chapter goes on to provide a narrative account of the development of new ways of working within the 'community of practice'. The final section interprets the history of the 'community of practice' in terms of the Working as Learning Framework and provides a brief conclusion.

Collecting the evidence

Our research adopted a variety of methodological techniques. Fifteen members of the 'community of practice' were individually interviewed in three sweeps, conducted over a two-year period. Most were interviewed at least twice. In addition, an interim feedback meeting, which evolved into a focus group discussion, was conducted with members of the 'community of practice'. Selected members of the health visitor teams were also given cameras and asked to take photographs to illustrate their working lives. These were used in the second sweep of interviews as catalysts for discussion about how their work was organized and the role of learning in their everyday activities. Members of the 'community of practice' were also asked to keep structured learning logs over an eight-week period (see Fuller and Unwin 2004 for details of this approach). The logs, which recorded the extent to which the health visitors felt they were learning through work and the extent to which they helped colleagues to learn, were also used as a basis for discussion in interviews and in the focus group meeting. Additional interviews were conducted with a senior operational manager, a front-line operational manager and an HR manager within the Primary Care Trust (PCT), and with the directors of two Children's Centres connected to the health visiting teams. In addition, members of the research team spent a total of seven hours, over several days, in non-participant observation in offices occupied by members of the 'community of practice'.

Role of health visitors

Health visiting has its roots in the philanthropic public health move-ment of the nineteenth century, which aimed to reduce mortality and morbidity by teaching hygiene and household management to working class wives and mothers (Symonds 1991; Davies 1988). These origins have influenced subsequent practice even to this day, but the employment status, organizational context and work tasks of health visitors evolved over succeeding decades (see Dingwall 1977 and 1983; Connolly 1980a and 1980b; Cowley 1996; Craig and Smith 1998; Kelsey 2000). Initially, health visitors were employed by voluntary organizations but were gradually absorbed into local authority service provision. From 1962, entry to health visiting required a nursing qualification, usually with some additional experience in a senior clinical nursing post. In 1974, health visitors became part of the UK's National Health Service (NHS). As a result of these developments, health visitors have become more closely associated with nursing and with the primary care provided by General Practitioners (GPs). They are employed on NHS scales and are among the highest paid clinical nursing personnel in the health service.

The NHS organizes and delivers healthcare through a complex network of agencies and institutions. Most primary care is provided through GP surgeries. Access to other aspects of the system, such as specialist hospital treatment, is predominantly via GP referral. GPs have their own contractual arrangements directly with the Department of Health (DH). Primary Care Trusts (PCTs), also funded by the DH, employ a range of ancillary health workers, including health visitors. Thus, the line of managerial responsibility for health visitors is to PCTs, not GPs. Nevertheless, nearly all health visitors are physically located within GP surgeries and their caseloads are usually derived from GP patient lists. In addition, over the past decade, a key government policy has been to bring public services for families and children closer together, partly through the 'Sure Start' initiative. At the centre of this policy has been the establishment of Children's Centres (for children under five years old), which aim to provide a 'one stop shop' of social and healthcare services for local communities. Children's Centres are the responsibility of the Department for Children, Schools and Families (DCSF). Initially located in deprived neighbourhoods, at the time of writing it is intended to roll them out to every community. A few health visitors have been seconded to Children's Centres, including one of our respondents, and this may become the future location of the service as a whole. As will be seen, the GPs, PCTs and Children's Centres of Mid City all shaped the history of the 'community of practice'.

Uncertainty about their role has dogged health visitors throughout their history (Brocklehurst 2004a and 2004b), reflected in the presence of radically different paradigms of practice within the professional literature (Twinn 1993; Craig and Smith 1998). A recent review of the functions of health visitors, commissioned by the DH, acknowledged that:

> For some time now, there have been concerns that health visiting had lost its focus, or rather, there seemed to be too many foci for anyone, even health visitors themselves, to be able to define what health visiting was about and what health visitors should be doing.
>
> (Department of Health 2007: 4)

The potential professional tasks of health visitors are broad, multiple and fluid. Unlike the overwhelming majority of health professionals in the NHS, health visitors focus on the promotion of health rather than the treatment of sickness. They work with the 'well' population, providing advice that aims to promote health, diminish risks and prevent disease. They adopt a holistic model of health that encompasses all aspects of physical, mental, emotional and social well-being. Their remit potentially includes not only the needs of individuals but also those of whole populations, such as neighbourhood communities. Frequently, health visitors provide links between their clients and other health and social care services, drawing on their extensive knowledge of, and networks with, other statutory and voluntary agencies. Health visiting is a universal service and potentially draws its clients from all age groups. However, in the time and place of our research, the focus was heavily on mothers and children under school age (0–5 years old). Health visitors play a major role in child protection (Taylor and Tilley 1989) and, in this capacity, they are not only sources of advice and support – 'mother's helper' (Davies 1988 and 1995) – but also of surveillance and discipline. One of our health visitor respondents remarked: 'we are the health police' (cf. Abbott and Sapsford 1990; Bloor and McIntosh 1990; Dingwall and Robinson 1990; Heritage and Lindstrom 1998; Peckover 2002).

The education and training of health visitors is widely regarded as among the most demanding offered to nursing personnel. It is grounded in theoretical knowledge as well as practical application (Symonds 1991: 257). In addition to placements with practising health visitors, students encounter conceptual and empirical aspects of medical science, public health, social sciences and psychology. Graduates of the course are expected to develop an analytical, reflexive and evidence-based attitude towards their practice. Their professional training was regarded by many of our respondents as the basis of their professional identity.

> We've got this history and this training that encourages us to be independent practitioners.
>
> (Hannah, Health Visitor seconded to
> Children's Centre A)

> I think there's something about that education that enables you to look at things much, much more broadly than perhaps you have in the past.
>
> (Bethany, Head of Children's Centre A and
> former Health Visitor)

Health visitors have a statutory requirement to assess all babies, usually via a home visit, shortly after birth. They are also expected to carry out up to four further home visits during the pre-school years, although in practice the extent of these reflects availability of time and resources, including PCT funding. As a result, a distinctive feature of the work of health visitors is the substantial amount of time they spend on their own travelling and visiting families within the home.

> I know people have remarked that, those who've not worked on the community before, how difficult it can be and how challenging it can be to work out there on your own, in the community, compared with being a team on a ward. . . . Going into people's homes is completely different to them coming into a hospital environment, for example, or a GP surgery. Because you are just a visitor . . . we have no right of entry.
>
> (Hannah, Health Visitor seconded to
> Children's Centre A)

> The knock on the front door . . . that's hard, really hard . . . knocking on someone's door and expecting them to let you in, that's actually a bit odd and scary.
>
> (Winifred, Newly Qualified Health Visitor)

> You are working on your own. You are quite autonomous and, at the end of the day, the bricks fall on your head.
>
> (Natasha, Newly Qualified Health Visitor)

Home visits and community outreach are, then, critical aspects of the work. In these encounters, health visitors monitor the development of the child, identifying any service interventions that might be required, and offer advice constructed around the concept of 'parenting' (Malone 2000). Parents themselves may initiate additional contacts – by phone, home visit or surgery visit – to discuss issues of concern. Mothers and babies also may attend clinics run by health visitors, and/or by health visitors in conjunction with GPs. At birth, babies are issued with a document ('the Red Book') that records the immunization history of the child and its weight at various stages in its early years. As will be seen, the responsibility of health visitors for these two tasks was a matter of contention in the 'community of practice'.

In contrast to these specific responsibilities, there is an enormous range of activities that can potentially be seen as central to health visitors' mission. The DH's (2007) recent report suggested that these include, *inter alia*, preventing social exclusion, reducing health and social inequalities, tackling key public health priorities (such as obesity, smoking, alcohol, drugs and accidents), promoting infant, child and family mental health, and supporting better parenting. Such open-ended and challenging roles leave scope for variation between health visiting teams in their daily practices and the inevitability of selecting between a vast range of possible tasks. It readily leads to a gap opening between, on the one hand, the busy schedule of visits, clinics and development checks that must be done and, on the other, a broad array of public health interventions that could potentially be regarded as professionally legitimate.

Another persistent problem is the relative invisibility of the outcomes of health visitors' professional activities. Many valued outcomes are difficult to quantify because they concern crises that have been avoided; for example, the prevention of post-natal depression, violence in the family or abuse of children. Moreover, the benefits of many interventions are long-term and outcomes are difficult to attribute to one particular action. In these circumstances, there may be an understandable temptation for health visitors to focus on measurable short-term activities, which have public and clinical recognition (such as weighing babies and recording the results in the Red Book), rather than 'big picture' long-term strategic work.

The connection of health visiting with nursing intensifies these dilemmas. Health visitors are often involved in delivering services that competent community nurses could do; for example, immunizations or routine secondary developmental checks. However, community nurses are not trained to undertake the broader public health remit of health visitors. Nevertheless, it is tempting for health visitors to be drawn into these more routine duties. They justify their position within the hierarchy of the GP surgery and help them feel more acceptable to colleagues, who are predominantly engaged in acute medical services. Research suggests that some health visitors respond to (real and perceived) threats to their profession by clinging to 'entrenched routines of dubious value', while newly qualified practitioners express 'frustration at their inability to put recently acquired public health skills into practice' (Brocklehurst 2004b: 216). As a result, the population-based, preventative and public health roles, for which health visitors are trained, are jeopardized. Health visitors become an expensive source of services that could be done by less qualified staff.

Uncertainties surrounding health visitors are further exacerbated by an absence of a strong professional organization representing their views, able to represent them at the highest levels of government and NHS administration. Health visitors do not have an equivalent body to the Royal College of Midwives or Royal College of Nurses. It is striking that of the 34 members of the DoH body recently charged to review the role of the profession, only one was currently working as a health visitor (Department of Health 2007).

In the light of these challenges, it is notable that the number of health visitors in employment has declined. Between 1996 and 2004 they remained static at a time when other nursing and midwifery occupations increased in size. In 2006 numbers fell by approximately 10 per cent and those in training fell by 40 per cent. Workloads in some health visitor teams soared (Campbell 2007). There is a wide-spread perception that PCTs have sought to reduce the number of relatively expensive health visitor posts and to substitute lower paid and less qualified staff for routine roles. There is a fear that, in a future era of commissioned services, purchasers will not wish to invest in the long term and unquantifiable benefits of public health out-reach work.

Productive system of health visiting

In this section we turn to an examination of the roles of health visitors through the Working as Learning Framework, developed in Chapter 2, with particular reference to the situation in Mid City at the time of our research. The productive system of health visitor teams is represented diagrammatically in Figures 4.1 and 4.2. The vertical axis outlines the main sources of regulation and management of the work of health visitors. The horizontal axis represents the sequences or stages of the productive system.

Turning first to the vertical axis of the productive system, the striking feature is the diversity and fragmentation of lines of managerial control and professional responsibility, as represented in Figure 4.1. Three different major lines of control bore down on the 'community of practice': General Practitioners, Primary Care Trusts and Children's Centres. For different reasons in each case, none of these was able to exert total control over health visitor teams but each had a claim on their services. Formal lines of managerial responsibility for health visitor teams were clearly anchored in the PCT. However, health visitor teams were located in GP surgeries, obtained their clients from GP lists and, on a day-to-day basis, were physically distant from PCT managers. Although there were extensive meetings between PCT managers and representatives of health visitor teams, the 'community of practice' felt that the PCT adopted a 'light touch' and that they had considerable scope to interpret their professional roles as they saw fit. For their part, GPs tended to look upon health visitors as part of the surgery workforce and expected

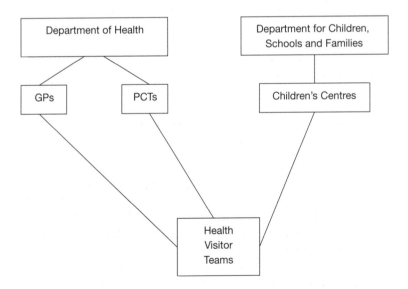

Figure 4.1 Structures of production in health visiting

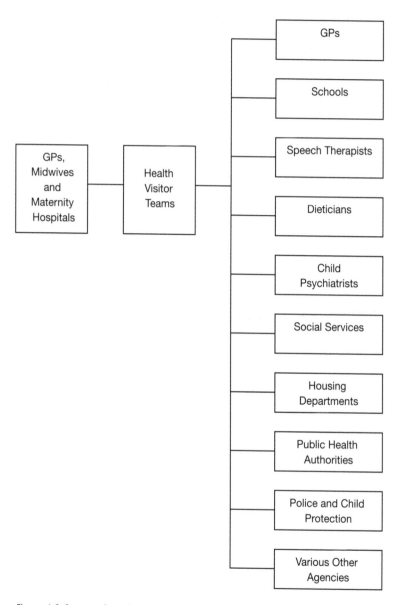

Figure 4.2 Stages of production in health visiting

them to participate in scheduled surgery activities. Children's Centres were engaged in devising a new kind of professional division of labour, which involved pulling together a wide range of health and social care specialists, within a single building. Health visitors had much to offer this project and, at the time of the research, were beginning to be drawn into its orbit.

The productive system of Mid City health visitor teams, then, incorporated a variety of different vertical lines of control. In addition, however, each was internally divided, adding to complexity and uncertainty. GP surgeries adopted contrasting working practices and had different expectations of health visitor teams. Different PCT managers issued contradictory messages concerning the scope and autonomy of health visitor teams in developing new ways of working. Each Children's Centre was relatively autonomous and open to negotiation in developing working relationships with health visitors. Moreover, at the time of the research, PCTs and GPs were both ultimately funded and organized by the DH, albeit through different and separate channels, whereas Children's Centres were ultimately responsible to the DCSF. The vertical axis of the productive system of health visiting is, thus, fractured and fragmented. As we shall see, in the case of the 'community of practice', it was these divisions which, ultimately, eroded the attempt to create an expansive learning environment.

Turning to the stages of the productive system, the left hand side of the horizontal axis in Figure 4.2 identifies the processes by which health visitor teams receive a supply of clients; that is, families with newborn babies. These channels are clear and unambiguous. New births are referred to health visitors from maternity hospitals and midwives. They are also formally notified of transfers into GP patient lists from overseas or elsewhere in the UK. These sources are precise, prescribed and formally organized. Once in the system, babies are tracked via the Red Book, GP medical records and health visitors' own filing systems. There is little ambiguity or scope for discretion, therefore, in the flow of clients to health visitor teams. However, following the horizontal axis of the productive system through to the right hand side of Figure 4.2, we can see that the outputs of health visiting teams are more varied and less predictable. Health visitors themselves render services to their clients by providing advice, support, information and, in some situations, prescription medicines. In addition, health visitors often act as a conduit to other healthcare professionals or occupations offering relevant services. They may arrange a GP appointment for mother and baby, to follow up concerns that have arisen during a visit or developmental check. They may refer families to speech therapists, dieticians, child psychiatrists or any of a host of other specialist services. They may liaise with social services, social workers or the police about children at risk. They may put families in touch with agencies that can advise or assist with housing, legal or welfare issues. When children reach school age, they typically pass out of the care of health visitors and into the remit of other professions and agencies, such as school nurses. In responding to the needs of families, then, health visitor teams are drawn into multiple relationships with other professionals, within and outside the NHS. They identify the distinctive problems and needs of each family and respond by delivering and/or organizing a unique set of responses. Health visitors, therefore, are often engaged in 'knot-working' across boundaries of professional expertise, knowledge and responsibility (Engeström et al. 1999; Engeström 2000). Their work calls for skills in communication, interpretation and negotiation between agencies.

> You are kind of like the middle of a wheel sometimes . . . You do know what's out there and you're able to let other people access it.
>
> (Natasha, Newly Qualified Health Visitor)

> Everybody wants a slice of health visiting because they know they can do something for them. So you end up having all the slices together.
>
> (Olivia, Senior Health Visitor)

> It's working across boundaries.
>
> (Morag, Senior Health Visitor)

In order to construct a package of appropriate measures, and enter into dialogue with relevant agencies, health visitors must first make an individual assessment of each family's distinctive needs. This calls for skills in creating and maintaining on-going rapport and non-judgemental empathy with different types of families in diverse circumstances, cultures and contexts. It requires reflexivity and emotional labour in engaging with clients who may feel vulnerable, stressed or, indeed, hostile. The type of relationships health visitors make with their clients, and the tasks in which they are engaged, then, call for sympathetic understanding, dispassionate analysis and creative invention. The horizontal axis of health visitors' productive system, thus, potentially promotes forms of work organization and liaison with colleagues that facilitate expansive learning.

The history of the 'community of practice'

This section traces the history of attempts by the 'community of practice', within the context of the productive system outlined above, to develop an innovative set of working practices and learning contexts. Inevitably, a brief narrative has to simplify what were often complex events. Nevertheless, the history of the 'community of practice' can be described as an initial period of gradual growth, followed by a series of challenges and obstacles.

The 'community of practice' operated from premises within four GP surgeries. Each surgery contained health visiting teams comprising two or three health visitors and one or two Nursery Nurses and/or Associate Nurses. One team also included a part-time administrative assistant. The four GP surgeries were located close to one another in a neighbourhood containing large numbers of disadvantaged families resident in social housing. As far as PCT management was concerned, these four teams were part of a larger organizational unit that comprised health visitors located in seven GP surgeries, stretched out along one of the main arterial routes into the town that ran from leafy suburbs to inner city.

Although each of the four teams had experimented individually with innovative ways of working, at the beginning of our two-year study they began to collaborate in developing a distinctive professional vision and, at the same time, began to refer to themselves as the 'community of practice'. They sought to transform their current way of working, which they believed limited their professional identity, joint learning and shared expertise. This shift was led by three long-established health visitors, who brought to bear wide-ranging personal experience (i.e. their expansive learning territories; see Chapter 2) in reinterpreting the professional mission of the 'community of practice'. Although they had a clear idea of how they hoped the 'community of practice' would evolve, they were keen for new ways of working to be the product of consensus and commitment generated from below, rather than instructions imposed from above. Consequently, the 'community of practice' emerged slowly, gradually building momentum, self-confidence and self-awareness.

During the first year of its existence, the members of the 'community of practice' developed a collaborative division of labour across the four surgeries. This enabled them to adopt more flexible working patterns, eliminate duplication of personnel in the delivery of services, and pool the specialist expertise of individual members. In order to facilitate the new division of labour, the 'community of practice' adopted a collective case load, serving clients across all four surgeries. By working more efficiently, time and resources became available for imaginative new services. These included user-friendly and heavily-subscribed 'mother and baby' and 'mother and toddler' groups, in which nursery nurses played a major role in devising innovative pedagogies. The 'community of practice' increasingly concentrated on families within the deprived neighbourhoods that constituted their immediate locality, rather than the more scattered geographical boundaries of the patient lists of the four GP practices in which they were located.

The new way of working offered enhanced roles for all members of the 'community of practice'. The more junior acquired more responsible and challenging roles; senior 'old timers' were freed up to deal with the most difficult cases. All shared their experience and expertise, learning together from one another. Enthusiasm and commitment soared, reflected in plans for further initiatives formulated by both senior and junior members. A collective identity began to emerge, transcending divisions between the four surgeries and fostering an egalitarian and informal ethos. This was reflected in the comments of a junior and a senior member of the 'community of practice' about working with each other:

> There's definitely no, sort of: 'who's better than who?'. We're all, sort of, on the same level. Obviously, I look up to [names two senior Health Visitors in the 'community of practice'].
>
> (Donna, Associate Nurse attached to Health Visitor Team)

> I don't think that she's inferior to me and I'm superior to her. I know I've got much, much more experience. And I'm trained and qualified. But that doesn't mean I see myself in a position of being the boss ... Everybody has the thing what they bring to offer to the team. .... It's a skill mix, not a rank mix.
>
> (Morag, Senior Health Visitor)

The ways of working adopted by the 'community of practice' are discussed within the professional health visiting literature (see, *inter alia*, Gastrill 1994; Jackson 1994; Ferguson 1996; Craig and Smith 1998; Houston and Clifton 2001; Hyett 2003; Rowe *et al.* 2003). In this sense, they were not new. Nevertheless, these developments were novel within the context of Mid City. Our interviews suggest that, initially, they were welcomed by PCT management. In part, this was because they promised cost savings. More generally, managers expressed satisfaction that a group of health workers was taking the initiative in shaping their own professional destinies, rather than waiting passively for instructions.

> We're not in a world where you can sit back and wait to be told. The leadership comes from yourselves. It comes from a professional group . . . Don't sit back waiting for somebody to tell you what to do.
>
> (Kimberly, HR Manager, Mid City Primary Care Trust)

Compared to many other public sector workers, health visitors in Mid City had historically enjoyed relatively high levels of discretion in setting and prioritizing job tasks.

> We don't see [PCT managers] very much. I think we are quite capable of self managing thank you very much. And they are there if we need them, if we get stuck . . . but I think that's our training. That searching out needs and saying: 'what can we do about it and what can we put in?' . . . We perhaps tell managers what we are doing rather than saying: 'is it ok?'
>
> (Olivia, Senior Health Visitor)

There was little formal performance assessment and annual appraisals addressed professional development rather than ranking of achievements. These arrangements afforded the 'community of practice' space in which to develop their ideas. However, as the scope and ambition of the 'community of practice' became more apparent, opposition began to be expressed in other quarters; in particular, by some GPs and by health visitors located in surgeries outside the 'community of practice'.

The opposition of GPs was not uniform across the four surgeries. Some were comfortable with health visitors developing their role as they saw fit; some were even sympathetic. However, there were several issues that concerned GPs, and in one of the four practices these became the subject of bitter conflict. Although GPs did not have formal managerial authority, some felt that they had customary rights over health visitors' activities. For example, some GPs expected health visitors to take a major role in running immunization clinics. Tough government targets with respect to immunizations were reflected in the incomes of GP practices.

> GPs became proprietary about anything that happened within their four walls. Because 'this is our business model', basically. So we found ourselves, sort of, grafted on to a business model, when we were a public health model really.
>
> (Morag, Senior Health Visitor)

The way of working introduced by the 'community of practice' was perceived by some GPs as breaking the link with 'their' health visitors. For example, some GPs expected health visitors to participate, in a subservient role, in the conduct of clinics where babies received medical checks (as distinct from the developmental checks undertaken by health visitor teams themselves). Some health visitors in Mid City had been willing to collaborate in this 'theatre of deference'. However, the new way of working developed by the 'community of practice' cut across all these expectations. The members of the 'community of practice' had a keen sense of their professional identity and professional autonomy. They were conscious that they were not employed by GPs (cf. Speed and Luker 2006) and they did not see themselves as supports or handmaidens of GPs. They envisaged themselves as engaged in a different professional task, albeit one which was closely related to the work of doctors.

> There was a very paternalistic relationship between the GPs and everybody else. . . . the GPs expected that we would do as they said . . . their expectation was that we would be doing things that would support them getting payments. . . . it means that the mothers don't see you as an independent practitioner. The mothers see you as being a sort of associate of the GP.
>
> (Nancy, Senior Health Visitor)

> For me, the status that you get being based in a doctor's surgery isn't that positive. It's more about being seen as the doctor's assistant – and I have no problem with giving that role up

[laughs], that status. Yeah, I would rather be seen as one of a group of professionals working together in an equal way. . . . There's always been this bit of friction between how health visitors see themselves and how GPs see them.

(Hannah, Health Visitor seconded to Children's Centre A)

The 'community of practice' collectively decided to stop carrying out many of the routine tasks expected by GPs, freeing up time to develop other types of services. In particular, the issue of weighing babies became a focus of debate. Many GPs (and mothers) expected health visitors to maintain a regime of regular weighing checks, at home and in clinics, with results recorded in the Red Book. Health visitors in the 'community of practice' were adamant that weighing babies was not part of their professional role and a gross misuse of highly trained and highly paid staff. They further argued that extensive weighing was of no value in most cases and that those babies in need of special care should be identified in other ways. They also felt it set up misleading and potentially damaging expectations among mothers. In this, the 'community of practice' was supported by the PCT.

If you've got a perfectly healthy baby, the baby is feeding well, the baby is thriving, there's absolutely no reason developmentally why you should be concerned about the baby, then I do not see the need to be constantly weighing babies.

(Melissa, Front Line Operational Manager, Mid City Primary Care Trust)

Weighing scales became devices that symbolized to members of the 'community of practice' an old way of working that they wished to shake off. They were perceived as artefacts which locked them into occupational roles that restricted their autonomy and demeaned their professional authority. Since members of the 'community of practice' could not find ways of turning the use of baby weighing scales to their advantage, they challenged their use directly. This stands in marked contrast to the reassertion of worker control in supermarkets over the 'symbol gun', as discussed in Chapter 8.

GPs in the most traditional of the four surgeries mounted vehement resistance to the new way of working. In a series of increasingly acrimonious exchanges and meetings, they tried to make the PCT replace the health visitors based in their surgery. However, the PCT held firm.

> Deep, deep hostility towards us from everybody, from everybody ... the first few months were absolutely terrible ... absolutely hell ... often to be found sobbing, together and separately. And if it hadn't been for the support of my colleagues.
>
> (Morag, Senior Health Visitor)

Eventually, over many months, most of the recalcitrant GPs were won over. They even began to recognize that the new way of working brought them benefits; for example, in the management of post-natal depression (cf. Carmel 2006). The 'community of practice' had persisted, not least as a result of support from PCT managers.

Although resistance by GPs was gradually diffused, that of fellow health visitors working outside the 'community of practice' was more difficult to overcome. Indeed, it persisted throughout the research period. Locality working meant that the 'community of practice' focused attention on mothers and babies within the deprived estates that constituted the immediate neighbourhood of the four surgeries. However, the geographical boundaries of GP patient lists did not match this focus. Not all patients registered with the four GP surgeries were resident in the immediate vicinity; some lived several miles away, on the other side of busy traffic systems. Furthermore, some families in the immediate locality were not registered with any of the four surgeries. Increasingly members of the 'community of practice' encountered clients who were not registered with the four surgeries, while feeling irked at making long journeys to mothers and babies long distances away. Accordingly, members of the 'community of practice' proposed that they would look after all mothers and babies in the immediate locality, irrespective of their GP registration. Similarly, health visitors in other practices would take on board families from the four surgeries living in their vicinity. However, this idea met with hostility from health visitors elsewhere in Mid City. Our interviewees suggested that the root of their objections was a desire to protect their personal case loads.

> There's also a very proprietorial nature, especially running a case load, that these are *my families*. That again is a nursing thing: these are *my* patients, *my* staff, *my* families. And I don't want anybody else looking after my families.
>
> (Nancy, Senior Health Visitor; respondent's emphasis)

Resistance to the new way of working by health visitors outside the 'community of practice' was not confined to this issue, however. They also feared that enhancing the roles of less qualified staff would result in the dilution of their occupational mandate and invasion of their professional territory.

> People feel it's actually deskilling health visitors if you delegate some of your work to other professionals.
>
> (Martha, Senior Health Visitor)

> A lot of my health visiting colleagues aren't happy about handing over their skills. They'd rather not do it at all than see somebody else do it.
>
> (Nancy, Senior Health Visitor)

> A lot of health visitors have this sort of hierarchical manner in their work and treat people such as myself or the Nursery Nurse as sort of like the dog's body.
>
> (Judith, Nursery Nurse)

Health visitors who resisted change were characterized by members of the 'community of practice', and some PCT managers, as sheltering in their 'comfort zone'.

> Some people obviously are not comfortable moving out of their comfort zone . . . And I think there's been a resistance from some staff about letting go.
>
> (Olivia, Senior Health Visitor)

Although some new births were delegated by the 'community of practice' to health visiting teams elsewhere in the city, during the course of our research not one baby was referred to the care of the 'community of practice' from outside the four surgeries. The situation was exacerbated by mixed messages from the PCT, as some managers initially endorsed the proposal only for others to change their minds as opposition grew. Consequently, the professional division of labour implied by locality working was never fully put in place.

Opposition from GPs and fellow health visitors tested the confidence of the 'community of practice'. However, further challenges were about to unfold. A year after its inception, the 'community of practice' discovered that the PCT had, without consultation, negotiated and signed a Service Level Agreement (SLA) with Children's Centre A in Mid City. The SLA committed members of the 'community of practice' to substantial hours of work, each week, within Centre A. Members of the 'community of practice' only discovered its existence when, at a routine meeting, they were asked by managers at Centre A how they proposed to fit in with the existing programme. The members of the 'community of practice' felt angry and betrayed by this development. Ironically, few if any, were opposed to Children's Centres in principle, and several suggested they could be the salvation of health visiting. Several aspects of the work of Children's Centres chimed well with their professional vision. Children's Centres were engaged in the promotion of healthy lives and the education of parents. They adopted locality working, supported imaginative new services (such as baby massage and yoga for mothers), and incorporated a wide range of other professionals with whom health visitors were already involved. Children's Centres, at least potentially, offered the opportunity to assemble large groups of health visitors in daily contact and to escape from the clutches of GP surgeries. Furthermore, Children's Centres were relatively well funded and, at the time of our research, were clearly favoured by government. Some members of the 'community of practice' also recognized that health visitors themselves had a great deal to offer Children's Centres, such as their reach into communities and access to mothers and pre-school children. There were some anxieties expressed by members of the 'community of practice' about whether health visitors based in Centres would be able to maintain their home visiting role and whether educational rather than health agendas would have priority. Nevertheless, their objection was neither to Children's Centres in general, nor to Children's Centre A in particular. Rather, it was to the manner in which the SLA had come into existence and its implications for the new way of working:

> That was not because we didn't want to work with the Unit. It was the way it was imposed. Essentially management agreed things without consultation. There were people within the PCT who think their role is to tell the health visiting service what they should be doing. And that's not always acceptable.
>
> (Nancy, Senior Health Visitor)

> So we were just informed . . . that was the objection. There was no consultation.
>
> (Olivia, Senior Health Visitor)

The 'community of practice' feared that working time diverted to Children's Centre A would jeopardize the continuation of some of the imaginative new services they had developed. The tasks assigned to them in Centre A would, they believed, duplicate, marginalize or undermine programmes they had already put in place. The 'community of practice' also felt that its expertise in identifying needs and appropriate services had been sidelined. It had been treated as a source of service delivery, but not of service design. Finally, it was argued that drafting members of the 'community of practice' into a Children's Centre on a part-time basis cut across organizational frameworks, lines of managerial responsibility and geographical boundaries. This last point was shared by Children's Centre management.

Protracted and sometimes difficult negotiations ensued over several months but, in the end, a compromise emerged. A senior health visitor was appointed by the PCT to be on the relevant liaison committee, thereby bringing the 'community of practice' into the communication and negotiation loop. Eventually, the 'community of practice' supplied some hours of work to Children's Centre A, but on its own terms and not to the full extent of the original SLA. Other health visitors, from outside the 'community of practice', were brought in by the PCT to cover the shortfall. Eventually, several months later, the SLA was replaced (again without consultation) by a 'partnership', which appeared to provide a looser and less prescriptive relationship between the 'community of practice' and Children's Centre A.

While negotiations were continuing with Children's Centre A, the 'community of practice' began to develop an alternative strategy. A programme of Children's Centres was being rolled out in Mid City and leading members of the 'community of practice' made contact with the Director of Children's Centre B, which was soon to be launched within the immediate vicinity of the four surgeries. Centre B had fewer resources than Centre A, but the Director was looking for ideas about how to make it a success. Becoming involved at the early planning stage enabled the 'community of practice' to shape the scope and format of services. Thus, the 'community of practice' proved itself willing to co-operate with Children's Centres, when the terms of the exchange respected their professional expertise and autonomy. It was a measure of their distrust of the PCT, however, that negotiations with Children's Centre B were kept secret for as long as possible. Relationships with the PCT had become strained.

I think we were now seen as the difficult bunch.

(Morag, Senior Health Visitor)

Struggles with GPs, the PCT, Children's Centres and fellow health visitors exacted a toll on the enthusiasm and energies of members of the 'community of practice'.

> You lose the morale. And I've picked up there's some really, really low morale among the health visitors.
>
> (Theresa, Nursery Nurse)

These pressures were magnified, however, by a more insidious drain on their confidence. Turnover of personnel in the health visitor teams in the four surgeries gradually diluted commitment to the new way of working. Several processes were at work here. Some less qualified staff became so enthused that they decided to retrain as health visitors, thereby leaving the 'community of practice'. Some of the most experienced health visitors, who had been among the prime movers of the project, reached retirement age; others went on to senior jobs elsewhere. Some replacements at team leader and other levels proved to be unfamiliar with, or overtly hostile to, the new way of working. They sought to reinstate the GP-focused, individual case load approach. This caused great stress among those who remained; at least one went on long-term sick leave.

Management of change, not to mention the reconfiguring of work, is challenging in any organization. However, for the members of the 'community of practice' there were particular difficulties. To fulfil the ambitions of their vision, they needed the consent and commitment of colleagues, both those elsewhere and those entering the team. Their history meant that they had few allies in management who they could call upon to compel compliance of outsiders and incomers. When new personnel came on the scene, and persisted in operating in ways fundamentally at odds with the new way of working, there was little the dwindling 'community of practice' could do other than seek to persuade (cf. Fuller *et al.* 2005). One of the main aims of the senior members of the 'community of practice' had been to generate and maintain a sense of collective identity and solidarity. They saw this as critical to the project and a source of the dynamism that would keep it intact. Lacking the managerial authority to compel colleagues to adopt new ways of working or sustain group identity, they relied upon consent and persuasion. This created a sense of enthusiastic commitment among those who were willing participants. However, when incomers refused to identify with their project, there was little they could do to prevent the network unravelling (cf. Callon 1986; Law 1986).

Conclusion

This chapter has examined attempts by a group of health workers in the NHS to reconfigure their work organization, expand their learning opportunities and collaborate more effectively. The evidence suggests that the success of such a project rested on several conditions. Long-standing 'old timers' inspired their colleagues to claim and to exercise discretion and autonomy in defining the professional mission of health visitors. Trust in the judgement and integrity of senior colleagues, who were prepared to undertake stressful leadership roles, was crucial in mobilizing the commitment, enthusiasm and initiative of more junior members of the 'community of practice'. Their leadership, which avoided didactic instruction, enabled a collective identity to emerge that permeated the group as a whole. This provided a practical and emotional bond that united the 'community of practice', transcending the geographical, social and personal isolation of members dispersed across four GP surgeries. A safe and secure learning environment facilitated the steady growth of a new way of working, which reflected the professional interests of participants.

The horizontal axis of the productive system of health visiting (cf. Figure 4.2) facilitated these conditions for the emergence of a relatively expansive learning environment. The sequences or stages of the work processes of health visitors encouraged reflexive involvement with a wide range of clients and colleagues. Collaborative team working – in order to share skills among colleagues, widen services for families and enhance co-operation with other agencies – was a logical response to the demands of the horizontal axis.

However, tensions and cross-cutting currents in the vertical axis of the productive system did not sustain these conditions (cf. Figure 4.1). The autonomy and discretion of the 'community of practice' was challenged from above by a variety of different sources of control. These divisions had both positive and negative implications for the 'community of practice'. Initially, fractures in the vertical axis of the productive system afforded sufficient discretion for an enterprising group of health visitor teams to seize the initiative and, without prompting from management, develop their own innovative way of working. Moreover, gaps between different sources of control generated a degree of autonomy. Opponents in one situation might be recruited as allies in another. However, in the longer term, the pressures of the vertical axis constrained their autonomy and eroded their confidence. The 'community of practice' was caught between the conflicting demands of different sources of authority, management and obligation. Members tried to renegotiate relationships with each of these, while at the same time asserting professional independence from all. This proved to be a difficult and debilitating task. Furthermore, fractured lines of control within the vertical axis of the productive system positioned the 'community of practice' across an array of different geographical areas, organizational units and professional missions. The PCT, Children's Centres and GPs all had their own notions of how health visitors should operate. Each had their own organizational frameworks, none of which recognized the 'community of practice'. Each had their own geographical area of operations, none of which corresponded to that claimed by the 'community of practice'. As a result of its ill-defined position in the vertical axis of the productive system, then, the 'community of practice' faced uncertainty, contradiction and unanticipated pressures. Members of the 'community of practice' could not discover an organizational context they could trust to respect the kind of professional discretion and self-directed expansive learning to which they aspired. Moreover, fellow health visitors outside the four surgeries were unwilling to collaborate with their project. As a result, the 'community of practice' remained localized and vulnerable to disruption, unable to roll out its vision across Mid City and beyond.

The combined effects of the vertical and horizontal axes of the productive system of health visitors in Mid City, then, were paradoxical. Some aspects promoted, or at least facilitated, the emergence of new ways of working; others undermined it. The potential for expansive learning, inherent in the diverse and multiples tasks that comprised the horizontal axis of the productive system, was smothered by forces generated within the fractures and fissures of the vertical axis of the productive system. The result was a pattern of indeterminacy; raised hopes followed by dashed confidence. Ultimately, the 'community of practice' could not overcome the systemic problems that beset the profession of health visiting. From this perspective, it is perhaps not surprising that health visitors outside the 'community of practice' sought to maintain traditional ways of working that appeared to offer a secure (albeit subservient) niche within the work organization of GP surgeries. Their approach to surviving the vicissitudes of the vertical axis of the productive system left them relatively isolated from one another, defending their personal case loads from perceived encroachments. However, it provided them with a source of occupational identification and a predictable professional role.

This chapter has added to the Working as Learning Framework (WALF) in several ways. First, it has highlighted the indeterminacy that often characterizes complex social networks, such as productive systems. Indeterminacy can take several different forms and is not necessarily synonymous with an absence of pattern to events. In this case, the indeterminacy of the productive system both promoted and impeded the advance of an expansive learning environment. Members of the 'community of practice' were apt to attribute uncertainty and sudden switches of fortune to the actions of individuals. However, seen from the perspective of the Working as Learning Framework, they can be seen as systemic properties.

Second, this case study highlights the importance of personal learning biographies – 'learning territories' referred to in Chapter 2 – of key individuals (Billett 2006; Hodkinson and Hodkinson 2004b). The emergence of the 'community of practice' was the brainchild of a small number of long-established health visitors. Each had distinctive learning biographies, stretching across a range of healthcare contexts and broader life experiences outside work. The significance of the dynamism and confidence of this triumvirate to the emergence of the 'community of practice' should not be underestimated. The productive system of community healthcare in Mid City had generated a number of potential learning possibilities; three 'old timers', who recognized and seized upon these opportunities, propelled the 'community of practice' forward.

Third, this case study demonstrates that, notwithstanding the above, some workers may be content to remain in a restrictive learning environment. This is particularly likely when their primary life interests lie outside the workplace or where they are more concerned to defend their existing terms and conditions in the face of perceived threats to their security. This is echoed in other chapters. For example, our analysis of commercial sandwich making, reported in Chapter 7, suggests that many assembly line operatives were not interested in stretching their learning horizons and that more expansive learning environments were confined to personnel engaged in new product development. Moreover, in this chapter, we have found contrasting attitudes among members of the same occupational group. Health visitors outside the 'community of practice' opted to remain within a medical division of labour that offered them less opportunity for expansive learning but, arguably, greater security of employment. Similarly, in Chapter 5, we will find that inexperienced aerobics instructors were happy to follow class scripts written and developed by others, while those with more experience preferred to devise classes of their own. Thus, while some workers may yearn for an expansive learning environment, others, in the same workplace or occupation, may be content to be restricted.

Fourth, this case study has illustrated how the cross-cutting pressures and tensions generated by the actions of diverse participants in a productive system shape the outcomes of learning initiatives of particular groups. The 'community of practice' seized the initiative and pursued an emerging set of intended learning processes. However, they increasingly encountered obstacles arising from the plans of other important groups within the productive system. Some, such as the GPs, ultimately came round to accepting their agenda. Others, such as health visitors outside the 'community of practice', continued to feel threatened and remained uncooperative. Yet others, such as PCT managers, were initially supportive but subsequently discovered that their own planned actions were impeded by those of the 'community of practice'. The outcome of the bid to develop an expansive learning environment by the 'community of practice' was determined by the interplay of all these forces, generated by and within the productive system. A fast moving and continually changing network of relationships created unintended consequences for all the participants.

Chapter 5

Exercising to music

Introduction

Membership of health and fitness clubs in the UK has grown rapidly since the early 1990s. Recent estimates suggest that there are around 4.5 million members of private health clubs in the UK, or 9 per cent of the adult population, compared to 6 per cent at the start of the new millennium and a fraction of the population in the early 1990s. The estimated value of the sector is £3.7 billion, with nearly six thousand clubs operating in the UK (Mintel 2005; FIA 2008). However, the era of spiralling membership levels and club openings has come to an end in recent years. In response, health and fitness club operators have switched their emphasis to increasing the productivity of existing estates. As a result, they are now devoting more resources to the retention of existing members than simply signing up new recruits (FIA 2003). This has led to a host of management initiatives designed to ensure that newcomers are quickly embedded as club members. These include: group inductions to introduce new members to those who joined at about the same time; appointments to devise exercise programmes; regular reviews of progress in the first few weeks of membership; free personal training sessions; social events; and group exercise classes, often promoted through taster sessions and in-club marketing. These group exercise classes – known as exercise to music (ETM) – are the focus of this chapter.

The chapter begins with a brief account of the types, sources and methods of data collection. This is followed by a section that identifies the two main ways of delivering ETM classes. These are designated as the 'freestyle' and 'pre-choreography' productive systems. In the former, instructors devise all aspects of the classes they deliver, whereas in the latter they deliver pre-packaged classes that minimize their decision-making. This has major implications for the discretion that instructors are able to exercise over music selection, choreography, and the image and style of the classes they lead. The chapter then goes on to examine the consequences this has for instructor learning and so demonstrates the analytical value of the Working as Learning Framework (WALF). Adopting such an approach, the chapter argues that the freestyle productive system produces a more expansive learning environment with boundary crossing possibilities in a wide range of spheres, whereas pre-choreography offers a restrictive learning environment in which boundary crossing is discouraged and instructors are simply expected to follow the set music, moves and style format. In other words, in the former instructors are 'recipe writers' who have to collect, assemble and create a class, while in the latter they are 'recipe followers' who are given all the materials they need and are told what to do. The chapter also examines how the individual biographies – or learning territories – of instructors shape their response to these quite different learning environments. This is used to explain why freestyle is relished by some and feared by others. Similarly, it helps to explain why pre-choreography frustrates the individual flair of the more experienced instructor, while for those who lack experience it provides an easy route to perceived instructor competence, and provides employers with a substitutable and large labour pool of instructors who can 'get by'. The chapter ends with a brief conclusion.

Collecting the evidence

The chapter draws on a range of different types of data collected in a variety of ways. However, the primary method of data collection was through interviews with a number of stakeholders in the sector. Some of these interviews were specifically focused on ETM, but in others ETM was just one of the subjects under discussion. The interview process began by focusing on sector-wide bodies responsible for skills, qualifications and business development. Three interviews were conducted at this level. From these informants, a list of organizational contacts was assembled, leading to interviews with human resource/training managers. These 11 respondents represented five operators – three stand-alone, multi-site, private chains and two contract-managed, local-authority owned, leisure centres. At club/gym level, we conducted nine interviews with general/studio managers based in private chains, publicly owned leisure centres and single site facilities (two of whom were also instructors). These interviews provided insights into the vertical axis of the productive system.

A member of the research team attended and participated in a two-day fitness convention and a two-day training event for ETM instructors. The latter provided a platform to draw up a list of instructors for interview. However, previous studies of service work – such as Leidner's (1993) study of McDonald's counter staff and insurance sales representatives – suggest that interviews alone can only give a partial account of the experience of doing and learning the ropes of service work. Participant observation is required in order to get more of an insight into working lives. Similar calls for observation have also been made by those studying workplace learning (see, especially, Eraut 2000). Both make the case on the grounds that workers' recall is often limited to the extremes and the extraordinary. This means that the routine, everyday and ordinary are taken for granted and therefore tend to be unreported in verbal accounts given to interviewers (see Chapter 4; Felstead *et al.* 2009a). As a result, in eight out of 15 cases, ETM interviews were preceded by the interviewer participating in one of the classes taken by the interviewee. All of these participant observation/interviews took place in the evenings and at weekends when most ETM classes are held.

The instructors interviewed were drawn from a variety of backgrounds: five had obtained their ETM qualifications over a decade ago; six were instructing as part of their current job and were employees; seven were freelancing for a number of operators; and two were employed on a casual basis by a single employer. Nine of the 15 interviewed were practising freestyle instructors but also held pre-choreographed licenses. These interviewees were, therefore, able to make direct comparisons between the discretion levels they enjoyed and the learning environments they faced in these two productive systems. This offered insights into the horizontal sequencing of ETM delivery and its consequences. However, even those who did not have direct experience of the two productive systems themselves were keen to offer observations and comments on these issues. In addition to the collection of interview data, artefacts (such as training videos, choreography notes and training manuals) were gathered in the course of the research. Where appropriate, insights gained from this material are presented below.

Producing exercise to music classes

The principal product of the health and fitness industry is the supervision of exercise in a controlled environment. This is realized in physical form by the provision of exercise equipment in a room that is supervised by staff (e.g. in a fitness studio or gym). In addition, around three-quarters of health and fitness clubs in the UK also provide facilities for group training in a dedicated room set aside and equipped with a music system, loudspeakers and full-length wall mirrors (Mintel 2005; SkillsActive 2004). By contrast to machine-based workouts, time is collectivized through the class timetable and participants openly share a wider field of vision, focus of attention and even physical space (cf. Goffman 1959). As a result, industry research suggests that participation in group exercise makes club attendance more habitual and is more effective at building social bonds between members. It is therefore an important means of stemming the outflow of members from private clubs and keeping membership levels high (FIA 2003).

The activity itself is led by an ETM instructor who is visible in front of the class or on a platform. Instructors wear headset radio microphones for large classes or simply project their voices for smaller classes (or when the headset does not work). Music is used to accompany the different stages of activity, and the instructor's voice is made audible above the sound tracks. Although usually in front of the class, either facing or with their back to them, instructors may also move around giving brief comments to participants. Instructors participate fully in the class and, therefore, direct, describe and teach movement sequences at the same time as moving their own bodies in time with the music (Maguire Smith 2001).

What the instructor says (Delin 2001; Collins 2002), how the accompanying music is used to structure human agency (DeNora 2000; Sayers and Bradbury 2004) and the ways participants react (Sassatelli 1999; Crossley 2004) are issues that have attracted the attention of sociologists in recent years. However, how the instructor's work is organized and the consequences this has for their learning has received very little, if any, coverage.

Viewed through the lens of the Working as Learning Framework (WALF), outlined in Chapter 2, the work of the ETM instructor is subject to vertical regulation by club managers who set class timetables and allocate instructors to particular slots (see Figure 5.1). The timetable is the equivalent of a restaurant menu in that it lists the type of exercise classes in which participants can take part (Korczynski and Ott 2004). This shapes the nature of the class and those who participate. One instructor characterized class participants accordingly. She referred to those who attend on a Monday night as 'our front row people who will like loud and fast music'; those who go to classes billed as high impact aerobics as 'your fitness junkies . . . they're going to want everything hard and fast'; and those who 'like it more gentle will go to legs, bums and tums . . . young mums or ladies that aren't that fit'. Timetables are constructed and reconstructed according to the popularity of classes. This is reinforced in large chains through head office issued ETM budgets which specify the costs of each class per participant. Classes that are not sufficiently popular are removed

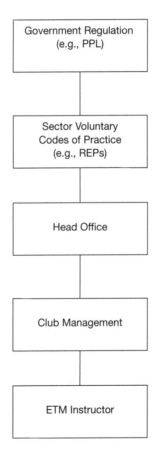

Figure 5.1 Structures of production in exercise to music

from the timetable and replaced with those that have lower costs per participant. However, club management cannot easily see and hear what goes on in classes since rooms are enclosed. They either have to trust instructors to deliver safe and effective group exercise classes of their own making, or require them to follow classes formulated by others (see p. 95).

Despite the health and safety risks involved in the industry, there is no legal requirement for instructors to possess a fitness qualification. In response, the industry set up the Register of Exercise Professionals (REPs) in 2002 in order to ensure that instructors (and personal trainers) had at least a National Vocational Qualification (NVQ) Level Two (or equivalent). These qualifications teach the basics of anatomy and physiology needed to deliver ETM classes and provide clubs with a defence against claims of negligence brought by members injured while exercising under their supervision (Lloyd 2005). In contrast, the use of sound recordings that have been modified for fitness use is tightly regulated. These can only be purchased by those who hold a Phonographic Performance Limited (PPL) licence to play them in public. Such licences are often included in the subscription packages purchasers take out when buying these special compilations. A license is also required if instructors choose to use unmodified shop-bought music for their classes (PPL 2004; Monopolies and Mergers Commission 1988).

While vertical regulation of ETM is relatively weak, there are many horizontal stages involved in the production of a class that can be either strongly or weakly regulated by third parties. This largely depends on the type of class that is delivered and where the locus of control for its production lies. Instructors who put their own classes together – hence the term freestyle – have to source their own music, ensure that it is fit for purpose, choreograph the moves, and create an appropriate atmosphere for the time and type of class they teach (see Figure 5.2). Pre-choreography instructors, on the other hand, have most of these decisions taken for them by concept developers

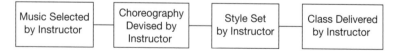

Figure 5.2 Stages of production in exercise to music: freestyle

Figure 5.3 Stages of production in exercise to music: pre-choreography

who are located earlier in the horizontal sequence of production (see Figure 5.3). In the former system, the instructor is the decision-maker at each stage of production process, whereas in the latter this is not the case and hence, for them, the sequence of production is compressed. We examine these two productive systems in more detail in the following discussion.

The concept of exercising to music in the company of others, rather than at home and alone in front of a video, was popularized in the late 1980s with the launch of step aerobics. This involved participants lifting their body weight onto and off a platform in time with music. The basic moves and floor patterns adopted were those originally used in floor aerobics. However, the addition of the step had the added benefit of strengthening the primary movers of the lower body (quadriceps, gluteals and hamstrings), while continuing to improve cardio-vascular abilities. At that time, the moves were uncomplicated and easy-to-follow, and the music was slow by today's standards.

Step classes quickly spread throughout the south east of the US with clubs constructing makeshift platforms out of wooden boxes or benches. However, these handmade devices were cumbersome and often unsteady. More robust and safer alternatives quickly became available. The first mass produced platforms were manufactured and sold by The Step Company in 1990. Their design remains much the same today and can be seen in many gyms, private health clubs and leisure centres around the world. In 1993, Reebok went on to design another version of the platform. Packaged with this platform was the first instructional step video that demonstrated basic moves and pattern variation. A year later the first manual was produced and instructors from the US began to give educational workshops to instructors in other parts of the world. However, step classes were never standardized and instructors were not expected to use particular music or follow a pre-determined routine. In other words, step instructors put together their own freestyle classes by using instructional videos and manuals, attending workshops or conferences and/or consulting other informational sources such as the internet.

An experienced instructor recalled this 'do-it-yourself' world in the following terms:

> No-one told you what to do on it, they gave you a step . . . you were given guidelines on what you couldn't do on it . . . But it was always down to the instructor as to how creative you were.
>
> (Steve, Instructor)

He also recalled how, in the past, he got a disc jockey friend to remix tapes to produce tracks with the appropriate tempo:

> There was no stereos around then [in the early 1990s] that had pitch control. It was how your tape played there and then. You couldn't make it go fast, you couldn't make it any slower, so it wasn't easy. He'd [a disk jockey friend] speed them up on the turntable and remix them for me and if I needed a certain beat he'd mix them for me.
>
> (Steve, Instructor)

However, the growing popularity of ETM classes has led to the emergence of music suppliers who serve the specific needs of the fitness industry, hence minimizing the need for illegal copying and remixing of sound recordings. These suppliers offer an extensive selection of high quality original artist music. Tracks are remixed to follow the 32 count structure required for simple choreography (see p. 98), grouped into particular styles such as step, combat, cycling and aerobics, and labelled according to their speed. In some cases, further support is built into the tracks with faint additional sounds, such as an extra drum roll or cymbal, introduced towards the end of each 32 count block. This helps freestyle instructors switch between different movement sequences but the sounds are so faint that they go unnoticed by class participants. Even so, freestylers still have to choose the music they use and add the moves to the music they select; hence they remain central to the production of the classes they deliver. As another experienced instructor remarked:

> OK, it's [remixing] made it easier with your music-wise, but it's not made it any easier for your own choreography, has it? Not really, because you've still got to work your own routines out.
>
> (Gwen, Instructor)

This is in marked contrast to pre-choreographed classes, which are highly prescriptive and therefore constitute an alternative productive system. The largest producer of these classes has several programmes in its repertoire, all marketed under a particular brand name (referred to here as 'Work Out'). They are offered in thousands of venues across the world, with millions of participants taking part every week. Each programme focuses on different activities in order to deliver contrasting workouts. These foci include stepping, dancing, kicking, punching, weight lifting and cycling.

Work Out tightly regulates the delivery of its classes by licensing clubs, training instructors and monitoring instructor performance on an on-going basis. All Work Out programmes are club-driven and instructors must be affiliated to a club that holds an agreement to operate the appropriate programme. Club licences run for 12 months with monthly payments being made to Work Out for each type of class regardless of the number of classes on the weekly timetable. In addition to the right to host particular classes, operators receive marketing materials to promote interest in the class and enhance awareness of the Work Out brand. These materials include large ceiling banners, wall posters and informational leaflets.

Instructor affiliation to a licensed Work Out venue is required in order to receive training and hence attain qualified status. Instructors can either be employed by the venue operator or be self-employed. Either way, the instructor needs to provide written confirmation to Work Out that they will be given a regular class to teach on completion of their training. In addition, instructors need to have an NVQ Level Two (or equivalent), which provides the underpinning knowledge of anatomy and physiology needed to teach exercise and meets standards set down by the Register of Exercise Professionals (REPs). After meeting these prerequisites, prospective instructors are required to complete two training modules. These are specific to each discipline. The courses last between two and three days and end with an assessment of whether individuals are able to teach on their own or only when accompanied by a qualified instructor. Within 16 weeks of completing the course, all participants are required to submit a video of one of their classes which uses a variety of camera angles to show the assessor the instructor's movements and facial expressions as well as those of some of the class. At this point, full certification is awarded or an instructor is invited to resubmit another video that corrects and addresses any failings identified. The certification received allows holders to teach in any club in the world provided it holds the appropriate licence. Thousands of certificates have been issued in the UK alone.

Every three months, fresh choreography and music is supplied to qualified instructors. These are known as Quarterly Releases and are issued without variation across the world, so that a boxing class following the current release in Swansea is the same as it is in Stirling or Singapore (cf. Gereffi and Korzeniewicz 1994; Kaplinsky and Morris 2001). As part of their continuing professional development, each year qualified instructors are required to attend three out of the four Quarterly Workshops staged to launch each new release. These are usually held over two consecutive weekends at locations across the country. The workshops for each discipline last between one and two hours; sometimes the complete Work Out repertoire runs back-to-back on the same day. At these events, instructors are required to participate in a Master Class for their respective programme in order to have their Work Out Passbooks validated. These may be inspected in cases of complaints received from other Work Out instructors, class participants or operators. At the end of the Quarterly Workshops instructors are issued with a choreography booklet for the new release, a DVD (comprising a Master Class and an Educational Update) and a CD of the tracks for the new class. Payments are made for each part of this package.

These arrangements mean that, to become a Work Out instructor, new entrants have to find an appropriate venue to ply their services, demonstrate a certain level of competence (through possession of a fitness qualification) and successfully complete a training course for each type of class they wish to teach (cf. Kleiner 2000). They can then teach at any venue that holds the appropriate Work Out licence. In turn, the Work Out organization licenses venues, maintains an instructor register, provides regular training updates, and collects fees from clubs and instructors for the services it provides.

Exercising discretion

The two distinctive ways of providing exercise to music classes to participants – freestyle and pre-choreography – cast the instructor in a profoundly different role. In the former, the instructor is trusted to make a number of decisions, including deciding what music to use, choreographing all the moves and presenting an image entirely of their own choosing. In making these decisions instructors have to call upon their knowledge of anatomy, physiology and musical form to deliver safe, effective group workouts for members of the public. However, in the pre-choreographed system trust levels are much lower. Here, the instructor delivers a package in which these decisions have been taken by other actors located earlier on the horizontal axis that constitutes the productive system. These include those who select the sound tracks, choreographers who fit movement to music, and image makers who promote the wearing of particular clothes and the use of certain dialogue to match the mood of the class. This section, then, considers how instructors in the two productive systems enjoy varying levels of trust and differing levels of discretion over these crucial aspects of the classes they deliver.

The sounds, style, tempo and lyrics of each musical track are used to frame the workout and distract participants from feelings of tiredness and/or boredom (cf. Sharma and Black 2001; DeNora and Belcher 2000). As such they act as an 'aesthetic prosthetic' by prompting the instructor's dialogue and the physical movement of the class (Sayers and Bradbury 2004). In most ETM classes, the sound tracks that accompany sessions are played at full volume. An hour's workout typically contains around ten sound tracks, each lasting about five minutes. The components of a class are structured around the musical tempo of each sound track which take participants' heart rate up and down the 'aerobic curve'. This begins with a warm-up segment, an aerobic core, isolation of particular muscle groups, and ends with a post-exercise cool-down and stretch. The tempo of the class rises, peaks and falls accordingly. In musical terms, tempo refers to the beats per minute (BPM) of a track. A pop song runs, on average, at 130 BPM. Warm-ups begin at or below this rate, core segments use quicker tracks running between 140 and 150 BPM, while cool-down/relaxation exercises are carried out using tracks that run at less than 100 BPM.

Both freestyle and pre-choreographed classes follow this structure. However, in a freestyle setting, the instructor has to choose appropriate tracks for each segment of activity, whereas in the pre-choreography situation these decisions are built into the CD that accompanies each new release. Moreover, the CD and accompanying notes do not indicate the BPM of the tracks used as the instructor's delivery of the class does not depend on this information. In analytical terms, this is an illustration of how pre-choreography separates the conception and execution of the labour process, and thereby reallocates knowledge to the few who design the class for worldwide delivery (cf. Braverman 1974). Freestylers, on the other hand, have to search fitness music catalogues and/or count the BPM of shop-bought music in order to design 'aerobically ordered' classes that have tracks running at a variety of speeds.

The music used for exercise to music also has to cope with other aerobic grammar rules. The most important of these is that the music is mixed into 32 count blocks, which makes setting moves to music easier to devise and enhances participants' ability to follow (a method known as 'music phrasing'). It is the repetitive pulsing sound usually made by the bass line, which is the element we normally tap to when listening. Just as words are put together to form sentences, so too are beats of music grouped together to form phrases. These consist of eight beats, with the first count in a phrase normally being the heaviest or loudest. As sentences together form paragraphs, groups of music phrases comprise blocks. Each block consists of four phrases. Often the music changes dramatically at the beginning of a block. Listening for the beginning of a new block is one of the major challenges facing instructors, but this is easier when blocks have different content such as verse, chorus or instrumental. However, these song segments may be more than 32 counts long and/or segments may not last for the entire 32 counts that comprise a block (this is referred to as a musical bridge).

Freestylers have to break down music according to these principles (a technique known as music mapping) before they add exercise sequences. Freestylers explained how breaking down the music can be difficult:

> As for picking up the first beat in a 32 count phrase, that took me a long time to find. I can always pick out the first beat of an 8 count phrase, but music comes in 32 count phrases and to get that first of the 32 that's taken some time to do.
>
> (Eve, Instructor)

> So, you can get lost in your music. I mean it's allowed, you're not going to get hanged if you do because it's your class.
>
> (Emanuelle, Studio Manager and Instructor)

Delivery of pre-choreographed classes, on the other hand, does not require instructors to break down the music themselves. Instead, the music is supplied ready-phrased and each block/segment of the track is formally indicated in the notes that accompany the CD (the first count in each block is often pinpointed by words used in the lyrics).

Music selection gives instructors the ability to stamp their own personality on the classes they teach and hence develop a class following. However, the sound tracks used in pre-choreography classes are someone else's choice that instructors have to use until the next quarterly release, whether they like them or not.

> My personality is so through the music and it's coming from you, isn't it. And you can project you, I think, better than you can project somebody else's programme.
>
> (Mandy, Instructor)

At the heart of exercise to music are a number of basic moves drawn from disciplines such as aerobics, karate, boxing, pilates and yoga. All these movements are performed in time with the beat of the music – sometimes slowly, sometimes quickly. So, for example, a bicep curl may take 16 musical beats to complete (eight up, eight down – known as 'four-four rhythm') or at the same time may be used to complete four repetitions of the same movement (two up, two down – known as 'one-one rhythm' or 'single-single'). Particular movements and repetitions are attached to each block of music. To further complicate the picture variations can be added. These include the direction of travel the body is moving towards while performing the basic move (i.e. forward, back or sideways) and the direction the class is facing (i.e. front, back, left side, right side and the diagonals).

Although 32 count music supply has taken out unhelpful musical bridges and other discontinuities of shop-bought music, the freestyler has to have good choreography skills because the moves still have to be fitted to the music. In practice, this means taking some of the basic moves – such as grapevine, v-step and knee repeater – adding variations and arranging them in different sequences. This often involves experimentation.

> I experiment quite a lot . . . each week my class is never the same . . . Because I've not pre-planned it, I've listened to some music and thought: 'right OK I could do this, I could do that'. So next time, I do things in perhaps a slightly different order.
>
> (Jade, Instructor)

It also involves taking ideas from a wide variety of sources and putting them together to create a routine of one's own.

You take a bit of theirs [well known presenter on DVD] and a bit of my own and a bit of somebody else's. And you put it together, and you've got your own routine – that's how I like it.

(Gwen, Instructor)

Furthermore, freestyling also involves watching how the class participants react to new moves and sequences, and adapting accordingly.

I like it because, you know, it's up to me . . . I can see how long, how long it takes people to learn it, you know, that is what I like.

(Rula, Instructor)

However, none of this is possible when delivering pre-choreography classes since all the moves are pre-determined, codified in booklets issued with each new release, reinforced at Quarterly Workshops and demonstrated in videos of 'model' classes. Even though it is acknowledged that these classes are well put together, instructors can feel alienated from the delivery of a product that is not of their own making:

As instructors I think they're fantastic and I think the style's fantastic, but I don't like teaching pre-choreographed classes . . . It doesn't give you a lot of scope, you feel brain-dead.

(Gwen, Instructor)

In contrast, freestyle classes allow instructors to do their own thing by devising their own moves, pattern variation and sequencing to musical tracks of their choosing.

With pre-choreographed workout, yes, the music leads you . . . this is how they design their workout. With freestyle you don't have to do that. You can start and finish whenever you want to. You're not restricted in any way.

(Emanuelle, Studio Manager and Instructor)

All of the instructors (and managers) interviewed entered the industry because of an interest in health and fitness. Of the 15 instructors interviewed, three were professional dancers, while the remainder described their prior interest in fitness in obsessive terms – describing themselves as 'a fitness junkie', 'catching fitness fever' or 'a gym bunny'. All were avid class participants prior to becoming instructors.

Most instructors, therefore, come to the job with a genuine interest in ETM as a leisure pursuit (Field 2006). However, unlike many other front-line workers in the leisure industry – such as bar tenders, restaurant staff, hotel workers and airline stewardesses – ETM instructors carry out their work while participating fully in the activity (cf. Guerier and Adib 2003; Kakavelakis *et al.* 2008; Kakavelakis 2008). Indeed, one of the main roles of an instructor is to lead class participants, not only in technique but also in terms of effort. This cannot be done from the sidelines (as in personal training), but has to be done from the front of the class through active participation. A key attribute of ETM instructors, whether using freestyle or pre-choreographed methods of class delivery, is to appear excited, happy and energetic in this role.

This applies to both freestyle and pre-choreography classes. However, authenticity is more difficult to maintain in the latter since there are a number of styles or disciplines each with its own brand image and associated emotional atmosphere. The Work Out boxing class, for example, provides a 'fierce, energetic experience'; the dance class 'unlocks everyone's rhythmic and dancing instincts'; and body conditioning 'brings the body into a state of harmony and balance' (quotes taken from the Work Out website). Instructors are expected to alter their personality accordingly:

> It's like putting on a performance . . . You have to put a different head on, you know, like Wurzel Gummidge [a children's TV character who changed heads to switch personalities] . . . One of the things that they [Work Out] drill into you is this playing a role, playing a character . . . It's like Wurzel Gummidge, you put on a different head, depending on what different discipline you're teaching . . . You've got [body conditioning], which is mellow, gentle person, so you've got be calm. [In-door cycling], you've got to keep them going. [Boxing] you're just like an animal, you're punching . . . You've got to be different in each class.
>
> (Jessica, Studio Manager and Instructor)

To help instructors step into character, different styles of dress are suggested. Master Trainers, therefore, encourage instructors to 'dress in programme costume' in order 'to stand in the spirit of the programme' (quote taken from DVD). This message is repeated again and again during initial training and via the Educational Updates included on the DVDs that accompany each Quarterly Release. This drilled behaviour begins at the first weekend of initial training with notable consequences:

> They say to you on the first weekend: 'In two weeks' time, it's a good idea if you come in something that looks the role, because if you look the part then people are going to want to copy you' ... Most people came back in combats and people had wraps and things like that, so yeah. And there were loads of people who ... had gone out and bought like the whole kit, like the proper combat trousers.
>
> (Samuel, Instructor)

Here, 'proper combat trousers' refers to a clothing range that is branded according to each of the Work Out programmes. Each has its own logo, colour scheme and dress code (e.g. bandanas for boxing and in-door cycling, calf length loose trousers for body conditioning and elasticated leggings for floor aerobics). The recommended clothing range follows these branding principles. Master Trainers at the Quarterly Workshops and on video are dressed in branded clothing as are many of their peers who they meet at these Work Out sponsored events. Once again, there is pressure to conform to the format with instructors becoming, in the words of some respondents, 'clones' or 'mini-mes' of the presenters.

Image making also extends to the use of language and particular phrases. While most of the instructional language relating to each exercise is taken from the various disciplines on which pre-choreography is based, the coaching cues are the choreographer's creation. These are codified in the choreography notes which have three columns – one breaks the music down into segments and blocks; another gives the exercise rhythm and repetitions; and the third gives verbal cues to be used at particular points in the class. Often these verbal cues are tied to the music but others are more generic, such as 'real slooooow', 'reach for the sky' and 'graze the knees'. The notes, video and Quarterly Workshops drill trainees into using this language.

Scope for learning

The freestyle and pre-choreography productive systems accord instructors different levels of trust and associated levels of discretion.

This has consequences for the type of learning environments instructors face and the degree to which they are expansive or restrictive (Fuller and Unwin 2003; 2004). Instructors react quite differently to the same circumstances; sometimes contented, sometimes frustrated. We argue that these different reactions are best explained by examining the individual biographies of instructors and, in particular, the level and variety of their experience (i.e. their learning territories).

Much of the knowledge to which instructors would have been introduced in their ETM qualification is not needed to deliver a pre-choreographed class. Sound tracks are selected and appropriately remixed and burnt onto a CD for unvarying worldwide use. The accompanying moves are codified in choreography booklets. Instructors are required to attend Quarterly Workshops and are supplied with DVDs of 'model' classes they are expected to follow. Yet, an instructor's initial training before they take up pre-choreography is about sourcing their own music, breaking it down and adding the appropriate moves. Sector representatives were acutely aware of this conflict:

> The focus of all exercise to music qualifications is all about designing your own choreography and doing it yourself – taking a range of movements and designing something around that. [Work Out] is completely different. It's completely pre-choreographed, there's no option to show your design skills and choreography.
>
> (Stuart, Sector Representative)

The danger, therefore, is that these skills degrade and wither through lack of use. This is a particular risk for recently qualified instructors who tend to take the easy route and copy what they are given, as the following examples illustrate.

> I won't ad lib as much in pre-choreographed classes, no, because it's already pre-done, so I just work to what they've got ... I won't deviate from what they've given me ... I won't no, because the easy option is just to follow it.
>
> (Jade, Instructor)

> It's all done for you and you don't have to think: 'what should I be doing now?'
>
> (Chelsea, Instructor)

> When you do ['pre-choreography'] you're doing somebody else's stuff, you're just a clone of somebody else.
>
> (Jordon, Gym/Studio Manager and Instructor)

> I would say 75 to 95 per cent of people that go into [Work Out] training are probably new instructors who've never made up their own class, so everything they [Work Out] do, they copy exactly . . . They have to learn verbatim.
>
> (Vanessa, Group Trainer, Multiple Site Operator)

In order to hone nascent choreographic skills, experienced instructors suggest that a period of freestyling is essential:

> Freestyle is you. How you are and what you're doing. It teaches you about all these different people. It gives you a chance to build on the information that you've had fed at you during the course to learn about the range of movements that people have. Pre-choreography doesn't allow you to do that. It's somebody else's ideas, somebody else's moves. But I think freestyle is important for you to just consolidate what you've learnt on a course. And I think everyone should freestyle, I would say, for two years before you go and do anything like pre-choreography because I think you lose the ability then to act on your own initiative because everything is programmed into you. You become a bit like a robot.
>
> (Tamara, Instructor)

However, in the pre-choreographed world, instructors tend to rote learn each of the tracks in the session. This means repeatedly listening to the CD, memorizing the choreography notes and watching the DVD time and time again.

> I'll probably watch it [the DVD], you know, like 15 times. And I'll probably watch that little bit . . . over and over again and then . . . watch it and listen to the music over and over again to try and get the beats to the music.
>
> (Mia, Instructor)

Repetitive viewing of the same video not only drills instructors into making the same moves at the same time, but scripts other behaviours such as winks, facial movements and posture. These pre-determined actions form a package (i.e. a script) that is an integral feature of the standard product that pre-choreographed classes are designed to deliver. These learning artefacts are, therefore, intended to have a limited role in enhancing the cognitive development of instructors in terms of their understanding and comprehension of the choreography (for a contrast, see the role of measurement devices in automotive manufacturing as discussed in Chapter 8). Instead, they are aimed at instilling, albeit subtly, behavioural conformity (Hall 1993). Several interviewees were aware of this tendency:

> You've always got to have a guard in Combat – a boxing guard. Now you see this on the videos. Because you're studying that video so it's like you're getting drilled . . . When you're watching the video, it's being drilled into you so you just don't pick up the moves, you pick everything up that they're saying. All the little moves that they do and everything, you pick it up.
>
> (Samuel, Instructor)

The emphasis on conformity begins at an early stage in the process of becoming a licensed Work Out instructor and continues via the Quarterly Workshops and the new releases that accompany these sessions. The initial training is almost exclusively studio-based. Two modules are normally completed over two separate weekends with the training lasting between two to three days in total. Most of the time is spent going over and over the current release with some technique work in between. These whole class sessions are taken by a Master Trainer. However, on other occasions participants are led by a fellow trainee whose performance is then discussed. This feedback tends to identify not only poor technique but areas where trainees vary the script, such as missing out or adding certain moves, not doing the specified number of repetitions or altering the sequence of the movements.

> After the first day you get given a track to learn overnight and then you have to teach it the following day. In the morning, first thing, they video you teaching that track. And when everybody's done their track you then watch the videos. Everybody sits around the video and you have to watch yourself and she tells you what you're doing wrong. You can see and hear everything you did wrong, and you can see and hear everything everybody else did wrong.
>
> (Eve, Instructor)

The fear of 'going wrong' and, therefore, delivering a non-standard product persists long after certification has been secured. The fear comes from the normalizing gaze of participants and other instructors. For example, new release launch dates are often used within clubs to promote interest in the studio timetable. This, in turn, puts pressure on all instructors in that club to launch the new class at about the same time. The content of the classes can also come under scrutiny by expert participants, who go to the same class led by different instructors. These participants are so well schooled that they can tell when an instructor makes a mistake and/or the new release is not being followed. Inventiveness is outlawed in this context.

> You can only stick to their rules, so it's choreographed absolutely. You buy their music, you follow their routine and you have to do their workshops . . . You don't have any inventiveness . . . What you're doing is delivering a format and that is it, full-stop.
> (Bill, Sector Representative)

From a club management point of view, standardization has a number of benefits. First, it routinizes the labour process and therefore minimizes its inherent unpredictability. What happens in a studio is not subject to direct or intrusive surveillance by club management since the studio is not always easily visible to those outside. However, with pre-choreography the content of each class is prescribed and well-known.

> If you buy in [to Work Out] you know what you're getting for your money . . . If you leave it down to the instructor, then really it's a bit of a lottery whether the classes are going to be great or whether they're going to be quite crap.
> (Victoria, Training Manager, Contract Managed Leisure Centres)

The second benefit is that the popularity of a class no longer wholly relies on the instructor and the specificity of their class since the product they deliver is the same. Instructors therefore become more substitutable. In these circumstances, finding suitable cover for instructors who fail to turn up, are off sick or are on holiday is much easier.

> With [Work Out] it's set [the content of the class]. They're going to come in with the same music and they're going to do exactly the

same thing. So, if one of my instructors can't do it and I get in another [Work Out] woman in there, I wouldn't expect to hear: 'Oh, she was rubbish, she didn't do this, she didn't do that'. Because they're expected to do it and follow a procedure . . . So, in that respect, it's better because . . . I can just phone them up and I know they're going to do exactly the same thing in the class.

(Sylvia, Studio Co-ordinator, Private Chain)

As a result, instructor bargaining power is reduced and their labour power is cheapened. It is noticeable, for example, that pre-choreography instructors are rarely able to negotiate their own rates of pay. Instead, pay rates are offered by club/leisure centre management on a take-it-or-leave-it basis. Our interviewees were on average paid £15 an hour for pre-choreography classes. In contrast, some freestylers were able to charge up to £40 an hour for freestyle classes and seek other rewards such as being given popular slots on the timetable and/or back-to-back classes (Felstead et al. 2006: Table A1 and 2007a).

Third, the advent of pre-choreography widens the pool of instructors since instructors are no longer required to devise classes themselves and draw on a range of music, movement and stylistic skills. According to one management respondent: 'in my day, if you couldn't music map, you didn't do exercise to music' (Vanessa, Group Trainer, Multiple Site Operator). However, this is no longer the case as the same respondent went on to explain that now 'you just copy what they tell you to do'. This quick fix solution means that newcomers:

Go out with the absolute basics and don't know really how to start working in the industry, which is why we end up with people maybe doing [pre-choreography] as opposed to going out and doing a freestyle apprenticeship.

(Jordan, Gym/Studio Manager and Instructor)

Standardization has other drawbacks. It is difficult, for example, to differentiate between instructors in terms of their own abilities since these are not really developed in a pre-choreographed setting that provides instructors – as one respondent put it – with 'exercise sessions to go'. The consequence is that instructor skills are not really developed or stretched. A management respondent suggested that class participants, or even club management, cannot always tell how long instructors have been in the industry simply by observing their performance in front of a class:

> You wouldn't be able to look and think that person's been teaching for ten years and that person's been teaching for ten weeks. Because the music will be exactly the same, the instructions should be exactly the same . . . [This] is a benefit to the industry, but also there's no learning curve for the person who's only been teaching for ten weeks.
>
> (Vanessa, Group Trainer, Multiple Site Operator)

Moreover, instructors face disincentives in honing their freestyle skills. Selecting music and breaking it down, putting routines together, going to workshops and fitness conventions to get new ideas, and tailoring the class to a range of abilities takes money, time and effort. This applies to even the most experienced instructor:

> Like tonight, I didn't have to prepare for that class, because I know the choreography, I just went straight in and did it. Whereas if it was freestyle, I would have to do a lot of preparation.
>
> (Jessica, Studio Manager and Instructor)

For the less experienced, these disincentives are even higher since their knowledge, skills and practices are less developed, and the prospect of teaching a freestyle class is nerve-racking and daunting.

> [The NVQ in ETM] is just a qualification that you get to show that you can teach a safe class, but there's just nothing else that goes with it. Then, you're on your own.
>
> (Eve, Instructor)

> I was really nervous for quite some time . . . but I got some hours under my belt because it's one of those things you've got to do. You've got to get out there and do it.
>
> (Tamara, Instructor)

While pre-choreography eases the entry of newcomers into the sector, it often frustrates those more experienced instructors who have to teach these classes because of their popularity with health club members and their widespread use (especially in the large chains, see Felstead *et al.* 2006 and 2007a).

Some of my friends, are pure [Work Out] instructors ... They love it because they can just switch off. They can do it with their eyes shut which is great, but for me that's not what I'm an instructor for ... I need a bit of creativity.

(Steve, Instructor)

These instructors have the confidence and ability to 'just do what the music tells me' as one of our interviewees repeated several times and are therefore frustrated by the restrictions that pre-choreography places on what is taught:

I absolutely love it ['freestyle' teaching], it's stimulating, it gets you to places where you've never been before and you learn it yourself, therefore it's not mechanical. It's not been given to you, you have to go there yourself and explore it ... Whereas in [Work Out], for example, you've got to do exactly the same thing to exactly the same count throughout the whole class, which is a real restriction.

(Emanuelle, Studio Manager and Instructor)

The choreography I teach will probably change every week ... So it makes me remain creative and it makes me want to keep doing it ... the reason that [Work Out] is there is to categorize everything and everyone the same. I want to be completely different to that. I want to be creative and do different things as much as I can, to stay fresh.

(Richard, Manager and Studio Co-ordinator,
Single Site Club)

Conclusion

This chapter has argued that the learning environments faced by exercise to music instructors differ markedly according to the nature of the productive system in which they operate. This, in turn, has implications for the trust they have and the latitude they are given in developing and delivering classes. In the pre-choreographed productive system, classes are manufactured and scripted by specialized workers located far away from the point of delivery. These include professional disc jockeys who remix sound tracks in accordance with the rules of aerobic grammar, choreographers who put bodily movement to music, Master Trainers who serve as role models, and marketers who package different types of class for sale. They are part of a productive system organized and managed by the owners of a concept that is duplicated throughout the world with no variation allowed. As a result, instructors delivering these classes operate in a restrictive learning environment in which they are discouraged from accessing a broad range of learning experiences that might cause them to alter or change components of the classes they deliver. In addition, the 'recipe following' nature of these classes means that they have a shallow engagement with the contents of the product (Braverman 1974).

The freestyle productive system, on the other hand, relies on the abilities of the instructor to select appropriate sound tracks, map this music and choreograph the moves accordingly (cf. Figure 5.2). This involves both crossing multiple boundaries and acquiring rich in-depth knowledge, skills and practices related to music, physical movement and co-ordination. With no set routines to follow, freestyle instructors roam widely and freely across these areas. Their ideas are sourced in a variety of ways such as attendance at fitness conventions, listening to music, browsing the internet, buying DVDs, attending other instructors' classes and practising new routines on their own. This places them in a learning environment that is expansive and casts them in the role of 'recipe writers'.

A management interviewee – Vanessa, a Multiple Site Operator – likened the contrast between freestyle and pre-choreography class delivery to driving a car with manual rather than automatic controls. She suggested that 'if you learn in an automatic, you'll never learn to go manual . . . because you won't know what to do'. On the other hand, she suggested, switching from manual to automatic is relatively easy, but tends to frustrate those who do so since they are unable to use the knowledge, skills and practices learned elsewhere. However, for employers the formulaic solution offered by the pre-choreography productive system cheapens labour, makes high labour turnover easier to cope with and minimizes the problems associated with high rates of absenteeism. It is therefore the productive system that dominates the class timetables of the large chains of health and fitness clubs in the UK and beyond. This produces a restrictive learning environment that makes it difficult for instructors to deploy their knowledge, acquire new skills and improve crucial aspects of their working practices. By contrast, the freestyle productive system offers instructors a more expansive learning environment in each of these respects (cf. Figures 5.2 and 5.3). However, opportunities for instructors to operate in such a world are shrinking fast as employers prefer the pre-packaged solution to the growing business need for more group exercise classes.

As far as the Working as Learning Framework (WALF) is concerned, this chapter illustrates how organizations which are far removed from the final destination of products and services can extend their reach to this – the ultimate – stage of production. This includes determining what consumers are offered, how services are delivered and who faces end-users. Here, the locus of control on the horizontal axis of the productive system is located at an early point in the stages that transform raw materials into finished goods and services for consumption. The chapter, therefore, provides an example of control being exercised forwards, with attendant consequences for trust, discretion and ultimately the learning environments of those on the front line. To underline the point, a later chapter, focusing on the manufacturing of pre-packaged sandwiches (see Chapter 7), provides a contrasting example of control being exercised in the opposite direction (i.e. backwards) with similar consequences. This provides further testament to the flexibility of the Working as Learning Framework as a useful analytical and diagnostic tool.

Chapter 6

Creating knowledge

Introduction

Use of the word 'knowledge' to preface the terms 'economy', 'work' and 'worker' is now commonplace in academic and policy-related literatures. From one perspective, these terms are associated with the creation of information, ideas and concepts that add value. From another, they are linked with those occupations that require high level (graduate) skills and qualifications. The assumptions associated with both perspectives underpin national education and training policies designed to create the more highly skilled and qualified workforce considered necessary to generate a competitive 'knowledge economy'. In this chapter, we explore evidence relating to these themes drawn from workers in two knowledge intensive organizations: a research-led university (The University) and a 'cutting edge' software engineering company (The Company). In the former, we investigated the learning environments of contract researchers; in the latter, we focused on the learning environments of software engineers.

Although there is much written about the development of knowledge work and those who carry it out, less attention has been directed towards defining and operationalizing the terms in empirical research (Brinkley 2006). Nevertheless, two broad, and often overlapping, perspectives emerge from attempts analytically to distinguish knowledge work from other kinds of economic activity. The first perspective – developed originally by the management theorist Peter Drucker (1959 and 1969) – takes its defining characteristic to be the creation of information, ideas and concepts which add value. Drucker identified a rise in the number of workers who were using and creating knowledge in their jobs. 'Knowledge work' was seen to be the mechanism by which knowledge was transformed into something (a commodity) that could be exchanged. Such work and workers were not new, but were growing as a result of the changing industrial, economic and technological landscape (Cortada 1998). Similarly, Robert Reich associated knowledge work with 'symbolic analytic services' comprising 'all the problem-solving, problem-identifying, and strategic-brokering activities' (1991: 177). These he distinguished from two other work functions: 'routine production' typically found in manufacturing settings; and 'routine services' performed, for example, in retail, hairdressing and hospitality roles. Reich argued that the demand for 'symbolic analysts' was rising in countries like the US, which needed to develop knowledge economies to prosper under conditions of technological and economic globalization. According to Reich, symbolic analytic work, requiring the manipulation of symbols, can be found in a range of occupations. These include, *inter alia*: research scientists, software engineers, civil engineers, bio-technology engineers, public relations executives, architects, investment bankers, lawyers, real estate developers and cinematographers.

The second perspective equates ideas of knowledge work with the activities of workers who have high level skills and qualifications (Brown *et al.* 2001; Brown and Hesketh 2004; Warhurst *et al.* 2004). For example, Brown *et al.* (2001) set current economic and industrial change within the context of a 'high skills' debate and the benefits accruing to countries, sectors and organizations competing at the 'higher' rather than the 'lower' end of the market. The former is associated with high skills and high 'value added'; the latter with low skills and low pay. The logic of this argument leads to demands for high levels of education and training for all workers, who are then able, through their skills, to contribute to the creation of value and improvements in productivity. This argument is often coupled with a social democratic view that education and training for all is the route to creating more wealth and, hence, provide governments with the opportunity to redistribute these gains to achieve a more equal society.

It is important to recognize that the concepts of knowledge work and knowledge workers (as well as knowledge economy and society) are hotly contested terms. Given the range of sectors and types of jobs covered in our project, some of which are discussed in this book, we reject the idea that conclusions about knowledge and skills can be easily read off from job titles or levels of qualifications (see, for example, Livingstone and Sawchuk 2003; Fenwick 2004; Fuller *et al.* 2007). In this regard, we are sympathetic to the critique made by

Brint (2001) of the term 'knowledge workers', which he sees as being used increasingly as a badge conferring prestige rather than an accurate description of the work people do. He argues that: 'The term "knowledge worker" is now far along the path of appropriation as a status term by scientific-technical experts and those who idealize them' (Brint 2001: 113).

Nonetheless, from either of the perspectives outlined above, contract researchers employed by The University and software engineers employed by The Company qualify as knowledge workers. Creating and producing new knowledge is an expected outcome of their work, even though the purposes for which it is generated differ. Both require high levels of qualifications. The possession of a good degree (first or high upper second) is a minimum requirement for employment in the software engineering organization, while university researchers are expected to have a post-graduate qualification. Our case study organizations also accord with Alvesson's description of knowledge-intensive companies (or organizations) as ones in which: 'most work is said to be of an intellectual nature and where well-educated, qualified employees form the major part of the workforce' (Alvesson 2001: 863). Despite these similarities, however, the chapter argues that the two organizations operate within different types of productive system and, hence, treat their knowledge workers very differently. This view challenges the current homogenizing narrative about the nature of knowledge work and the extent to which such workers are able to develop their expertise and pursue their career goals. The Working as Learning Framework (WALF), outlined in Chapter 2, enables us to highlight and to analyse these differences.

In the following section we outline how we collected the evidence. Drawing on the Working as Learning Framework, the chapter then examines the contrasting productive systems within which The University and The Company operated. This is followed by two substantive sections, in which we present evidence from the two case studies. The chapter ends by drawing some conclusions about the similarities and differences between the way knowledge workers are conceptualized, employed and supported in the two organizations.

Collecting the evidence

In The University, our research was conducted in two stages. First, a series of face-to-face key informant interviews were undertaken with senior HR, personnel and staff development managers as well as with the Deans in three faculties spanning the 'hard' and 'soft' sciences. The purpose of these interviews was to obtain contextual information and to gain an institutional perspective on how recent contractual changes affecting researchers (stemming from the implementation of European legislation) were being perceived and implemented. The second stage of the research focused on three departments, one from each faculty. The aim here was to investigate how the new contractual arrangements were being received and interpreted in diverse departmental and disciplinary settings, with different traditions of research funding and notions of the career trajectories of contract researchers (CRs). Interviews were conducted with Heads of Department, Principal Investigators and CRs of different levels of seniority and experience, and with a mix of males and females. This allowed us to collect the views of respondents located at different levels within the vertical relations of the productive system of The University. A total of 54 interviews were carried out across the two data gathering stages.

In The Company, interviews were conducted with 26 members of staff, including the chairman, directors, a sample of software engineers, staff from Human Resources (HR) and employees in other departments. In addition, non-participant observation was conducted at the head office, focusing on everyday work activities, and at a 24-hour recruitment event to select new software engineers. The latter enabled us to compare the way in which potential recruits conceptualized their personal identities as software workers with those of existing employees, and to listen to the corporate narrative fed to interview candidates over a 24-hour period. It also revealed the very high value that managers placed on technical competence, to the extent that they were prepared to recruit candidates whose communication skills were poor, and even those who were not particularly innovative or adventurous thinkers. This complemented the insights we were able to gather from the interviews we carried out at a variety of levels within the organization.

Two contrasting productive systems

The University is located in England and is a member of the 'Russell Group'; that is, a cluster of 20 leading universities in the UK which describe themselves as 'research intensive' and as achieving 'research excellence' on the basis of their performance against a variety of indicators such as research income, numbers of doctoral and overseas students, and the proportion of top-rated departments. The University is governed by a Royal Charter, administered by the Privy Council, to whom it must apply to amend its statutes or constitution. All universities with Royal Charters are technically, therefore, independent institutions. Since the 1980s, however, and in particular since the 2004 Higher Education Act, universities in the UK have become subject to more intense monitoring and accountability regimes exercised by central government and its agencies. As Salter and Tapper (2002) argue, the state has increasingly adopted the role of the guardian of the consumers of higher education (HE) and has imposed a raft of targets and league tables to expose the performance of universities to the general public.

As Figure 6.1 indicates, the productive system for research within which The University operated has complex vertical structures of production, revolving around a number of lines of control and accountability. Although ultimately responsible to the Privy Council, a variety of state bodies hold the purse strings. The Department for Innovation, Universities and Skills (DIUS) funds the Higher Education Funding Council for England (HEFCE) and seven Research Councils that cover the full spectrum of academic disciplines. HEFCE provides core funding to the universities for research and teaching. The research councils provide discretionary grants for specific research projects, programmes and centres, which are allocated in competition between universities. Thus, much of the funding for research, and hence for the employment of contract researchers, comes from state directed or controlled bodies. These exercise controls over policy-making, and regulate a range of activities, within higher education research. In addition to government policies, ministerial directives and national legislation, universities must also comply with legislation and directives emanating from the European Union (EU). As we shall see later, it was European legislation implemented in 2006 that required institutions to introduce new contractual arrangements for staff on fixed-term contracts, such as researchers. The EU is also a potential source of discretionary grant funding for research. However, as Figure 6.1 also indicates, not all university income is derived from government sources. It is an important aspect of the status of a research intensive university, such as the one in our case study, that it attracts non-governmental funding to increase its income in order to try bolster its independence. These sources include industry, charities, endowments and investments. In addition, Figure 6.1 shows that not only are the external controls over The University complex but also internal managerial structures are extended and hierarchical.

Contract researchers are at the bottom of tiers of institutional relationships that include established academic staff (such as Principal Investigators), Department managers and heads, Faculty managers and heads, senior management (such as Pro-Vice-Chancellors), Senate, Vice-Chancellor and Council.

The stages of knowledge production in universities likely to employ contract researchers are set out in Figure 6.2. Essential overhead

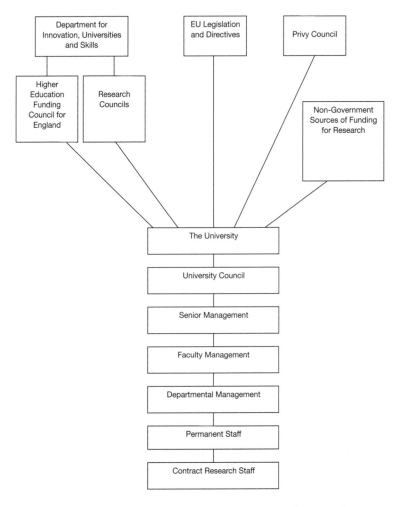

Figure 6.1 Structures of production of contract research in The University

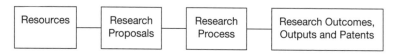

Figure 6.2 Stages of production of contract research in The University

resources – such as laboratories, libraries, academic staff, administrative systems, buildings, IT and so on – are gathered, organized and managed by the institution. Drawing on these facilities, some established academic staff make bids to funding bodies for additional resources to carry out specific research projects. Others may undertake (usually smaller) projects drawing solely on existing resources in the institution, without bidding for external grants, but these examples of personal scholarship rarely generate sufficient funds to employ contract researchers. Successful externally-funded teams, led by the Principal Investigator, but often including contract researchers, carry out the research. The final stage in the sequence is the production of research outputs, such as books, journal articles and patents.

The software engineering organization (The Company) had a very different history. It was established in 1981 by a group of seven colleagues, who decided to split away from their employer at the time and start a new business. At the time of the research it employed between three and four hundred people. Most were located in the head office on the outskirts of London, with smaller teams in the north of England and Scotland, and a sales force of about 50 in the US. Just over half were (predominately male) software engineers. The company is owned by an Employee Benefit Trust. Profit share arrangements mean that all employees receive an annual share of profit based on their performance. Some 90 per cent of sales are generated in the US, but all the products were made in the UK. Staff turnover was very low (around 5 per cent) and one third of employees had been with The Company for over 10 years. The Company had built an international reputation for being both cutting edge and able to deliver on time. The structures and stages of the productive system vary accordingly.

Figure 6.3 indicates that, compared with those of The University, the structures of production characteristic of The Company were relatively simple and truncated. The Employee Benefit Trust was the most senior external source of regulation. Employees were represented in the membership of the Trust, which operated and managed the

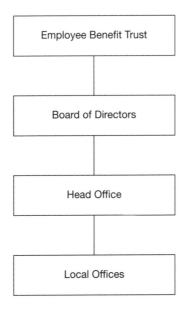

Figure 6.3 Structures of production of software engineering in The Company

profit sharing scheme with staff. The next level of control was that of the Board of Directors, appointed by and answerable to the Trust. Below the Board came senior staff at head office, followed by those in local offices.

The stages of knowledge production in The Company, which provided employment for software engineers, are set out in Figure 6.4. Initially, The Company gathered together, and made available to staff, background and overhead resources necessary for intellectual production. These were not dissimilar to those assembled by The University and included an array of texts, devices and artefacts (see Chapter 8 of this book for further discussion of the role of artefacts in productive systems). Sales staff employed by The Company formed relationships with clients that resulted in contracts to undertake work.

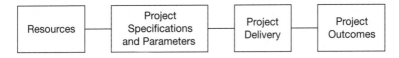

Figure 6.4 Stages of production of software engineering in The Company

Teams of software engineers in The Company made bids to clients with specified project parameters and costs. Members of teams successful in the bidding process undertook the delivery of the project by working closely in collaboration with one another and with their opposite numbers in client organizations. In addition, some teams in The Company worked on 'blue sky' projects that were not driven by client contacts, but instead involved the development of completely new products that would eventually attract business (cf. contrasts between 'new to the firm' and 'new to the market' sandwiches discussed in Chapter 7). Teams typically were composed of full-time established staff and rarely, if ever, employed software engineers on short terms. As will be seen, leadership within these teams was flexible and did not revolve around a hierarchy of occupational ranks. The final stage in the sequence was the completion and commissioning of software products for clients.

The stages of the productive systems of The University and The Company were, thus, broadly similar (cf. Figures 6.2 and 6.4), although fixed-term contract researchers are used extensively in the former but not in the latter. However, it is clear from a comparison of Figures 6.1 and 6.3 that The University had far less autonomy than The Company in determining the scale and nature of its business strategy and was subject to far more interference from external agencies. While The Company had to be very alive to developments in the marketplace and to nurturing its customer base, it was in charge of its own destiny. This chapter will explore the implications of these contrasts for relations of discretion in the management of staff in the two settings and the implications for their respective learning environments.

University contract researchers

It was not until the mid-1970s that contract researchers (CRs) became regarded as a specific category of university staff. Since that time, and alongside the general rise of fixed-term employment within HE, numbers of CRs have substantially increased. Data provided by the Higher Education Statistics Agency shows that in 2004/5 there were 36,100 CRs, compared to just 5,886 in 1978. Although the current research base is small, studies have identified a range of negative effects associated with the employment status of CRs, as compared with those categorized as 'academic' and 'established' staff whose salaries are paid out of core funding provided by publicly funded agencies such as the Higher Education Funding Council for England (HEFCE). These include job insecurity, inferior standing and the lack of a clear career structure (see, *inter alia,* Williams *et al.* 1974; Freedman *et al.* 2000). Such problems have impacted adversely on researchers' careers and identities as well as on recruitment into the HE sector, particularly in the areas of science, engineering and technology. In terms of the structures of production, outlined in Figure 6.1, CRs are distant from the locus of control at the top of the institution. They are employed by universities, but their salaries are paid out of funds derived from the external agencies, research councils and organizations that commission specific projects. In this sense, CRs have relatively little control over what they do and how they do it. Moreover, they have few rights to bid for projects or to hold budgets of their own. Historically, employer commitment to them as employees has been low.

In recent years, there have been a number of initiatives designed to improve matters, such as the Concordat (CVCP 1996), the Research Careers Initiative (OST 1998), and the review carried out by Sir Gareth Roberts (Roberts 2002). In addition, new employment legislation specifies that anyone who has completed four or more years continuous service, and has had their contract renewed, must be moved onto an open-ended contract, unless the use of a fixed-term contract can be 'objectively' justified by the employer. Employers must also show that they have considered contract researchers for other positions available within the organization, provided they meet the requirements of the job. Moreover, career and staff development opportunities now have to be made available to all research staff. A member of the personnel department, involved in the early stages of developing The University's response to the new requirements, commented on the Concordat as follows:

> An important foundation document really . . . It lays out . . . broad areas of good practice in terms of managing and developing research staff in higher education . . . All the major players in terms of universities signed up to it.
>
> (Brendan, Personnel Manager, The University)

For The University, highlighting negative aspects of the way contract researchers have traditionally been employed, and the introduction of the Concordat, led to a reassessment of the roles of contract research staff. It was felt that the contribution of CRs to the research intensive and excellence dimensions of The University's goals might be enhanced by improving their terms and conditions of employment. For example, it might result in a reduction of high levels of researcher turnover, which was perceived as detrimental.

> A lot of researchers are leaving the profession for all sort of reasons ... security, having to move around the country ... and largely not having a really defined career structure to move up and have a sort of way of going towards. So we've got sort of a huge number of people who are extremely qualified, and a lot of them who are absolutely passionate about what they do and would stay and would make a career out of academic research if the circumstances made that more possible for them ... From the university point of view all the investment has gone into these people and it's a very, very high turnover. And if you're really wanting to get the best research – and, you know, aim to be one of the research led institutions – then why have this really high turnover? ... So I suppose that's why we're trying to change things.
>
> (Hillary, Personnel Officer, The University)

The University's Human Resources (HR) Director suggested that CRs should not be conceived or treated as a homogeneous group. He made the distinction between the impact of fixed-term contracts on new researchers, perhaps working on their first externally-funded project following completion of a doctorate, and those who have remained on such contracts for many years. He argued that the second category should be treated as 'proper employees', who were committed to The University and who The University needed to retain if valuable experience and skills were not to be lost. In effect, he suggested that such CRs should be aligned with other employees in the vertical axis of the productive system, rather than continuing to occupy a peripheral position. In the following quotation, he makes a connection between the way people are managed and their ability to perform the knowledge work necessary for the institution to compete at the high end of the HE market:

> If we can get it right, then we will be able to both attract and retain very good people, which is just absolutely critical to the future of the institution ... When you come to a research-led university you need some brilliant people, and there's no two ways about it.
>
> (George, HR Director, The University)

The HR Director went on to stress the importance of recruiting and retaining researchers who conform to the definition of knowledge workers or symbolic analysts outlined earlier in this chapter:

> However brilliant the PI [Principal Investigator] is, they need to be surrounded by really, really good researchers, because actually it's the dynamic of all that that works. And a sort of almost dumb researcher, who says: 'right I can run those 50 tests and I can give you the results', is far less useful than somebody who does the test while they're thinking about it and evolve the thing and comes back and says: 'oh ... and I changed it in the middle and this happened, da-da-da'. And the whole thing moves on from there.
>
> (George, HR Director, The University)

The University had put in place three areas of activity designed to provide researchers with more and better support: staff development and training; careers guidance; and mechanisms for improving communication and feedback between researchers and central management. It also used the introduction of the new legislation to start to rethink how it employed researchers and had been transferring people with four or more years of service onto open-ended contracts. This shift challenged the basis of the fixed-term model by undermining the explicit link between a specific source of funding (e.g. gained through winning an externally-funded research contract) and the employment of an individual researcher. It began to bring the employment conditions and expectations of CRs more into line with that of their peers on permanent contracts. However, as yet there is little sign that CRs and core funded academics will both be paid out of the same income streams. The association, on the one hand, between the employment of CRs and external soft funding and, on the other, academics and core funding remains strong. As the personnel manager in the following quotation observes, moving away from the fixed-term approach requires a cultural as well as contractual shift in the way the role and contribution of researchers is conceptualized, valued and managed:

> We need to start thinking more like Tesco. In terms of, we have a whole load of income and really – although I think many people don't believe this – we can do whatever we want with it ... How we contract our employees ... it's our responsibility ... To change

requires a massive change in culture, within a sector that changes very slowly and is really quite bureaucratic . . . I think if Tesco wanted to radically change the way which they contract their employees, they could probably do it quite easily.

(Brendan, Personnel Manager, The University)

The challenge of implementing changes across The University was illustrated through the different levels of resistance and scepticism expressed by managers in different departments. For example, the decision to encourage researchers to attend courses and make use of careers advice and guidance was not always supported by those who managed CRs on a daily basis.

I can think of one department where the researcher just has to do the work. 'What do you mean, look at their future career? What do you mean, give them time to go to a workshop? Well that's crazy, who's going to do the project?'. You know it's almost a factory mentality.

(Hillary, Personnel Officer, The University)

The above quotation illustrates an approach to work organization associated with the fixed-term model of employment, whereby the degree of discretion CRs are expected to exercise is limited. This, we discerned, was a result of management attempts at reducing uncertainty in the securing and delivery of externally-funded projects as well as protecting Principal Investigators' reputations. From the corporate perspective, the organization's mission to compete successfully with other top universities around the world had raised awareness of the tensions between, and different priorities of, the parties involved in the vertical structures of production (Figure 6.1). These included the central administration, discipline-based departments and individual academics, who historically had pursued relatively detached relationships from one another (see Chapter 8 for another example, in a supermarket chain, of tensions between groups within the vertical axis of the productive system). A personnel manager commented:

Some academics are interested in the global ambitions of the organization, but probably it's fair to say that many are more interested in their own ambitions . . . But that's changing a bit, I think, slowly as the culture changes. And, indeed, the university as a whole is trying to get people more engaged, at all levels

> ... [The Vice-Chancellor] sees that kind of ... global approach
> – all employees broadly pushing in the same direction – as being
> a strong future for the organization. As opposed to, you know,
> an organization where many of the employees are just pursuing
> in their own directions.
>
> (Marie, Personnel Manager, The University)

In addition, it was pointed out that the 'performance indicators'
traditionally used to determine the career progression of academics
have focused on their ability to gain external research funding and
produce high status academic publications. They had not paid
attention to their skills in developing the careers of others, particularly
those on fixed-term research contracts. For some academics, the
adoption of a management strategy that allowed CRs more discretion
over, and autonomy in, their work carried risks that they may be
reluctant to take. The following comment stands in stark contrast to
the management ethos developed in the software company, described
later in this chapter:

> The fact that somebody might be really a quite appalling manager
> ... isn't necessarily going to affect their seniority. Which, I think,
> is probably quite different in other organizations, where at that
> sort of level of seniority in management there's some evidence
> of your management ability. It has to be part of the criteria. And
> it's not necessarily the case. That's one of the real difficulties.
>
> (Dougal, Personnel Officer, The University)

As already indicated, The University displayed a strong commitment
to improving the working conditions of CRs and enhancing their
career prospects. This was evident across The University's promotional
and recruitment literature, most of which was publicly available on
the website. It was also made apparent through staff information
web pages, intranet/message board facilities, training and career
development programmes, communication strategies and the annual
CR conference. The information, development and communication
strategies that were in place for CRs were generally well received by
our interviewees. One of the main areas which they found valuable
was increased access to training. This included practical generic
courses, such as those concerned with the use of information technology, and others that were more tailored to the needs of researchers,
including specific topics such as the use of data analysis software and

proposal writing. In this respect, the changes were creating new opportunities for learning and were enhancing the quality of the workplace
as a learning environment.

The creation of an advice and guidance service specifically tailored
to the needs of CRs was also valued. The support available included
one-to-one career guidance as well as more general workshop sessions.
Some interviewees considered that the most useful form of support
being offered to them was advice and practical help in gaining new
employment once their contracts had ended:

> I think the careers advice here is very good and they do seem
> to have a whole section to help . . . I think it's fantastic they do
> that. They do tend to look after their staff, even if they're losing
> them.
>
> (Janice, Research Assistant, The University)

Despite what they saw to be the commitment of The University,
however, many CRs felt that the new contracts were as yet bringing
few positive and meaningful changes to their employment and career
prospects. As the following quotations indicate, the new arrangements
did not appear to have been accompanied by the sort of additional
core funding that could, for example, routinely bridge researchers
between projects:

> The problem is money. You know, you should have funding, and
> you can have an open-ended contract, but when there's no
> funding then you're on the street. So it's nice on paper but in
> reality it doesn't really change anything.
>
> (Edward, Research Fellow, The University)

> The implementation phase of this agreement is resulting in people
> still connecting individuals with individual streams of funding
> . . . because there's a six-month redundancy period now, once
> you're six months away from the end of your contract, I think
> you're being put forward for redundancy instead.
>
> (Linda, Research Associate, The University)

It is clear that contract research was still dependent on competitive
bidding for fixed-term grants from external funding sources. It is
perhaps not surprising then that CRs felt that genuine security of
employment would not be forthcoming. The majority also considered

that the new contractual system was doing little to change their second-class status in relation to lecturing staff:

> So all the lecturers are referred to as 'academic staff' and then you're 'a contract researcher' . . . If you look up the definition of academic you are an academic but you allow these people to make you feel crap . . . rather than being proud of your achievements, ability and having the feeling of self worth.
>
> (Sean, Research Associate, The University)

Four main concerns were raised by CRs in relation to the new employment arrangements. First, although open-ended contracts could keep research staff in post longer, and so enable them to gain experience and progress, individuals would inevitably become more expensive to employ. Over time this would make it more difficult for them to gain new research posts and many would find that they would have to take a reduction in salary in order to secure employment. Second, if researcher salary costs increased, then projects would become more expensive. Ultimately, this could mean a reduction in the number of projects successfully securing funding. It could also encourage PIs to reduce costs, in order to make their bids more competitive, by employing only new and inexperienced researchers. Third, the move to open-ended contracts was encouraging a system of redeployment, which, it was feared, could lead to some CRs becoming underemployed, with the consequent risk of becoming deskilled as skill obsolescence set in:

> My understanding with the change in contract was that at its heart was a move to make provisions for contract research staff better . . . the university will seek to find some other grant that's currently available that you can work on. . . . What I wouldn't want is for the university to say: 'Well, we have nothing in the area that you study but there's a test tube washing job going in Chemistry and we'll put you on that so you can continue your job'. That would be non-productive in many ways.
>
> (Roger, Research Associate, The University)

Fourth, some CRs suggested that open-ended contracts would discourage young researchers from gaining the sort of experience and expertise that would help them build successful research careers. According to these respondents, career building depended on learning highly specialized skills and techniques that they were unlikely to acquire if they stayed in one department or research group. If the availability of open-ended contracts resulted in them staying in one workplace, there could be unintended detrimental effects on their progression. Such a theme has echoes with our sandwich making research, discussed in Chapter 7, in which learning environments were categorized by the breadth and depth of the relationships to which employees had access. In this respect, CRs were conforming to the image of the knowledge worker as a highly desirable expert who can trade their skills in the marketplace and float free of organizational structures and loyalties. The University's treatment of CRs could be said to have fostered and even traded on that image.

The majority of our interviewees were relatively experienced researchers who hoped to remain in research-only posts, pursuing a research career trajectory in an academic environment. Most were not keen to become involved in teaching. This sort of trajectory has been labelled and described by Roberts (2002: 150) as 'the Research Associate Trajectory – for those who want to continue in research within a university but who do not want to pursue an academic lecturing career'.

> I just want to do research. You know, that's what I'm good at. I don't particularly enjoy teaching. But there's no facility within the university to allow you to do that and you're actively discouraged from doing that. So once you've done one Postdoc, they pretty much tells you, you know, you need to start thinking about teaching or leaving.
>
> (Norman, Research Fellow, The University)

At the time of our research, our evidence suggested that the contractual changes had not been sufficiently radical to enable the development of secure professional identities, and to create a defined and recognized career path, for CRs. Although CRs had access to training and careers advice, this could be perceived as a 'bolt-on', rather than integrated within day-to-day supervision and mentoring, linked directly to the department's or institution's business plan. Although the rhetoric of the contractual changes suggested that The University wanted to create a 'safe working culture' in which research careers flourished, the reality was that CRs still had to learn to survive in a labour market characterized by a culture of individuality, displayed through macho-style, workaholic behaviours. In this model, the burden of employment insecurity and uncertainty was essentially displaced from the employer to the individual CR. The University sought to minimize risks by pursuing a twin-track strategy: retaining control over who does what and how in the labour process; and maintaining a relatively elastic pool of expert labour in the labour market. As the comparison with the case study presented in the next section will indicate, this approach inhibited the sort of expansive learning environment that the software engineering company was able to create.

Software engineers

The history of modern software development is rooted in the production of early computing hardware during the Second World War, which built on the Babbage principle of breaking production down into smaller and smaller segments. Over the years, the industry's complex and continued evolution has resulted in two labour process paradigms. These have been referred to as the 'formalist' and 'pragmatist' paradigms (Quintas 1994). In the formalist paradigm, software development is regarded as an engineering discipline in which product development follows set procedures and stages. In the pragmatist paradigm, on the other hand, software development is an 'ad hoc process of "hacking" (i.e. writing code without rigorous planning and then hacking at it to remove bugs and achieve results)' (Barrett 2001: 26).

Other authors (e.g. Robinson *et al.* 1998) conceptualize this dichotomy as a 'hard/soft' division, where 'hard' relates to the designing of systems with a precise function, and 'soft' to the need to make a system compatible with the 'human system' that surrounds it. As Robinson *et al.* (1998: 372) argue, however, the need to reconcile the needs of multiple stakeholders in an information technology system means that the 'modernist' foundations of computing (emphasis on form and function and a belief in the existence of a rational solution to a problem) have to be transcended by a more pluralist approach. This requires facilitating teams that operate across the divisions of manager, user and developer, combined with an end to the 'single hero and the single voice' model in which lead designers and system architects passed down their instructions to subordinates. These paradigms have consequences for the way software engineers see themselves and are treated by their employers. They also have consequences for the way in which researchers conceptualize software workers. Marks and Lockyer (2005: 148), for example, argue that software developers operating under the pragmatist paradigm can be described as professionals, since 'they have an implicit set of professional codes and common beliefs, values and ceremonies' and are viewed as such by many employers. This is exhibited in the way work is organized, such as the opportunity developers have to work closely with peers, and their ability to exercise autonomy and discretion.

An alternative view conceptualizes software engineering as an artistic endeavour in that the programmer applies skill and ingenuity, the products themselves have an aesthetic quality, and the programmer takes pleasure in the construction of the product (see Knuth 1974). Austin and Devin (2003) portray software development as 'artful making', drawing comparisons with theatre production. This dimension was fostered to some degree in The Company by the freedom and time provided for teams to develop 'blue skies' products. The Company presented itself as in tune with the pragmatist model of software development described above, but also as being strongly anchored in the formalist paradigm in that rigorous planning formed an essential part of its product development. The commitment to planning, and the associated rigour of systematic quality assurance procedures, meant that The Company placed a high value on academic and technical ('hard') skills. Thus, its software engineers were all recruited to permanent contracts on the basis of excellent academic achievement at school and university. New recruits were also expected to demonstrate the ability to work in a team and show initiative. The belief in The Company was that these 'soft' skills were best developed within the workplace through collective engagement in work tasks and interaction with clients. It is noticeable that during the recruitment exercise observed for the research, one young man with a PhD was given a job because, despite his poorly developed inter-personal skills, his academic and technical abilities were regarded as outstanding.

The Company was founded in a spirit of entrepreneurship coupled with a desire to create a community that enjoyed working together with the ambition and expertise to be successful at the cutting edge of software engineering. This dual emphasis on collegiality and high level business success underpinned the design of the physical environment, the review and reward system, the recruitment strategy, and the positioning of learning at the centre of everyday workplace activity. At the time of our research, the Chairman, who was one of

The Company's original founders, was the driving force behind the organization and appeared to be actively involved at all levels. In particular, he was central to the review and feedback process that was the basis of the organization of work, monitoring of performance, allocation of rewards, and sharing and creation of knowledge. He was highly visible and approachable by all staff, regardless of their role and status in the company. To that extent, his position was comparable to that of a senior professor in a university department, though a crucial difference lay in the structures through which he could reward his staff.

The physical environment of The Company helped to sustain and enhance a strong spirit of collegiality (see Felstead *et al.* 2005a for other examples of comparable spatial arrangements). The two head office buildings (five minutes walk apart) were organized around open plan offices, with one or two glass-fronted offices for senior managers on each floor. Each floor also had a kitchen stocked with drinks, biscuits, fruit, fridges and microwaves. The subsidized canteen (in the main building) provided freshly cooked meals and sandwiches from early morning. The engineers could work flexible hours, but were expected to work late and for longer when pressure was on. The accent was on professional autonomy and discretion. Employees could take 'sabbaticals' and could work less than five days a week. A special fund (at team, business unit and corporate levels) supported a large range of social activities such as annual trips overseas, garden parties, children's parties, summer barbecues and dinners in London restaurants to celebrate new products. Employees received healthcare insurance and gym/tennis club membership. They were encouraged to play sport at lunchtime and racquets and other sporting equipment were frequently on display. In addition to the reward structures, then, the investment in The Company's physical environment was in marked contrast to the conditions in which many HE contract researchers work.

The valuing of academic and technical ability was articulated in a variety of ways, from pre-recruitment materials through to in-house briefings. During our interviews, the single most common way in which the software engineers identified themselves was as 'highly intelligent' people. Many cited the chance to join an 'intelligent' community as the key reason for accepting a job in The Company. Some described themselves as 'techies', in that they had been interested in computers from an early age and spent time out of work designing software posted on 'open source community' websites. Others, however, confined their software interests to the workplace. The following comment, from an engineer who joined the organization straight from university four years ago, was typical:

> The kind of people we have, this will sound arrogant and elitist, but they're sort of, a long way above the average you might encounter. If you go on a 'how to program course', the people working on that course generally would be of a lot lower ability than the people here.
>
> (Damian, Software Engineer, The Company)

The following comment is from a senior software engineer who had joined the organization ten years previously and had recently decided to work four days a week:

> I do lots of things that I don't have time for if I work five days a week ... I'm learning Chinese ... for the mental exercise ... I like keeping my brain busy ... I picked Chinese because it was, it's very much one of the most difficult languages and that was the most challenging ... Other kinds of things ... I do board games ... there's a group of people who come up to my house and we play ... Again it's solely about intellectual exercise, but then there's also an aspect of competing against other people rather than as against a computer or something. It's like computers are not as clever, so there's more satisfaction.
>
> (Isaac, Software Engineer, The Company)

The belief among software engineers that they comprised a highly intelligent community was shaped in several ways. It began with The Company's recruitment brochures for potential applicants, which sought young people with 'A' grades at A Level and destined for First Class Honours Degrees from top universities. It was fostered at the interview stage, where applicants spent time together as a group listening to presentations from software engineers who had recently joined The Company stressing that standards were very high but rewards were great. It was also reinforced by software engineers themselves. They appeared to internalize this aspect of their identities in order to cope with the pressures of problem-solving for high profile customers, while, at the same time, believing that they could trust their equally intelligent peers and managers to provide appropriate, collegial support. One recently employed engineer remarked:

Well you've got to be clever enough technically to do it, to have a technical/problem-solving set of skills. Determination to carry on in the face of this going wrong. Resolve kind of thing. And confidence. Yeah, I guess that's very strongly attached to determination isn't it ... I guess belief in one's own ability ... but I knew when I'd need help the help was there.

(Andrew, Software Engineer, The Company)

The Company's sensitivity to the ways in which many of the engineers pursued intellectual interests in both their professional and personal lives partly explains the deliberate construction of a working environment that mimicked, to some extent, an Oxbridge college, while also giving consideration to work–life balance needs (see Scarborough and Swan 1999; Felstead *et al.* 2005a). For example, an office in Scotland had been established despite the fact that the company had – and continued to have – no Scottish clients. It was set up solely because, as one of the directors said, he and a small group of other employees 'were very happy to stay in the company, but basically could not settle in the South East of England'. The determination of the Directors to find ways to retain valued staff by enabling the creation of the new office is in stark contrast to The University's management of CRs outlined earlier in the chapter. More significantly, the performance review system and annual profit share arrangements served the important functions of visibly and concretely rewarding expertise. It stitched employees into the fabric of the company, even though they could easily get employment elsewhere. The power of this self-reverential and self-referential community spirit is manifested in the apparent absence of worker resistance. The only critical remark we encountered was the view that the lack of off-the-job training for managers meant that the management was not sufficiently exposed to new thinking.

According to Barrett (2005: 3–4), exaggerated claims that software workers are destined to become the 'future aristocrats of the labour market' have 'served to obscure much of what the people developing software actually do from day-to-day at work'. Despite the hyperbole surrounding the excitement of software engineering, interviewees in The Company spent a great deal of time applying their technical know-how to a range of diagnostic activities such as writing thousands of lines of computer code, testing software systems and computer routines, and designing new software architecture for new products. They also had to demonstrate their technical intelligence on a daily basis with customers seeking updates and progress reports. For many, therefore, the label 'engineer' aptly described the reality of their occupational role and captured their professional identity. They were also working in a relatively stable and very successful commercial environment where employee turnover was low. In that sense, they conformed more to the Japanese model of the loyal company career professional, who progresses through a highly structured internal labour market, than to the highly mobile, risk-taking 'knowledge worker' in the new economy. A company director explained this as follows:

> We're talking about a lot of propeller heads here you see. And they want to know what the next exciting technology they're going to be working on is. They don't particularly want to know that I have recently negotiated so and so with customer X or whatever . . . I think that culture comes partly because . . . the company is full of engineers. It's very engineering dominated and they tend to not really be that interested in business an awful lot. But also it comes from the fact that they've grown up with a company that's always successful, that's always stable, that always makes its targets. And so there's not that underlying paranoia, if you like, that I think exists in the real world – you know, is our company going to go bust next year or whatever?
>
> (Lawrence, Director, The Company)

Another software engineer, who had spent four years as a researcher in particle physics, also reflected the desire of several colleagues to find a job that offered stimulation but also stability:

> I wanted something a little bit more stable. I wanted a job that wasn't, you know, some city job where you're, you're working all hours. Something a little bit more balanced, something a bit more interesting.
>
> (Patrick, Software Engineer, The Company)

The evidence presented here suggests that some so-called knowledge workers find themselves in (and may deliberately seek out) workplaces where they can enjoy applying their expertise, but at the same time find the conditions to sustain the type of work–life balance that becomes more important with age. To this extent, the software engineers of The Company may have much in common with the career aspirations of HE contract researchers in The University. For the engineers, the sense of being 'top of the class' had been forged early on in life, at school and then again at university. Becoming part of an intelligent, technical community at work was the next natural step. The organization they had joined was managed by people from the same mould, who used their understanding of their own personal identities to develop structures and an over-arching cultural narrative designed to attract and retain engineers with a similar outlook. In effect, the technical and social relations of production of The Company appeared to have created collective organizational and personal identities that were generally mutually constituted and reinforcing.

The software engineers worked in teams on projects that run for 6–12 months, although teams might exist for more than one project. Team rotation facilitated innovation and a sense of energy, and served to counteract potential boredom. Knowledge and expertise were captured within the teams, but disseminated through everyday interaction in the form of discussions and consultation across teams. The performance review system also acted as a mechanism for capturing ideas. The development process was organized hierarchically in that every project began with the design of an architectural plan, which was then broken down into smaller and smaller units by the project teams. The development of engineering expertise was, therefore, integral to the production process.

The articulation of the production levels provided the benchmarks for The Company's performance review process and was the basis of the workplace curriculum. Together, the review process and the curriculum enabled employees to teach each other and receive feedback on their performance. Teaching was seen as a constant part of workplace activity and an important function of management at all levels. The explicit foregrounding and integration of staff development within the work process, and in pursuit of business goals, generated a dynamic and distributed approach to learning. It also created awareness of the link between learning and knowledge production, which helped maintain the organization at the leading edge in its market. Although job levels within The Company were organized hierarchically, there was movement between them. For example, a 'second line manager' who was the best 'techie' in his team might stop managing for a period of time in order to provide the team with the necessary technical expertise. It is important to note here, therefore, that the hierarchy of skills did not translate across to a personnel structure. As one director explained:

You would never say you were, therefore, moving from priority level one to level two. I've got 73 people in my unit and I've got 72 grades in effect, because everyone is in a unique place.

(Lawrence, Director, The Company)

The success of these arrangements contrast sharply with the health visitors discussed in Chapter 4. They, too, attempted to cultivate a similar ethos and set of working practices, but were thwarted by the absence of appropriate managerial and institutional supports, such as those found in The Company.

The role of managers was seen as central to the on-going success of the business and to the reproduction of its ethos. In contrast to university academics and Principal Investigators, managers in The Company were expected to devote the majority of their time to people development. New software engineers spent 50 days of their first year being closely supervised by their managers as they learned on-the-job. The concept of 'management' thus incorporated expertise in 'teaching'. The following comment from a software engineer with some five years' experience captures the way in which new recruits were supported through their immersion in real work activities:

My first few weeks and months . . . I was put into a team of one. So I was given to a guy who was an experienced techie and someone who had management aspirations and I was given to him to manage initially. And I worked with him on supporting a major customer. Actually, I think it gave me a very good start in the company because it put me immediately in a position where I was very much in the deep end. Because I didn't really know the ropes and I had all this incredibly obscure and difficult code to support. And I had one guy who was a clear expert to guide me through it . . . That kind of environment meant that I had to learn to stand on my own two feet quite quickly.

(Terence, Software Engineer, The Company)

Knowledge, then, was distributed throughout the company through the use of teams and the central role played by everyday interaction within and between teams. All software engineers began by learning the core technologies involved in their area of the business and used this as a platform on which to build their expertise. As ideas were developed and problems solved, engineers placed this information in a series of 'public folders' on the company's intranet. There was a sense from some interviewees that The Company could make more of this by giving the folders greater status and visibility. The organization of work enabled employees to create new knowledge through the everyday interaction with customers. Solving problems resulted in new ideas and there was a constant building on the learning that was done from day-to-day. The approach to teaching and learning at work in The Company, then, differed from that in The University, where workplace learning was considered an *ad hoc*, tacit and individual aspect of work. In The University training was provided to individuals in the form of off-the-job courses that appeared to address individual needs, but which did not form part of an organizational workforce and business development plan.

Conclusion

Given the nature of their jobs, and their associated level of education and training prior to and during employment, contract researchers in The University and software engineers employed by The Company conform to current definitions of 'knowledge workers'. Both worked in knowledge-intensive organizations, in communities of talented professionals, and engaged in the creation and application of knowledge within a problem-solving environment. Both had chosen careers that would enable them to become experts and apply their knowledge and skills at a high level. In both cases, this commitment to their identity as experts took precedence over the desire for financial reward. It was clear, however, that the environments in which the two groups functioned, the ways their work was organized and the nature of their employment relationships were very different. We have utilized the Working as Learning Framework (WALF) to analyse and highlight these differences. The contrasting circumstances of contract researchers and software engineers reflected the character of their respective productive systems. Figures 6.1 and 6.3 reveal the complexity of the vertical structures of production characteristic of The University and the relative simplicity of the vertical relations associated with The Company. We saw that this, in turn, had profound implications for the learning environments of contract researchers and software engineers.

Universities, as employers, face considerable challenges in creating the conditions in which both researchers and universities can achieve their long-term goals. Over the past 20 or so years, the productive system of the higher education sector has intensified its demands on universities to widen access to courses, become more accountable for their large receipts of public money, diversify their funding base, increase research productivity and meet externally-set targets. This expansion of activity, however, has not been accompanied by an equivalent requirement for the substantial and necessary reform of the way work, career structures and reward systems are organized, which would lead to adjustment of the vertical and horizontal relations in the productive system. This is exemplified in the case study by the failure to think through the potential of contractual changes to act as a catalyst for the re-organization of the way CRs *and* so-called 'academic staff' are categorized, employed and supported. If a key purpose of the change to the employment relationship was to improve CR retention, our research evidence suggests that it will have a minor effect unless attention is paid to the way in which employee discretion is currently conceptualized in the CR role and trajectory, as compared to that of their permanent peers.

Achieving significant change in the way CRs are employed and managed is a challenge for universities that, in comparison to successful private sector companies, lack autonomy and flexibility within their vertical structures of production. There are, however, interesting parallels between The University and The Company with respect to the aspirations and motivations of the knowledge workers they employed. In both organizations, interviewees wanted to work in intelligent communities, where the quality of the work was of prime importance. In the case of The Company, a sophisticated system of performance review and constructive feedback, together with the conceptualization of management as a key vehicle for the transmission and development of knowledge and skills among software engineers, had created an environment in which talented individuals could flourish, but only to the extent that they served the needs of the team. The profit share arrangements were clearly a major weapon in The Company's ability to attract and retain staff, whereas The University was more restricted in terms of the reward incentives it could use. There are, however, ways in which universities could be much more creative in the ways they support and reward staff, including the improvement of the physical environment. The University was ahead of most in beginning to rethink how the contribution of CRs to its success can be better recognized and supported. The new legislative framework, together with growing awareness of the negative effects of job insecurity and limited employee discretion in the retention of 'the best' researchers, were pushing some changes in management strategy. However, this had yet to lead to a fundamental reconfiguration of the vertical relations of production.

Knowledge workers in the two organizations had different experiences of work. For the CRs in The University, work was dominated by their concern to secure more long-term security of employment and the dilemma of whether to switch to the standard academic track where they will be required to teach and contribute to the wider life of their department. Under the new contracts, this concern had been compounded by the worry that they may be asked to work in areas outside their main research interests. In contrast, the software engineers in The Company exhibited a much greater sense of security and confidence about their long-term future. It could be argued that the software engineers conformed more to the stereotype of the loyal company professional, whose long-term commitment and conformity is rewarded through both the pay structure and the supportive paternalism of like-minded bosses. Ironically, CRs, however, exemplified the image of the knowledge worker living at the sharp end of the contemporary economy, despite the fact of their being employed in the public sector and, moreover, in higher education.

Chapter 7

Making sandwiches

Introduction

While the sandwich is nothing new, its commercialization certainly is. In the UK, the first factory-made sandwich appeared on the shelves of Marks & Spencer as recently as 1981 (Dunn 2006). Since then, an increasing proportion of sandwiches have been produced commercially and sold through retail outlets. Industry estimates suggest that, in the UK, approaching two billion are purchased every year. The UK sandwich market is worth around £3.5 billion and is over three times bigger than that for UK pizza (Winship 2006). The most rapidly growing part of the market is the 'pre-packed, bought in' sandwich as opposed to those made on site. Two-thirds of these are 'pure sandwiches' – that is, two slices of bread cut into triangles and packaged for sale – as opposed to other formats, such as baguettes, rolls and wraps (Hunter 2007). This chapter focuses on the traditional 'triangle' part of the market.

Like other foods, such as cook-chill meals (Glucksmann 2008), the pre-packed sandwich was developed and launched by supermarkets (for a discussion of other 'convenience' foods, see Warde 1999). This, coupled with the huge numbers of products they sell, has given supermarkets an advantage over the manufacturers they contract to assemble, pack and deliver sandwiches. Supermarket chains continue to play a pivotal role in directing and overseeing manufacturers.

It is central to our analysis that sandwiches sold through retail outlets can be divided into two categories, generated within two different productive systems. We refer to those sandwiches that leave manufacturers' premises labelled with the supermarket's brand, rather than that of the manufacturer, as 'retailer label' sandwiches. The label printed on the container is emblematic of the power retailers are able to exercise over their suppliers, and their suppliers' suppliers. This, in turn, determines the parameters within which producers operate and the learning environments within which innovation takes place. Production for supermarkets (and other large purchasers, such as coffee shop chains) is 'buyer-driven' (Gereffi 1994 and 1999). However, although supermarkets sell huge volumes of sandwiches, there are nevertheless other locations where consumers can buy sandwiches, such as corner shops, garages and small restaurants. These provide more numerous outlets, although their average sales volumes are far lower. They offer sandwich producers an alternative route to market and, moreover, opportunities to sell sandwiches under the brand of the manufacturer rather than the retailer. These we designate as 'manufacturer label' sandwiches. Where sandwiches take this route to market, there is a greater potentiality for the horizontal axis of the productive system to be 'producer-driven', with more push from the manufacturer and less pull from the retailer (Burch and Lawrence 2005).

This chapter examines the consequences of these two distinctive productive systems for the discretion exercised by those whose responsibility it is to develop and launch new sandwiches (known as New Product Development or NPD for short). This, in turn, has implications for the learning environments in which NPD takes place. The chapter provides another illustration of the usefulness of the Working as Learning Framework (WALF) in revealing connections between productive systems, work organization and learning. In addition, it further develops the 'expansive–restrictive' continuum outlined in Chapter 2 (Fuller and Unwin 2003). We argue that NPD does not have the same characteristics across these two productive systems. Each incorporate elements of both expansive and restrictive learning environments; neither can be placed at either of the extreme ends of the expansive–restrictive continuum. Both fall somewhere in the middle of the spectrum. However, it is also apparent that their particular combinations of expansiveness and restrictiveness are not identical. As a result, NPD personnel in each of the two productive systems are characterized by different strategies of innovation and patterns of learning. This chapter, therefore, makes a contribution to illuminating the characteristics of some of the points along the expansive–restrictive continuum, which stretches from wholly expansive learning environments at one end to wholly restrictive ones at the other.

In addition, the substantive empirical focus of the chapter allows us to make a contribution to the food processing literature, since we examine the development of a particular food category rather than the emergence of the retail brand in general (cf. Harvey *et al.* 2002; Burch and Lawrence 2005; Jones *et al.* 2006). The product development focus of the chapter also makes it distinctive from much of the existing literature on the sector which gives a shop floor perspective. This emphasizes the monotony, low pay and racialized nature of factory work. We, too, observed these conditions, but do not focus on them here (e.g. Holgate 2005; Edwards *et al.* 2007; Lloyd *et al.* 2008).

The chapter begins with a brief account of the research methods used in generating the empirical data presented here. It goes on to outline the productive system of sandwich making, focusing in particular on the two contrasting forms associated with retailer and manufacturer labels. This is followed by an examination of the different ways in which these two productive systems shape patterns of innovation and learning by NPD personnel in manufacturing firms. The chapter ends with a short conclusion that highlights how elements of both 'expansiveness' and 'restrictiveness' characterize the learning environments of NPD workers in retailer label and manufacturer label firms, thereby giving an insight into what constitutes the mid-points along the expansive–restrictive continuum.

Collecting the evidence

Detective work was required to uncover where sandwiches for supermarkets were made. The location of manufacture was not evident from examining the fine print on the triangular packing in which they were typically sold; only the retailer's head office was printed on the labels. However, further investigations generated a total of ten interviews conducted in four of the largest retailer label manufacturers. Together they supplied all of the major supermarkets. In addition, we carried out 19 interviews with manufacturer label producers, covering eight brands. We also traced the horizontal stages of production backwards to include suppliers of bread, chicken, flavourings and packaging; three interviews were conducted with suppliers who had experience of both productive systems. A further 13 interviews traced the stages of production forwards to retailers. In this context, we interviewed chief buyers for large chains, coffee shop managers responsible for daily orders and corner shop owners. These interviews gave us insights into the two types of productive system from the perspective of retailers, both large and small. The vertical pressures under which sandwich manufacturers operate were frequently discussed in all the interviews. Accordingly, we conducted three interviews with stakeholders responsible for overseeing the industry by offering advice, providing training, disseminating best practice or verifying hygiene standards.

In addition to carrying out interviews, members of the research team also spent time observing the production process in three sandwich factories and accompanying sales staff as they sold sandwiches directly to the public. This entailed short periods working on the shop floor, several days spent shadowing sales staff, and observation of product tasting sessions organized by manufacturers.

Sandwich production

This section begins with a general overview of the productive system of commercial sandwich manufacture and then goes on to distinguish between retailer label and manufacturer label sandwich making. The horizontal axis of the productive system of commercial sandwich manufacture includes a series of sequences or stages (see Figure 7.1). Primary producers generate raw materials, such as vegetables, fish or meat. Suppliers purchase raw materials from primary producers and assemble some or all of a range of ingredients specified by particular sandwich recipes. They may also partially process some ingredients; for example, cooking chicken, baking bread or chopping vegetables. Manufacturers purchase ingredients from a variety of suppliers. They frequently undertake further processing of ingredients, prior to assembling a range of specific sandwiches. Sandwich assembly may be a labour intensive process or may be mechanized to varying degrees. When done by hand, taylorized assembly line techniques are often employed, breaking the job down into a series of small discrete tasks. However, some hand-made sandwiches are assembled from scratch by just one person. The latter is more likely when production runs are short, frequently changed and involve ingredients that are difficult to manage other than by hand. Mechanized assembly lines incorporate electronic weighing scales, overhead hoppers and metal

Figure 7.1 Stages of production in commercial sandwich manufacture

detectors. Fully automated production is typically confined to sandwiches with a few easily managed ingredients or those incorporating viscous fillings (known as 'splodge and dollop'). Automation facilitates the production of high volumes of basic sandwiches. The manufacture of premium priced sandwiches, however, is usually labour intensive and undertaken by hand. Finished sandwiches are packed into 'skillets' (i.e. triangular plastic or cardboard cartons) for distribution to retail outlets.

As far as the vertical axis of the productive system is concerned, we are particularly concerned here with the constraints exercised by regulatory bodies that bear on sandwich manufacturers (see Figure 7.2). Manufacturers are subject to several potential and actual sources of regulation from above. All are required to comply with health and safety legislation governing food production, which has increased in specificity and scope in recent years (Kjaernes *et al.* 2007). Many also seek to gain accreditation from industry-based regulatory organizations, which set rigorous standards, conduct site inspections and

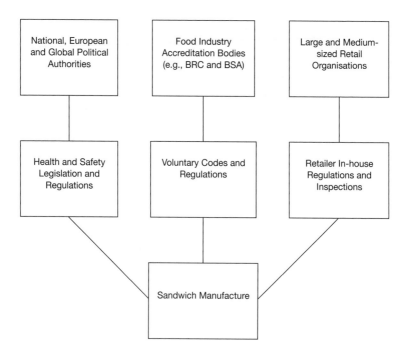

Figure 7.2 Structures of production in commercial sandwich manufacture

monitor voluntary codes of practice. Among the most respected is the British Retail Consortium (BRC). Another important agency is the British Sandwich Association (BSA). A further source of regulation that impinges on some manufacturers derives from retailers. Many small and medium-sized retailers are content to rely solely on requiring manufacturers to obtain BRC, BSA or similar accreditation, rather than undertaking investigations themselves. However, large retailers, such as national supermarket chains, usually have their own intensive in-house inspection processes. These address detailed aspects of the operations of manufacturers. In addition, they also regulate all the steps in the horizontal axis of the productive system. For example, supermarkets frequently inspect suppliers of ingredients and require manufacturers to buy only from approved sources. The controls imposed by large retailers, therefore, do not simply focus on manufacturers' operations but also regulate their relationships with others located earlier in the productive system.

These, then, are the horizontal and vertical axes of the productive system that constitute sandwich manufacture. However, we discern two different forms, or variants, of this productive system. These are defined by differences in the balance of power and locus of control. The key indicator, or marker, of difference is the brand name under which sandwiches are presented to consumers. Where sandwiches carry the brand name of the retailer, the balance of power in the productive system as a whole is weighted towards retailers, who impose stringent controls on manufacturers. We designate this variant as the Retailer Label Productive System or Retailer Label (RL). In contrast, where sandwiches carry the brand name of the manufacturer, not the retailer, the balance of power within the productive system is less heavily weighted towards retailers. Manufacturers typically have greater scope for independent action and innovation. Regulation of manufacturers is less likely to be under the direct control of a small number of retailers. We designate this variant of the productive system Manufacturer Label Productive System or, simply, Manufacturer Label (ML).

The overwhelming majority of sandwiches sold in supermarkets carry the retailer's label, not that of the manufacturer. They are RL products, manufactured in very large numbers and delivered to retailers on a daily basis. Manufacturers may produce sandwiches for more than one retailer, but the volumes demanded by supermarkets usually mean that manufacturers in this productive system are heavily committed to one or two retail chains. Supermarkets, in turn, often develop a close relationship with a limited number of manufacturers and play a significant part in the distribution process. The huge volumes of sandwiches required means that manufacturers are able to automate assembly lines. Relatively few are of sufficient size and capital intensity to compete in this market.

The RL sandwiches sold by large retailers, such as supermarkets, are those with mass appeal. Although supermarkets often also carry a premium range, they tend to concentrate on a standard menu of predictable fillings and breads. This suits large-scale manufacturers who can automate, simplify and maintain long production runs.

> Supermarkets ... they've probably got maximum sort of ten, twelve sandwiches on the shelves. They've got a lot of each filling but, you know, they haven't got that many varieties.
>
> (Julie, National Account Manager, large ML Manufacturer A)

> The standard range is pretty much cut and dry ... Like cornflakes. Everyone does there own version of cornflakes and they are all pretty much the same. So it is the same with tuna and sweet corn sandwich. There is no creativity in it.
>
> (Nigel, NPD Specialist, RL Manufacturer C)

Where huge numbers of sandwiches are being produced and sold, marginal savings on time and resources can be important to manufacturer and retailer alike. Thus, innovations in production processes and marginal cost savings may be as, if not more, significant as creating a new sandwich filling.

Within the RL productive system, power balances favour retailers; the retailer is the predominant locus of control. Retailers award huge contracts, calling for tens of thousands of sandwiches each day. As monopsony purchasers (that is, sole buyers), they are in a position to define product parameters, dictate terms and drive down margins. For their part, manufacturers are vulnerable to shifts in demand from the retailer.

> The retailers are notorious for squeezing the suppliers as much as they possibly can because that's where they make their profit.
>
> (Howard, Senior Manager, Industry Regulation Authority)

> Everybody tends to say that we're very [supermarket name] driven, and that we're almost a slave to [supermarket name] ...

> We are an extension of [supermarket name] really. . . . We do a lot of liaising with them, you know, and obviously presenting new products to them as well. So they're very much heavily involved in the business.
>
> (Abigail, Senior HR Manager, RL Manufacturer B)

> [supermarket name] have a number of policies, which we have to comply with as a supplier, but that's part of doing business. . . . You work within those parameters.
>
> (Owen, Senior Production Manager,
> RL Manufacturer B)

Retailers vary the amount of product they purchase on a daily basis and impose fines on manufacturers who fail to meet quotas. They demand rigorous standards in every aspect of manufacturers' factory operations, employment policies and product handling, enforced by a regime of rigorous in-house inspections. They frequently specify a limited list of suppliers that manufacturers must use.

For their part, manufacturers in the RL productive system necessarily commit themselves to supplying products attuned to the needs and requirements of one or two retailers. They make efficiency savings by building large factories, investing in automated production and employing large workforces. Their plants become dependent on the business provided by just one or two purchasers.

> Dedicated [supermarket name] facility. So we mould ourselves to what [supermarket name] want . . . we do a lot of work to try and make sure that [supermarket name] stay ahead of their competitors. Rather than us staying ahead of our competitors, we make sure [supermarket name] stay ahead of theirs.
>
> (Samantha, Financial Manager,
> RL Manufacturer B)

> The retailers like to have dedicated facilities concentrating solely on their needs.
>
> (Owen, Senior Production Manager,
> RL Manufacturer B)

Periodically, RL manufacturers pitch a range of new product lines to retailers. In this bidding process, manufacturers are in competition with one another and may incur loss of business.

> We compete among ourselves for business and innovation . . .
> [supermarket name] will get their prices that they're looking for
> by making the three of us compete against each other.
>
> (Owen, Senior Production Manager,
> Manufacturer B)

'Category management' is integral to this process. Category management involves manufacturers undertaking market research, and
spotting future trends, in order to appraise retailers of likely shifts
in the demand for products. Much of the costs of this process are
born by manufacturers themselves and, clearly, manufacturers have
an interest in foregrounding their own wares. However, only advice
that proves to be impartial and accurate will be of value to retailers
and, hence, worth retaining by the award of further contracts for
products. Thus, category management involves a delicate balance of
trust and instrumental calculation of self interests.

> So the retailers . . . expect the suppliers to do the work for them
> . . . At the end of the day, the products are vitally important to
> us, we are happy to do that.
>
> (Greg, National Account Manager,
> RL Manufacturer D)

> You are supposed to be making recommendations to the retailer
> as a totally independent body . . . It shouldn't be any concern of
> who's supplying the product. It's . . . what you believe is best for
> the consumer. . . . The benefits are that obviously if you are very
> good at category management, the retailer wants to work with
> you extremely closely. And then obviously bonds a stronger
> relationship . . . over your competitor.
>
> (Eliot, Senior Financial Manager,
> RL Manufacturer B)

The intensity of the controls exercised by supermarkets and other
big retailers reflects the enormous commercial value attached to
their brand names. A consumer scare about just one product carrying
a supermarket's brand can threaten the sales of all. Thus, isolated
problems with a RL sandwich line could damage retailers' entire
business. In response, retailers seek to retain customer loyalty by highlighting reassurances about ethical trading, corporate responsibility,
ecological credentials and hygiene standards. They also minimize risks

to their brand by maximizing their surveillance over manufacturers and suppliers. In so doing, however, they also transfer the legal responsibility, and hence risk, for much 'due diligence' to themselves. Thus, for example, fall-out from a problem with raw materials might well be the legal responsibility of the retailer who specified and inspected the supplier, rather than the manufacturer who was required by the retailer to use this source of ingredients.

In practice, then, the RL productive system is confined to mass production of a limited range of products by a small number of manufacturers for a few national retail outlets. Retailers are mostly national supermarket chains with an established reputation for quality and service. Manufacturers catering for this market operate large plants producing high volumes of a standard range of popular products.

Sandwiches produced within the ML productive system, on the other hand, are sold under the brand name of the manufacturer, not the retail outlet. Packaging carries the name of the producer. ML producers are more varied and heterogeneous than RL producers in scale and character. At one extreme, there are many small producers, often operating out of cramped premises with a handful of staff, servicing the immediate geographical area. Their production rarely involves capital intensive methods. Frequently, firms such as these sell a high proportion of their stock directly to the public from peripatetic company-owned vans travelling between localities, such as industrial estates, where it is known that customers purchase snacks and lunch-time food. Small-scale ML producers also often seek to place sandwiches on the shelves of corner shops, newsagents, garages and similar outlets. Typically, their relationships with these retailers are informal, short-term and involve placing a few products in many different locations. There is often intense competition between small ML manufacturers over price and access to retail outlets, with rivals undercutting one another (see Fuller *et al.* 2006 and 2007).

Medium-sized and large-scale ML producers – with more staff, better premises and operating at a regional or even national level – are less likely to rely on van sales and more likely to sell their sandwiches through shops and restaurants. Some of these retail outlets are similar to those sought by small-scale ML firms; consequently, garages and corner shops may carry sandwich brands that are nationally known alongside those that are highly local. However, medium and large-scale ML producers are also likely to seek formal contracts with larger, established retail outlets, such as universities or hospitals. Usually, such contractual arrangements tie a small number of ML sandwich manufacturers to the retailer over a number of years. Volumes purchased by retailers may vary over time, and shift between firms, but only contracted manufacturers will be used. However, to enter the competition for such contracts requires higher levels of external accreditation than is common among small-scale producers. The investment, expense and trouble involved in attaining and maintaining these accreditation standards restricts the numbers of ML producers who can compete for contracts of this kind.

Some medium and large ML firms consciously adopt a policy of preserving their autonomy from retailers by maintaining a broad customer base, avoiding dependence on a few purchasers. Where manufacturers do business with many retailers, each of whom represents a limited proportion of total sales, retailers are less able to dictate terms to manufacturers.

> It's better to have a diverse customer base . . . it's just spreading your risk.
>
> (Susanna, Senior Operations Manager,
> medium-size ML Manufacturer E)

> We have always said as a company we'd never have a customer more than 10 per cent of our sales . . . if you have something like a supermarket, they'd be sort of 90 per cent of your sales. And they hold you over a barrel with prices. And it's just something we don't want to get into.
>
> (Julie, National Account Manager, large ML Manufacturer A)

Thus, within the ML productive system the balance of power is not so heavily weighted in favour of the retailer. In general, ML manufacturers enjoy a greater degree of discretion in their business activities and are less at the beck and call of retailers.

> The fact it is our brand allows us to do what we want . . . And the fact that we don't have our eggs in one basket also contributes to that.
>
> (Geraint, Senior Production Manager,
> large ML Manufacturer A)

> Everything we do is our decision. We decide we want to move in that direction, so we can do. Although some of our customers do lead us, it's still sort of our decision because it is our brand.
>
> (Ewan, Senior NPD Manager, large ML Manufacturer A)

ML producers are also freer to seek alternative suppliers, rather than those prescribed by the retailer. They are more able to develop products according to their own criteria, without having to seek authorization from monopsony retailers, and to find new and additional retail outlets. The corollary is that, within the ML productive system, each member of the supply chain is more likely to be responsible for due diligence with respect to their own specifications and standards. Greater autonomy is matched by greater legal accountability.

Thus, whereas the RL productive system is, in practice, fairly homogeneous, the ML productive system is more diverse and heterogeneous. ML manufacturers differ in the size of their output, workforce and range of products. Their sphere of operations varies from local through regional to national markets. There is also diversity in the way their products reach end consumers.

Learning to develop new products

In the previous section, we examined the overall characteristics of the productive system of commercial sandwich making, and identified power balances within the RL and ML variants. This section draws out the implications of the two types of productive systems for processes of NPD, and the learning environments of NPD personnel. We will begin by briefly describing the core elements of the NPD process, before moving on to examine ways in which the two productive systems shape patterns of learning and innovation.

NPD specialists, in both RL and ML manufacturers, are in the business of innovation. They draw on a wide range of sources for new sandwiches. They monitor the products of competitors, attend trade fairs and professional venues, compete for industry awards, study culinary texts and seek inspiration from their personal experience of cooking, eating out and holidaying in exotic places. They are acutely interested in interpreting the direction of consumer tastes. They liaise with retailers of their products and involve them in future developments. NPD personnel, then, enjoy opportunities for learning in the workplace that entail crossing boundaries between bodies of knowledge, skill and practice both within and outside the firm.

The NPD process involves strategic and regular changes in products offered to the market, often following a seasonal and/or annual cycle (Akgün and Lynn 2002; van der Valk and Wynstra 2005; Bakker *et al.* 2006; Mikkola and Skjøtt-Larsen 2006). New sandwiches are introduced, existing products amended and established items 'delisted'.

Regular and consistent NPD cycles may constitute a formal and explicit, or informal and implicit, condition of a contract with a retailer. RL manufacturers and larger ML producers employ specialist personnel engaged in NPD and their work constitutes a distinct business function within the organization. NPD work may lead to the development of products that have never before appeared on the shelves of retailers ('new to the market' products). However, it may also involve the development of products that have already proved popular in the marketplace but which have not previously been offered by the firm ('new to the firm' products) (Tether 2000). The latter approach is reactive; it involves identifying and matching market trends. The former is proactive; it generates products that create and lead market trends.

> It could be something completely new sort of blue sky development . . . or it could be that they are taking it from someone else and they want just to match.
> (Rhiannon, Senior NPD Manager, Ingredients Supplier F)

Not least because of labelling regulations, it is difficult for manufacturers of 'new to the market' products to prevent other firms creating 'me too' products within relatively short time periods. Thus, NPD is a continuous and competitive process. Manufacturers like to maintain a degree of secrecy around the work of their NPD departments.

However, notwithstanding similarities between NPD personnel within the two variants of the productive system, there are important contrasts in their roles that have implications for their learning experiences. Differences in the structure of the RL and ML productive systems shape the direction, contents and form of their learning. NPD personnel within the RL productive system, for example, are constrained in their work by the technologies of production used by their employing organizations. Thus, profit maximization requires them to take advantage of the capital investment typical of RL firms. This directs them towards innovation at the high volume, low cost end of the market, where automated and mechanized assembly lines are most effective. These are unlikely to be 'new to the market' products.

> If you've got a certain piece of machinery that you know performs in a very good way and produces sandwiches in a certain way,

but it's a big, big machine and you've spent a lot of money on it, then your NPD could be swayed to always producing or bringing in sandwiches that are able to go down that machine.

(Malcolm, Senior NPD Manager, National
Supermarket Chain)

The high degree of control that retailers exercise over the RL productive system also means that retailers play an active and directive role in the development of new products. NPD personnel often work to specifications generated by retailers that guide the direction and timetable of the innovation process. Initial suggestions for the development of new products may come, wholly or in part, from retailers. Retailers may set specifications for NPD initiatives, and play a part in organizing the NPD process, within the manufacturing company. Signing off a new product typically requires the agreement and approval of the retailer.

[In RL] you are told what you are selling, these are the prices, this is what you've got to sell, this is the promotional activity and this is what you've got to do . . . You've got to work closer with the retailer.

(Eliot, Senior Financial Manager, RL Manufacturer B)

We give them a brief . . . We kind of guide them into what we want.

(Jesse, NPD Manager, National Coffee Shop Chain)

In addition, retailers shape the NPD process through the controls they exercise over suppliers and primary producers located earlier in the stages of sandwich production.

That's the inhibiting thing is that, when you, sort of, develop a sandwich, you have to make sure you've got the right ingredients in it so that [supermarket name] have approved or meet their specs, their minimum specification.

(Samantha, Financial Manager, RL Manufacturer B)

So we don't have much of a choice in certain areas and so that does constrain us a little bit . . . It does narrow who you can work with.

(Nigel, NPD Specialist, RL Manufacturer C)

Because purchasing decisions have such huge potential ramifications for supermarket chains, ML retailers seek to evaluate all the risks and explore the implications of NPD decisions by sandwich manufacturers. This entails co-ordination between a series of stakeholders across manufacturer and retailer companies. As a result, development times can be extended. Furthermore, retailers within the RL productive system are unlikely to opt for untried and unusual products. They are more likely to try to spot emerging market trends, rather than to strike out in wholly new directions. Innovation then tends to be skewed towards 'new to the firm' rather than 'new to the market' products.

> What people are expecting to see . . . is traditional with a twist rather than really wild and whacky flavour combinations.
> (Samantha, Financial Manager, RL Manufacturer B)

> If the product is incredibly popular, it then becomes a commodity product. The minute it starts to become a commodity product people start producing it in mass volumes and the larger manufacturers jump onto the band wagon.
> (Dylan, Managing Director, medium-size ML Manufacturer H)

NPD personnel are at the forefront of managing the relationships of ML manufacturers with monopsony retailers. They engage in extensive consultation and collaboration with retailers and form on-going relationships with their opposite numbers in retailers' organizations. NPD teams within RL manufacturers are often dedicated to working with specific retailers, seeking to match their organizational structures. Category management, in which NPD personnel play a prominent part and which is more extensive in RL than ML firms, plays a major role in these relationships.

> We all man mark different people within [supermarket name]. So we all have different people that we talk to . . . and obviously build a relationship with them.
> (Eliot, Senior Financial Manager, RL Manufacturer B)

NPD personnel in the RL productive system thus acquire knowledge about the culture, style, image and plans of their retailer, both directly and indirectly. They advise retailers but also learn a great deal about their businesses. They become aware not only of trends in the sandwich market but also of how retailers see sales of sandwiches fitting into their market offer as a whole, now and in the future. NPD personnel know that they have to bring forward products that not only conform to the strict regulations imposed by manufacturers but also realize the aspiration of retailers to develop a certain kind of business and to be perceived by consumers in a certain light. NPD personnel, thus, gain a great deal of broadly-based knowledge about the business of their designated retailers and of how their retailer is positioned in the food market as a whole. Not surprisingly, relationships with retailers can be an important source of identification for NPD personnel in RL firms.

> I mean the main job satisfaction probably comes with working for retailers. Because . . . selling just a bacon butty to, you know, some petrol station somewhere, you know, well it is not quite the same as getting a product listed with one of the retailers.
>
> (Nigel, NPD Specialist, RL Manufacturer C)

Within RL firms, NPD departments often contain a number of different specialists, engaged in a variety of roles and ranked in a hierarchy of responsibility and authority. The internal division of labour of the NPD function tends to be more complex, differentiated and stratified in RL than ML firms. NPD personnel learn to co-ordinate and co-operate with colleagues in a corporate process that embraces a range of stakeholders. They are often organized in teams that include specialists not only in food preparation but also other functions such as marketing, category management and sales. RL firms are characterized by relatively structured and formalized NPD processes, with a series of separate steps. NPD personnel thus tend to develop specialist knowledge that is relevant to their particular roles.

In summary, then, new product development by sandwich manufacturers within the RL productive system is heavily influenced by relationships with monopsony retailers, who are involved in devising, developing and signing off new products. The NPD function within RL manufacturing organizations tends to be relatively specialized, differentiated and professionalized. The NPD process is often formalized and organized in a series of steps which involves retailers. There is a tendency to spot and follow emerging market trends rather than shape and lead the market, resulting in a focus on 'new to the firm' products. Hence, the learning environments of NPD personnel are likely to overlap with a wide range of aspects of the learning environments of specific retailers, encourage the development of a broad awareness of industry-wide developments, facilitate the emergence of corporate-based team working with other specialists, generate skills in negotiating formalized procedures, favour 'new to the firm' innovations that match emerging trends in the market, and reward cost-conscious use of mass production technologies.

Turning now to ML manufacturers, many of these are small producers catering for a local market. Elsewhere we have explored the crucial role within small-scale ML production played by van drivers directly involved in selling sandwiches to consumers. We have acknowledged their potential for expansive learning, generated by the range of tasks they undertake and their role as transmitters of marketing information to managers and firm owners (Fuller *et al.* 2006 and 2007). Small-scale sandwich manufacturers are often highly sensitive to shifts in demand for their products and may pride themselves on the speed and care with which they respond to customer requests. However, this usually occurs on an opportunistic and *ad hoc* basis. Van drivers may ensure they carry the favourite sandwich of a particular customer or feedback to managers their experience of selling through particular shops and retail outlets. However, this does not constitute a regular review of the overall product range of the company and the likely direction of market trends. There is no routine cycle of renewal, or process of seasonal launch, of a menu of new or amended products. Rather, changes are short-term and episodic. Thus, small-scale firms in the ML productive system do not commonly undertake systematic, regular and strategic new product development.

> If [van drivers] do come back with any ideas, then we could do that . . . We've got a board out there for orders . . . It doesn't always work cos obviously sometimes we haven't got the ingredients or whatever . . . it's the same people that [van drivers] see, and if one of their customers say: "Oh I would like something", then we'll do that. No, we don't expect them to go out and say: 'Right, new fillings!'.
>
> (Sydney, Owner/Manager, small-scale ML
> Manufacturer J)

Thus, small ML firms rarely have dedicated NPD departments or employ NPD specialists. Furthermore, most of the sandwiches sold by small-scale ML producers fall into a highly predictable range of familiar favourites. Changes to product runs are normally within these parameters and reflect contingent circumstances. Small-scale ML producers are market sensitive, then, but do not engage in NPD. The source of competitive advantage for small-scale ML manufacturers lies not in NPD but in employing alert, personable and able sales staff.

> Oh, you've got to be able to get on with the people haven't you. Definitely . . . Because they buy off *you*, don't they, as opposed to the company. So true.'
>
> (Sydney, Owner/Manager, small-scale ML
> Manufacturer J; respondent's emphasis)

> Basically you've got to have someone who can smile, someone who can actually say: 'You alright? What are you up to at the weekend?'.
>
> (Karl, Owner/Manager, small-scale ML Manufacturer K)

For these reasons, our analysis of NPD within the ML productive system excludes small-scale firms and concentrates, instead, on large-scale organizations.

In contrast to the RL productive system, many larger ML manufacturers perceive profit maximization strategies to include the creation of unusual 'new to the market' products at the premium end of the price range. Cheaper and more predictable sandwiches do also appear in the portfolio of ML firms and are a staple aspect of their offer. However, 'new to market' sandwiches are projected by ML manufacturers as a mark of the quality, added value and versatility of their products, reflected in higher prices. Such sandwiches enliven and enrich the menus offered to retailers. Even when not sold in large numbers, they are perceived as conveying to retailers and consumers a strong and valued image. They also enable manufacturers to aim their menus at lucrative niche markets, such as vegetarians and consumers of 'ethnic' foods.

> We have our core range of our regulars and our premiums . . . When you go with your sample set, it's always lovely to go and see a client and show them something they haven't seen before . . . It is definitely a USP [unique selling point] of ours, you know, that we do innovate and we do try new things.
>
> (Olwen, NPD/Marketing Manager, large ML Manufacturer L)

We've got a range of probably about four hundred products, something like that. So, we can afford to have a few which tell nice stories, are interesting. So when you see the buyers you can show them a sandwich and say: 'Well, that's got broccoli shoots in it, no-one else is using broccoli shoots'.

(Ewan, Senior NPD Manager, large ML
Manufacturer A)

Since unusual new items on the menu are seen as contributing to profitability, NPD personnel enjoy scope to develop a wide range of products, encompassing not only the old favourites but also variations on standard sandwiches and some items that incorporate unexpected ingredients and taste sensations. As a result, large ML producers tend to have a broader range of products on offer than RL firms, even though they produce some of them in relatively small numbers. They are also likely to have a higher proportion of their product range at the premium end of the market, where consumers are more interested in unusual fillings. This approach to innovation is facilitated by the labour intensive modes of production often found in medium and large-size ML firms. Handcrafted production favours short runs of speciality sandwiches.

It would certainly be wrong to suggest that NPD personnel in large ML firms do not consult and liaise with retailers. They monitor patterns of demand from retailers, seek retailers' advice before introducing new products and maintain close contacts through occasions such as product tasting and marketing events. Sales roles are often undertaken by national or regional accounts managers who keep close relationships with retailers. Nevertheless, in the ML productive system the initiative for new product development appears to be more firmly rooted in manufacturing firms themselves, rather than in retailers. Retailers expect ML manufacturers to take the lead in devising new sandwiches and launching new products on the market. This is reflected in a sense of independence and autonomy among NPD personnel in ML firms. Contact with retailers is confined to a limited range of activities that are specific to marketing. Extended partnership relations between retailers and manufacturers – widespread in the RL productive system and covering a broad range of employment policies and practices – are not typical of the ML productive system. Thus, NPD personnel in ML firms engage in more specialized and focused relationships with retailers than do those in RL. Whereas NPD specialists in RL firms cross boundaries with retailers, those in

ML confine relationships with retailers to narrower channels. For example, intensive category management is rarely actively undertaken by ML firms and the decision to launch a new product is typically signed off internally.

> [ML firms] would go out, choose how they're going to do it and then just go and present it to the retailer. Whereas when you're working with the retailer, you've got to get their involvement with it.
>
> (Eliot, Senior Financial Manager, RL
> Manufacturer B)

> [ML firms] decide whether it's right or wrong and go with it or not ... If you're dealing with a [supermarket name] or a [supermarket name] or anything like that ... then it goes up and down the line to technical people and management and then more senior management ... It's very long winded.
>
> (Gordon, Owner/NPD Manager, Supplier M)

Indeed, retailers within the RL productive system, such as super-market chains, may even perceive ML manufacturers as potentially 'difficult', precisely because they are committed to acting independently.

> [ML firms] would look after their brand and would be more prescriptive about what they want to do ... The branded people have quite a bit of power in terms of what they want to do ... [ML] brands can be quite difficult because they just want to do it how they roughly want to do it ... won't do much category management.
>
> (Malcolm, Senior NPD Manager, National
> Supermarket Chain)

While large-scale ML firms frequently employ specialist NPD personnel, our research suggests that their NPD departments are often smaller, less specialized and less stratified than in RL firms. The NPD department may consist of just one or two individuals, often with experience across the business. As a result, NPD personnel within ML firms are more able to roam across all aspects of the product development process. They are also more likely to work informally with colleagues in other parts of the business, since the NPD process is less often divided into a series of fixed, discrete and bounded steps. Thus, for example, NPD managers are more likely to be responsible for taking the product right through the development and launch phases until it reaches the market. They are also likely to carry high levels of responsibility for all aspects of NPD within flattened organizational hierarchies, dealing directly in cross-functional communications with senior managers in other parts of the business that require rapid responses.

> We don't have massive tiers of management . . . Just go straight to the top really, you get the best results that way.
>
> (Julie, National account Manager, large ML Manufacturer A)

Wide-ranging professional roles and a lack of specialization mean that NPD personnel in large-scale ML firms are likely to develop work process knowledge that is specific to the firm and engage in opportunities to participate in multiple roles within the firm (cf. Boreham et al. 2002). Their learning environments cross boundaries within the firm, rather than outside the firm with retailers.

Although NPD within ML firms may take the form of matching the products of other manufacturers, leading to 'new to the firm' innovations, for successful large ML firms 'new to the market' products play a significant part in determining their market share and market profile.

> There is more innovation at the top end . . . People aren't worried about spending more on sandwiches now. So you can do a lot more at that end . . . I'd say there's less innovation at [the cheaper] end . . . There are price points people want and there's limits to what they'll pay . . . There's only so much you can actually take out ingredient-wise, or put in ingredient-wise, to produce a 60p sandwich.
>
> (Ewan, Senior NPD Manager, large ML Manufacturer A)

A focus on 'new to the market' NPD allows ML firms to differentiate their wares from the standard products that dominate supermarket shelves. Unusual 'new to the market' products may not always sell in high numbers but serve to establish a perception of the firm as a high quality market leader.

We're definitely kind of top tier sandwiches. That's what we market it as . . . And the client base that we have almost demand a kind of more exciting sandwich . . . We have to keep our image fresh . . . You retain your customers by showing that you're continually evolving.

> (Stanley, Operations Manager, large ML
> Manufacturer L)

The wow factor . . . people add it onto their order just to have a look at it. So it just gets people talking.

> (Olwen, NPD/Marketing Manager, large ML
> Manufacturer L)

A sort of all singing all dancing sandwich . . . it's a bit too wacky, so it's de-listed this year, but we weren't really expecting it to be a top seller. It was there to be on the menu, to be interesting and to show.

> (Ewan, Senior NPD Manager, large ML
> Manufacturer A)

Less specialization, fewer hierarchies, more attenuated relationships with retailers and less differentiated stages in the NPD process mean that product development and launch can take place quickly in the ML productive system.

We can make a decision in the morning and . . . by the afternoon it's well on its way. Which is great for product development and things like that.

> (Olwen, NPD/Marketing Manager, large ML
> Manufacturer L)

In summary, then, new product development within the ML productive system is heavily influenced by profit maximizing strategies that prioritize 'new to the market' innovations at the premium, or top end, of the product range. There is a greater willingness to create market trends, rather simply follow them with 'me too' or 'new to the firm' products. A focus on premium sandwiches and less capital intensive production methods afford NPD personnel in larger ML firms greater scope to create unusual, pioneering and imaginative products. While consulting and liaising with retailers, NPD personnel enjoy a greater degree of autonomy, independence and initiative in devising

and developing new products. The NPD function within ML manufacturers tends to be less specialized, differentiated and stratified.
The NPD process is often less formalized. Hence, the learning environments of NPD personnel are less likely to overlap and meld with
those of retailers, but may be more likely to offer opportunities to
work fluidly and flexibly with colleagues inside the employing firm.

Conclusion

In this chapter we have deployed the Working as Learning Framework
(WALF) to analyse and explain the roles, constraints and opportunities
encountered by staff engaged in new product development (NPD)
within the commercial sandwich making industry. We have seen that
contrasts in the balance of power within the Manufacturer Label (ML)
and Retailer Label (RL) productive systems shape learning environments and patterns of innovation. Small ML firms have few incentives
to engage in systematic NPD processes; their profit maximization
strategies revolve around the marketing abilities of sales staff in face-
to-face interaction with retailers. However, the dynamics of the
productive system ensure that both RL and large ML manufacturers
have a keen interest in product innovation and development. In the
case of RL producers, NPD is primarily focused on massproduced,
mass marketed, 'new to firm' products, which pick up emerging market
trends. Larger ML manufacturers, however, place a greater weight
on 'new to the market' products, which set new trends in consumer
tastes and may be hand-made and premium-priced as a result. Each
approach offers NPD specialists distinctive spheres of discretion and
autonomy in developing their skills and in forming relationships with
colleagues. These differences are explained by the contrasting power
balance between retailers and manufacturers in the ML and RL
productive systems.

NPD specialists in RL firms cross boundaries between their firm
and the monopsony retailer. However, they are limited in their
opportunities to cross boundaries within their employing firm by
functional specializations, managerial hierarchies and procedural
protocols. Their creative energies are also channelled toward 'new to
the firm' products as a result of the dependence of RL firms on high
volume, highly automated production runs. In contrast, NPD personnel
in the ML productive system are in contact with many more retailers
but have more specialized and narrowly-focused relationships with
them. They know less about a greater number of retailers (there are

interesting parallels here with the patterns of expertise developed by contact centre operators discussed in Chapter 3). Moreover, the character of their contacts with retailers affords them greater autonomy in developing new products. The role of NPD personnel in devising and launching 'new to the market' products is central to the establishment of credibility of ML firms with customers and profitability in the marketplace. Furthermore, within ML firms, the organization of NPD work is more informal and less specialized than in RL firms.

In addition to demonstrating the utility of the Working as Learning Framework, this chapter has extended our conceptualization in two respects. First, this case study further highlights the importance, for understanding processes of learning, of tracing relationships of authority, power and control across productive systems. In particular, the contrasting work organization, investment patterns, product development and marketing strategies characteristic of RL and ML manufacturing firms must be understood in terms of the sources of power and control – reflected in processes of surveillance and discipline – within the industry as a whole. Monopsony purchasers of RL products were able to exert huge influence over business operations located further back in the stages of the productive system. Their control over the channels through which products reached consumers enabled them to determine many aspects of the ways in which NPD specialists in RL manufacturing firms envisaged and realized their work roles, and hence their learning environments. Where retailers were less dominant in regulating access to markets, as was the case with ML manufacturers, those engaged in NPD faced different kinds of constraints and opportunities but enjoyed more autonomy. In commercial sandwich making, then, powerful controls over the 'early' stages of the productive system are exercised by participants strategically positioned relatively 'late' in the sequence of activities. As such, this case study provides interesting contrasts with aerobics classes, discussed in Chapter 5 of this book. Aerobics instructors teaching 'pre-choreographed' classes found themselves subject to intense regulation and discipline exercised from the 'early' stages of the productive system by companies that had successfully developed and marketed high profile work outs. Their opportunities for self-directed learning were curtailed as a result of the standardization imposed by these global providers of class routines. In our interviews, both aerobics instructors who hankered after the greater autonomy offered by 'freestyle' teaching, and senior personnel within ML sandwich manufacturers, spoke of the freedoms and the challenges of being independent from stringent controls wielded by those elsewhere in the stages of production.

A second contribution of this chapter is the opportunity it provides for us further to explore aspects of the expansive–restrictive continuum; in particular, to specify some of the intermediary positions occupied by different types of learning environments along the continuum. In Chapter 2, it was emphasized that expansiveness and restrictiveness are relative terms and not discrete variables. Thus, not all learning environments are wholly expansive or restrictive; some entail a mixture or combination of elements. Indeed, our case study has detected elements of both expansiveness and restrictiveness in the occupational roles and learning territories of NPD personnel in RL and ML firms.

Differences in the combination of expansive and restrictive elements in the learning environments of NPD specialists are a reflection of the overall structure, or configuration, of the networks of relationships that characterize the two productive systems of commercial sandwich production. NPD specialists in RL manufacturers have rich and complex relationships with dedicated retailers that span a broad range of professional activities and employment processes. They are engaged in partnership relationships which, in professional terms, are varied in nature. The balance of power within the RL productive system, which favours large retailers, makes the assiduous cultivation of such relationships a necessary and important task. Processes such as category management, product development, site inspections and NPD pitches provide important venues where engagement with retailers takes place. However, the number of retailer organizations with which NPD specialists conduct such relationships are few; indeed, often they are confined to just one organization. We may, then, characterize the social networks of NPD specialists in RL firms as involving in-depth relationships with a small number of specific outside bodies. In colloquial terms, their networks relationships, and learning opportunities, are 'fat but few'.

In contrast, NPD specialists in ML firms have more narrowly defined and circumscribed relationships with retailers. Although they consult and liaise with retail outlets, gleaning market information and advice, they do not form relationships that span a wide range of professional activities and employment processes. They are not required to co-ordinate their employment policies with retailers, seek approval for NPD initiatives and decision-making from retailers, or source their ingredients from suppliers nominated by retailers. ML manufacturers rarely pursue category management and do not dedicate their plant to a few customers. They often seek to avoid dependence on a few monopsony retailers by maintaining a large number of customers, preventing one purchaser from becoming the dominant source of their business and keeping a balance between different types of retail outlets. NPD becomes critical in differentiating the products of larger ML firms from one another and in creating a reputation for quality and high standards. NPD personnel in large ML firms are engaged in relationships with retailers that are intense but narrowly focused on specific business issues. We may, then, characterize the social networks of NPD specialists in large ML firms as comprising relatively narrowly-defined relationships with a relatively large number of external organizations. In colloquial terms, their networks relationships, and learning opportunities, are 'thin but many'.

This analysis, therefore, allows us to cast further light on the concept of expansive and restrictive learning environments and the expansive–restrictive continuum. In its classic sense, expansiveness embraces the 'many' and 'fat' dimensions of learning affordances. It involves both crossing multiple boundaries and acquiring rich in-depth knowledge, skills and practices. In contrast, restrictiveness is a product of 'few' and 'thin' learning environments. It entails lack of access to a broad range of learning experiences and a shallowness of engagement. The two types of NPD specialists in sandwich making who are the focus of this chapter do not conform to either of these categorizations. They are not located at either of the extreme poles of the expansive–restrictive continuum. Rather, they occupy intermediary positions. However, their learning environments are not identical. Their contrasting combinations of expansive and restrictive elements – fat and few, thin and many – generate different types of innovation and patterns of learning.

Chapter 8

Utilizing artefacts

Introduction

All workplaces contain resources of various types that have been created internally as part of the work process or have been introduced from external sources. These resources are created, used, refined, updated, discarded, and sometimes rediscovered, as part of everyday workplace activity. Some take the form of pieces of equipment provided by employers, such as scissors in a hairdressing salon (Lee *et al.* 2007), knives in a restaurant kitchen (Kakavelakis 2008) or the headsets used by the call centre operators discussed in Chapter 3. Some are fashioned by workers as personalized tools of the trade: for example, musical compilations copied onto CDs and choreography notes written by the 'freestyle' exercise to music instructors discussed in Chapter 5. Some resources, of course, are designed by management to exert control, such as wall charts displaying daily targets or devices for checking faults which may be computerized to make the storage and transfer of performance data easier (for the use of wall charts in commission-based sales, see Kakavelakis *et al.* 2008). Other resources may have a more symbolic purpose, such as in-company newsletters, designed to encourage a sense of community and shared purpose.

All of these resources are captured by the term 'artefact' (which can also be spelt as 'artifact'); a term used extensively in the literature on Cultural Historical Activity Theory (CHAT) as one of the three elements of an activity system (see, *inter alia*, Engeström 2001; Chaiklin and Lave 1993). In its simplest form, such a system comprises a subject (an individual or group of people who are the focus of study), an object (the raw material or problem towards which the subject's activity is directed), and a set of mediating artefacts that can be used to mould the object into the desired outcome. The concept of mediation comes from the work of the Russian developmental psychologist Vygotsky (1978), whose contribution to social science was his thesis that the human mind cannot be understood in isolation from the social world. Human beings exert agency by producing and using tools, which then form part of what Engeström (2001: 136) has called the historical 'sediment' that characterizes all activity systems, including workplaces: 'the activity system itself carries multiple layers and strands of history engraved in its artifacts, rules and conventions'.

Workplace artefacts also form a key part of Actor–Network Theory (ANT), which is concerned with how power, control and organization are established and reproduced in diffuse social networks (see, *inter alia*, Law and Hassard 1999; Mutch 2002). ANT suggests that such networks comprise and are held together by the relationships between human and non-human 'actants', such as texts, devices and disciplines. This theory is particularly helpful to our analysis of the relationship between the different structures and stages of production that are central to the Working as Learning Framework (WALF) outlined in this book. Some artefacts can also take on the role of what CHAT theorists refer to as 'boundary objects', in that they can be used to mediate between different spheres of activity (see Tuomi-Grohn *et al.* 2003), propagate knowledge within and across different contexts (Beach 2003) or, as Wenger, drawing on Star (1989), puts it, 'co-ordinate the perspectives of various constituencies for some purpose' (Wenger 1998: 106).

In this chapter, we acknowledge the important insights provided by CHAT's and ANT's use of the concept of artefacts, but we argue that the role of artefacts in the workplace is more complex and problematic than the way it is sometimes portrayed. The chapter examines their influence on both participation in and access to learning. We argue that those involved in particular structures and stages of production can extend their reach by designing or redesigning artefacts to create new 'practices of use' and meanings (Wenger 1998: 108). Artefacts have the potential, then, to facilitate learning between people in different parts of the productive system across and within workplaces and jobs. However, this capacity can only be fully understood by situating artefacts in a network of relationships and perspectives which differ in character. Whereas the CHAT concept of artefacts as boundary objects focuses on their ability to mediate relations, we argue that because they are embedded in and arise out of the productive system, they are often at the interface of perspectives which are hard to reconcile. For example, our case study of a group of health visitor teams (see Chapter 4) indicated that key artefacts associated with their professional practice, such as scales to weigh babies and hypodermic needles to immunize them, were seen by some health visitors as contested symbols of the restrictive nature of their working lives and learning environments. However, their attempts to change the way they used these artefacts was strongly resisted by doctors and other health visitors (Jewson et al. 2008). In line with ANT, we recognize artefacts as instruments of control but also highlight their Janus-like ability simultaneously to expand as well as restrict worker involvement.

To address these themes, the chapter draws on evidence from two contrasting sectors: automotive component manufacturing and super-market retailing. The chapter begins with an outline of the research sites and the data gathering techniques we used. It then presents the results in two substantive sections. The first of these focuses on how workplace practices within two automotive component manu-facturers were reified in order to demonstrate to parent companies and/or clients that the workforce was competent. In one case workplace assessors wanted to take their learning further but were prevented from doing so, while in another key artefacts were widely shared and utilized well beyond their intended target group. The second substantive section of the chapter also shows that artefacts may be used in ways not always intended by their immediate creators. It shows how, in supermarket retailing, a managerial tool of long-distance control could, under certain circumstances, be used by subordinate employees to reassert their influence on the productive process. The chapter ends with a conclusion that outlines how studying artefacts can provide researchers with another way of using the Working as Learning Framework (WALF). This highlights how opportunities for teaching, learning and assessment need to relate to how such resources are used in practice.

Collecting the evidence

Although no major British-owned vehicle manufacturers remain, the automotive sector still employs over half a million people, with a further 100,000 in related occupations, and 'comprises 70,000 businesses with a turnover of over £130 billion per annum accounting for 3 per cent of UK GDP' (SSDA and Automotive Skills, 2004: 1).

The performance of the automotive industry has been criticized because productivity has been considerably lower than in similar companies in competitor nations, such as Germany, the US and, in particular, Japan. British firms were seen as being too slow to adopt and embed new modes of working and best practice techniques (see, inter alia, Barlow and Chatterton 2002; Mason and Wagner 2002; LSC 2007). Particular criticism has been levelled at the automotive supply chain. UK suppliers are being edged out due to 'perceived weak performance in innovation [and] engineering' (SMMT 2002: 12) and fierce price competition from firms in low-wage economies (Rhys 2004). Boer et al. (2005: 356) have observed that, in the automotive industry, 'the battlefield of competition is increasingly moving from the level of individual firms to that of supply chains'.

We draw on evidence collected in two companies involved in this sector (referred to as Green Company and Brown Company). Both are based in the UK and make parts for global car manufacturers (for a more detailed discussion, see Unwin et al. 2008a). The results presented here focus on production workers involved in the manufacturing process. Both companies have introduced initiatives aimed at accrediting the skills and knowledge of production workers through the use of competence-based National Vocational Qualifications (NVQs). These initiatives provided the focus of our research and enabled us to investigate the role of artefacts in a manufacturing context. Those implementing the new programmes found themselves engaged in the task of reifying workplace processes and procedures and designing 'products' for use in new forms of participation (e.g. workplace assessment) linked to the introduction of the NVQs. As we will show, existing workplace artefacts became imbued with new meaning as a result of their role as pedagogical resources in the accreditation process.

This evidence was collected over a period of three years. We visited both companies eight times for one or two days at a time and also corresponded with managers via email and telephone between visits. Initially, face-to-face interviews were held with senior and line managers to gather information about business and Human Resource Development strategy and challenges. Samples of employees were then identified for interview. As well as face-to-face interviews with individuals and small groups, data was gathered through work shadowing and observation on the production floor, and through reviews of company documentation. A total of 25 people were interviewed in Green Company and 26 in Brown Company. At the end of the planned fieldwork phase, the opportunity arose to work with the Open University on a DVD of workplace learning for a new module in the Master's in Education. Green Company agreed to participate in the filming. This enabled us to carry out further non-participant observation and a further eight interviews over an intensive two-day period.

The research reported in this chapter also collected evidence on the use of artefacts in supermarket retailing (see Fuller *et al.* 2008). This illustrates how a focus on the role and utilization of workplace artefacts can shed light on the changing relationship between central management control and local employee discretion. Ordering and managing stock is a key function in retailing in general, and in food retailing in particular. In large chains, such as supermarkets, as corporate management seeks ways to optimize performance, the task is increasingly mediated and facilitated via information technology and electronic systems. From the perspective of Head Office, individual stores can be viewed as the transmitters of customer demands into the supply chain, thus enabling continuous replenishment of stock and feedback into purchasing strategy. Other authors argue that the use of computerized information systems in retailing 'begs for, and facilitates, more centralized management' (Kinsey and Ashman 2000: 86). An important artefact here is a device known as the 'symbol gun'. This electronic device is used in stores to check that the physical stock available on the shelves accords with what the computer states the store should have. This information is then used to replenish, collate and write off stock.

Our research in this sector was based in a nationwide chain of supermarkets in Britain which, at the time of our research, employed over 50,000 staff and had a multi-billion pound turnover (referred to here as 'The Supermarket'). In the first phase of the study, we conducted 18 interviews with personnel at all levels in two similarly sized stores in the English Midlands, as well as with the area manager who had overall responsibility for several outlets. For the purposes of our subsequent study (the main focus of this chapter), we conducted two interviews with staff at Head Office to get their perspective on the issues surrounding stock management and the relationship between individual stores and the Head Office. These were followed by 13 interviews with store managers, trading managers and stock management supervisors in four stores, two in Wales and two in Southern England, as well as with the area managers responsible for the stores in these two localities.

Depending on size, stores typically employed three trading managers. Each was responsible for a major area of stock – such as, 'ambient' (e.g. tins and dry goods), and 'fresh' (meat, dairy, fruit and vegetables) – or for 'customer service'. They reported directly to the store manager. In addition, we had the chance to shadow some of the research participants as they performed their day-to-day jobs, and to collect a range of documents, such as 'planograms' (instructions on how stock should be laid out and presented) and weekly stock offers and promotions.

Accrediting learning in automotive manufacturing

Since 2002, Green Company has been a wholly-owned subsidiary of a foreign car manufacturer, but has a long history of independence dating back to the 1920s when it was established as a supplier to the then British car industry. Since its establishment, Green Company has weathered a commercial roller coaster of take-overs and mergers. At the time of the research, it employed around 1,000 people. Brown Company employed a similar number and operated as a wholly-owned subsidiary of an overseas company which fabricated components for a number of car manufacturers in plants in France, Canada, Spain, Mexico and the UK.

In both cases, therefore, plant level management in the UK reports, via its own Head Office, to an overseas owner located in the higher echelons of the vertical axis, or structures, of the productive system (see Figure 8.1). These, in turn, have to follow international standards agreed by the International Automotive Task Force (IATF), a group of large vehicle manufacturers and national trade associations. This standard (referred to as TS-16949) addresses the development, design, production, installation and servicing of automotive-related products; in short, it covers all aspects of what we have referred to as the stages of production in our Working as Learning Framework (WALF). International regulation of the supply chain began in 1994, led by Daimler-Chrysler, Ford and General Motors, but has developed significantly since then to become the globally accepted standard in the automotive industry.

Both companies produce component parts for car manufacturers located at a later stage in the sequence, or stages, of production (see Figure 8.2). These manufacturers can exert significant control over how the components that make up a car are produced. Viewed from

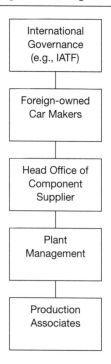

Figure 8.1 Structures of production of two automotive component manufacturers

the perspective of the productive system, this control is exercised backwards along the supply chain (for a similar example of backward control, see sandwich making reported in Chapter 7). The level of control is at its most pronounced in the case of Green Company, since it is owned by its one and only customer. By supplying a number of car manufacturers, none of whom have an ownership stake, Brown Company enjoys a little more leeway in how it conducts business. However, as we will show, both companies came under pressure – mainly from those located at later points in the stages of production – to demonstrate worker competence. In the UK, the NVQ was the most obvious artefact to use for this purpose.

Figure 8.2 Stages of production of two automotive component manufacturers

Competence-based qualifications were introduced in the UK from the late 1980s onwards as part of government attempts to reform the existing provision of vocational qualifications. The new NVQs (or SVQs as they were referred to in Scotland) posed a major challenge to existing qualifications in several respects. Their content was based on national occupational standards identified by sector-based, employer-led bodies, which were described in terms of 'competences' rather than a syllabus of theories and techniques. Moreover, their assessment was based on criterion-referencing, conducted in the workplace. The worth of the associated certificates lies in their claim to attest to employees' occupational competence. However, NVQs remain highly controversial, with commentators questioning the validity and reliability of the processes that lead to the award of the qualification. Particular concerns have been raised about the relatively low emphasis placed on the testing of underpinning knowledge (see, *inter alia*, Wolf 1995; Hager 2004).

The NVQ initiative in Green Company arose when it was asked by its foreign parent company – located higher up the vertical structure of production – to bid for the contract to supply up to 90 per cent of the parts for a new model of car. The General Manager of Green Company saw the contract as an opportunity to 'prove competence' to the parent company and, hence, put the relationship on a solid footing. There were two key areas where he felt Green Company had been paying lip service to standards: health and safety, and training and development. When interviewed, he said that 'it was difficult to know if the unskilled part of the workforce [the majority] was really competent'. The use of the term 'unskilled' (which actually meant unqualified) is indicative of the lack of recognition of shop-floor workers' expertise, and the privileging of certified skills and knowledge.

In recent years, the introduction of automated press lines and the need for workers (known throughout the industry as 'production associates' or just 'associates') to be able to operate flexibly across lines led to substantive changes in the way work was organized and to reductions in the size of the workforce. Historically, when lines were manual and labour intensive, associates tended only to work on one line. This resulted in groups of associates with a wealth of experience in restricted line-related tasks, but lacking a shared understanding of the work process and a wider set of skills and knowledge. However, the latter was increasingly seen as crucial to the facilitation of flexible working, boundary crossing, and, above all, as a means of ensuring quality standards and the elimination of faults.

The company decided to develop a Competence Assessment Programme (CAP). This was built around the NVQ Level Two in Process Manufacturing Operations (PMO). This was in line with the automotive industry's global quality standard (TS-16949). Car manufacturers, including the owner and sole client of Green Company, insisted that all those involved at earlier points in the horizontal axis of production adhered to this standard. The company could have contracted out the CAP to an external training provider, but decided to work in the spirit of the competence-based approach. As such, it created an in-house programme that drew on the expertise of experienced associates as well as the company's training department. Three experienced employees were selected to work full-time on devising a practical framework for implementing the CAP. They were also given the responsibility of assessing their peers (other associates) and ensuring that the target number of NVQs was achieved. In line with the approach embedded in the NVQ model, the focus in creating the new system was on the assessment of existing skills and knowledge, not on the teaching and learning of new skills and knowledge. Despite this somewhat restrictive remit, the work of the CAP team included the development of new forms of participation enacted through engagement with either new artefacts or the new uses to which existing artefacts were put (see p. 167). For the period that the CAP operated, then, the workplace became a more expansive environment for associates and, particularly, for the members of the assessment team (Fuller and Unwin 2004).

To carry out the assessment process, the team utilized a range of resources that we have categorized in two ways. In the first of these, the assessors identified existing workplace artefacts (such as written quality specifications, tools for checking tolerances and measurements, and instructions on computer screens) that could be used in the on-the-job assessment process. The team's rationale for this approach was that observing associates' everyday engagement with these sorts of resources would enable them to conduct authentic and meaningful assessments of associate competence in carrying out day-to-day tasks in the workplace. Through the implementation of this strategy, the artefacts maintained their original workplace function, but gained new meaning (for assessors and those being assessed) as devices for assessing competence. The second category of artefacts consisted of those that the team deliberately created to facilitate and record the assessment process. These included tracking sheets, photographs and portfolios for filing documentation. The associates' engagement with both these types of artefacts generated opportunities for them to show their assessors that they had the skills to perform the required operations to the required standard. However, in addition to these strategies, the assessors decided that a further method, which they termed the 'professional discussion', was also needed to draw out the extent of associates' knowledge.

> This [the professional discussion] involved taking the candidate into a quiet room, because it's very noisy on the shop-floor, and we, we had a, a couple of pages of, of notes or questions. Not really questions as such but topics that we wanted to talk about. And we recorded this just, just to save ourselves a lot of pen work writing it all down. And we covered, in a professional discussion we covered, again, all six units of the assessment.
>
> (Bob, Assessor, Green Company)

The professional discussion was recorded onto CD and associates received a copy to put in their portfolios. As an artefact, the CD was the means to capture the outcome of the discussion that enabled workers to make explicit their tacit knowledge (cf. Nonaka and Takeuchi 1995). More importantly, it provided a public record of the formal process of assessment, manifested through an observable and consistent process of questions and answers. The creation of the professional discussion provides a good example of what Wenger (1998) refers to as the duality of reification and participation. In this case, the reification that characterized the professional discussion enabled a new form of participative practice to emerge.

From our observations of this new form of interaction, it was clear that the professional discussion had more than symbolic meaning as a testament to associate competence – it also had value as a pedagogic practice. The three assessors employed high levels of pedagogical skill, including the ability to structure their questioning in a supportive way, the use of cues and prompts to help the associates reflect on their knowledge, and provide praise and encouragement as a means to keep associates motivated. The assessors said that both they and the associates were surprised at how much knowledge was revealed through this process, and that the majority of associates appeared to enjoy the discussions. Some associates were very nervous and a minority were resistant to the process, but the majority felt that they had reminded themselves of how much they knew and that this was empowering. The new form of participation enabled through the professional discussion provided an example of what we have called the 'elasticity of NVQs' (Unwin *et al.* 2008a). The assessment team was able to use the model to create an innovative form of practice that helped surface and explore associates' knowledge and understanding. In so doing they created a collective confidence in the assertion of workforce competence, symbolized through the award of NVQs.

Some workers expressed ambivalence in that they went along with the process, but regarded it as having more meaning for associates who were newer to the job. Moreover, the assessors revealed that some line leaders were less enthusiastic about taking part in the CAP than the people they supervised. The NVQ process placed them back on an equal footing with associates whom they managed. In these circumstances, some line leaders felt that they were under more pressure than associates to 'prove' their competence. This reminds us that experienced workers who are asked to 'prove' competence in tasks that they have been performing day in, day out, for several years may find the process threatening or even demeaning.

As far as the company was concerned, the CAP initiative was very successful in that it achieved its main goal of demonstrating to the parent company its workers' competence. In addition, the process itself led to quality improvements by sharpening associates' quality checking skills. For example, although new tools had been introduced to check components, not all workers were using them precisely. The ability to use the tools correctly was included as a key competence in the CAP and, as a result, faults were dramatically reduced. Despite this success, however, the company failed to build on the CAP in terms of creating opportunities for associates to progress to the next level (Level Three). By running the CAP and introducing new forms of participation for both the CAP team and the associates, the company raised employee expectations. The three assessors were parachuted into roles for which they had had very little training, but developed considerable and wide-ranging expertise (including organizational, pedagogical and social) as a result of their experience. In addition, everyday workplace artefacts were transformed into assessment devices and in the process new ones were created. Both were used in the new practices of assessment and participation that they designed and introduced. However, sadly, at Green Company the assessors were sent back to their production jobs when the CAP finished.

The trigger for Brown Company's use of NVQs came from increasing and intensive competition from other producers, particularly from those in Eastern Europe. At the same time, one of its major customers ended the company's status as a 'tier one supplier' due to weaknesses in product quality. Raising the skill levels of the workforce was seen as a crucial way of responding. A further important driver was the introduction of a new global quality standard, which required companies to show how the workforce was developed to ensure competence. The Training Manager commented:

> They don't tell you what competency means. There's no definition of competency. And competency, as you know, is one of those concepts there's a lot of argument around: What it is? Can you describe it? What does it mean? ... the [NVQ] national framework [is used] as a protection against third party audit. So, when an order comes in that says how do you train your guys? We tell them. What's the standard? We can show them ... it's the national standard.
>
> (Derek, Training Manager, Brown Company)

In contrast to Green Company, the senior managers at Brown Company gave the Training Manager and his three full-time trainers the responsibility for constructing the competence-based programme. Unlike Green Company, there was an explicit training focus stemming from a recognized need to improve workforce skills and not simply to accredit existing levels of competence. Accordingly, 95 production operators were selected for training as 'Skills Tutors'. Initially, the 'tutors' themselves were put through a programme to achieve the NVQ and 30 also acquired the necessary competencies to perform the role of assessors. The introduction of the initiative provided an opportunity, then, for a significant minority of the workforce to engage in new forms of participation as workplace tutors and assessors. Each tutor was assigned one or more operators to train on the shop floor as part of everyday workplace activity. The tutors prepared action plans for their tutees and gave written as well as oral feedback following assessments. Given the varied nature of individual dispositions to learning, not all employees approached the competence-based initiative in the same way (see Chapter 5 for another example of how individual workers respond to different learning environments according to their own personal backgrounds; also, Hodkinson and Hodkinson 2004b; Evans *et al.* 2006; Billett 2007a and 2007b).

The training team developed one key artefact as the focus for their programme. This took the form of a 'tutor pack' comprising detailed descriptions of the shop-floor tasks and associated quality checks. The pack was to be used for two main purposes: to provide a guide for production workers (particularly new entrants) to all the tasks they would be required to perform; and to act as a vehicle for discussions between workers and assessors when competences were being assessed. The packs comprised A4 files containing sheets of text and diagrams, located on every work station throughout the plant. They were described by the trainers as 'live' documents that were being continually updated and improved through the input of employees at all levels, including specialist engineers and operatives. The Training Manager insisted that the key driver for using a competence-based approach was the need to prove everyone was working to a clear standard. However, the 'live' nature of the tutor pack meant that discussions (and to some extent negotiations) were taking place on a regular basis. These were about how to convey through the pack that better ways of practice were being identified through everyday workplace activity. In this sense, this artefact could be seen as a boundary object as 'it lends itself to various activities and purposes' (Wenger 1998: 107).

The Training Manager argued that the involvement of employees in the continued development of the pack led to the creation of a shared vocabulary for production staff, which enabled employees to talk about skills and knowledge, negotiate meanings and develop collective understanding. This was reinforced through daily team meetings at which supervisors discussed how the different shifts were meeting the plant's key performance indicators in relation to production targets, quality checks and the minimization of waste. As in the case of Green Company, workers in Brown Company were surprised at the extent to which the competence-based process had made them aware of their skills and knowledge. At the same time, however, there was more evidence at Brown that the process had sought and had revealed competence gaps. The motivational benefit of achieving a qualification is illustrated by this comment from a worker who progressed on to the NVQ Level Three and then worked as a supervisor:

> I mean I was just like any other production operator. I'd come in, done the job and go home again until I done this NVQ. And from that I thought to myself: 'Well, I could do better for myself than here I can and I can maybe step on to the rungs of the ladder' ... And that's where I was glad that the company give me opportunities to do the next NVQ level 3.
>
> (Reg, Supervisor, Brown Company)

Our evidence supports some of the concerns expressed in the literature about the NVQ-related model of competence and the instrumentalism that now characterizes assessment practices in many education and training settings (see Torrance 2007). We would note, in particular, that the model's permissiveness means that it is more likely to be used for restrictive than expansive purposes. Hence, on the one hand, NVQs can be used as artefacts in an accounting process to produce perceived 'proof' of competence to customers and external regulators (or by governments as targets for organizations to meet or as evidence in international league tables of qualification stocks). On the other hand, they can be used as a means to stimulate the motivation for learning, as platforms for further learning, and as boundary objects in an expansive approach to collaborative workplace learning. In today's target-driven and highly pressurized economic climate, the former approach has considerable appeal for employers in both the public and private sectors.

In Brown Company, the tutor pack, created as an artefact of the competence programme, proved to be a very effective boundary object because it was used by all grades of workers in the plant as a shared space for articulating expertise that could be used on a daily basis. In addition, the competence programme was seen from the start as much more than simply a vehicle for auditing existing skills and, hence, was underpinned by a more expansive concept of workforce development. This meant that progression opportunities were seen as central to the initiative. In Green Company, the professional discussion that was created as an artefact of the competence programme introduced a pedagogical aspect to the assessment system, which was valued by assessors and those being assessed. However, the perspective of the company's senior management team – that the CAP was simply a tool for proving competence to its customer which could be removed once all associates had been assessed – meant that the potential for work-force development that had been opened up through the generation of new participatory practices was subsequently lost. This reminds us that although forms of reification, such as the professional discussion, 'can take a life of their own, beyond the context of origin', nevertheless 'their meaningfulness is always potentially expanded and potentially lost' (Wenger 1998: 62).

Managerial control in supermarket retailing

Our initial interviews in supermarket retailing suggested that the use of computerized systems was centralizing the stock management function. This was having the effect of reducing local employees' involvement in the process and their ability to influence the range and quantity of products being ordered for their stores. Some longer-serving staff were concerned that having less personal and collective discretion to tailor stock requirements could have an adverse effect on the achievement of key performance indicators in the areas of sales, waste and availability. In addition, declining discretion was associated by some employees with less skill and, therefore, lower job satisfaction. Some interviewees identified the 'symbol gun' as a key device in controlling the 'stock store management' system. As one observed:

> These little guns obviously are controlling . . . Obviously we're putting all the information in to that, which takes it to the computers. So, I mean, without these in this store, we wouldn't know what our stock levels were and we'd be in a bit of a mess. We do rely on those.
>
> (Barbara, Systems Manager, Store A, The Supermarket)

It is important, however, to locate the stock control process in the productive system of food retailing. This draws attention not only to the relevance of the vertical relations of regulation and control between the constituent networks but also to the stages of production (horizontal interconnections) by which raw materials are transformed into goods bought by those who shop at supermarkets. One of the contributions of the Working as Learning Framework (WALF) is that it enables us to characterize the learning environments of any particular group of workers by the distinctive intersection of vertical and horizontal relationships under which work is conducted. To put it another way, work can be characterized by its location in the productive system; it can come earlier or later in the sequence of production and higher or lower in the hierarchy of regulation and control.

In this chapter our interest is in understanding where store management teams are positioned, how their work is organized via devices, and what opportunities for discretion and learning are thereby generated – a set of relationships captured by the Working as Learning Framework. ANT's notion that such networks comprise and are held together by the relationships between human and non-human 'actants' provides a complementary perspective. In the case of supermarket retailing, it allowed us to explore how the use of artefacts, such as the symbol gun, enabled long-distance control to be exercised across the supermarket chain as a whole, and also the effects this had on the discretion enjoyed by store staff. Here, long-distance control was exercised from the top of the vertical axis of production over those at the bottom (see Figure 8.3). It stretched from Head

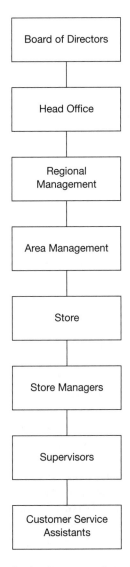

Figure 8.3 Structures of production in supermarket retailing

Figure 8.4 Stages of production in supermarket retailing

Office, through regional and area management down to those located in the stores, and, in particular, those involved in managing the stock – store managers, trading managers and supervisors. Furthermore, the symbol gun not only regulated stock ordering by store managers, but also gave Head Office management greater control over orders placed with suppliers, manufacturers and wholesalers located earlier in the horizontal axis of the productive system (see Figure 8.4). There are parallels here with the analysis of commercial sandwich making presented in Chapter 7.

ANT allows us to address the relationship between different aspects of the productive system and, in particular, how it is mediated in a distributed and dispersed process, such as stock management in a large chain of supermarkets. When an actor-network is produced, the networks of human and non-human elements of which it consists are, in some cases, hidden from view for an outside observer and the network seems to act as a single entity. This is what ANT writers call 'punctualized order', a term which signals that 'order' should be conceived as contingent and precarious. Law (1986) argues that long-distance control (and thus punctualized order in a network) is afforded by three elements: texts, machines or other devices, and 'drilled people'. It is possible for control to be lost over network constituents, for example, through forms of resistance. Although in his analysis Law illustrates how various artefacts can facilitate control, what is less obvious in his work and that of other ANT writers is how artefacts can not only be tools of control but also, as our evidence will show, provide opportunities for local intervention. In the rest of our discussion of the supermarket, we discuss the way in which our evidence reveals how workplace artefacts provide a window on employee discretion and the central part they play in setting the parameters of learning environments.

Control over the management, ordering and presentation of stock within our case study supermarket chain was exercised through a range of technological tools, texts and mechanisms that were designed by

Head Office with the aim of improving efficiency. These were linked most closely to ambient products, which have a relatively long shelf life and do not require refrigeration, and also to items that were on promotion in stores. Apart from occasional exceptions, stores could not adjust quantities ordered through this system. Similarly, through market research, the company identified 500 core items that were always in demand and thus must be available at all times to maximize sales. The orders for these items were 'locked down': that is, they could not be adjusted by store staff. A centralizing approach to stock control was achieved by supervisors and managers following specified procedures to identify the reasons for, and subsequently to eliminate, gaps on the shelves. This strategy allowed the system to generate orders automatically, avoiding store interventions that might slow down stock replenishment and thus affect availability. Finally, precise instructions for the presentation of stock in stores were conveyed through 'planograms'. These documents depicted, through diagrams, the exact positioning and layout of merchandise by type of shelf, display cabinet and refrigerator. An updated planogram was issued to each store every two weeks by Head Office. From the perspective of senior management, located in the higher echelons of the company's productive system, a tightly controlled approach to stock management was justified by the performance gains to be made across what was described as the 'ordering through to sales process', and through the exercise of more tightly controlled and timely purchasing and throughput decisions.

Local store managers had more discretion to adjust fresh (in comparison to ambient) produce orders as the scope for creating and reducing waste was high. Fresh food ordering was accomplished under a different system, which gave store and trading managers the opportunity to alter or cancel orders and to tailor the range and quantity of products they required for their particular store or department. They were aided in this process by the availability of reports, which traced the sales and waste of each product in stock. A produce supervisor described this process as follows:

> Head Office, they track the sales of each product and they track the waste of each product and then every two weeks they send you a whole list out of this, broken down into departments . . . And you need, then, to decide . . . There's one there, Caesar Salad. The average sales weekly were £29.82 and the waste was £9.20.

> So we've wasted £9.20 but we sold nearly £30 worth. Now, I need to take a decision . . . is that really worth having it in the building because of the waste?
>
> (Millie, Supervisor, Store C, The Supermarket)

Product ordering systems and devices, such as the symbol gun, resonate with Law's argument that network order is maintained through the deployment of texts, devices and trained people. However, our evidence shows that artefacts were not only operating as tools of central control but were also providing the means for local intervention, discretion and improvisation. Store level decisions about whether to intervene in stock ordering were based, at least in part, on the context-specific or situated knowledge of staff (for example, knowledge of local events and customer groups), but the means of executing this discretion relied on their ability to use the tools designed by Head Office. There was, however, tension and dynamism in the relationship between Head Office and stores, which was indicative of the indeterminacy of productive systems and the different perspectives and priorities of groups located at different points in the vertical structures and horizontal stages of production.

Employees' compliance with the display specification set out in the planogram provided another example of control exercised from above in the structures of the productive system over staff behaviour, in this case, with reference to stock layout. As a Trading Manager remarked:

> Beforehand we used to be able to juggle it about a bit, but they don't want that anymore. They're telling you what they want in there and that's what you put in there [cabinet].
>
> (Adam, Trading Manager, Store D, The Supermarket)

Store management, then, had limited discretion over the conception of their work, in that they were not in a position to specify the aims and objectives of their work process. However, they did have some discretion over how they executed their work tasks. Their ability to exercise this discretion draws on both tacit and codified sources of knowledge. In the following quotation, a Trading Manager points out that 'rough judgements', utilizing only on-the-job experience and tacit knowledge, could be inadequate:

> More or less it's done on judgement . . . We sort of, like, roughly judge how much we would need to get in compared to last week,

whether we've sold enough of it . . . Doing that way has its pluses
but it also has its minuses . . . It does need, I think, more
analytical information to judge – to say, right, this is actually
how much you've sold, this is what percentage you've done, you
know. And then get more accurate figures to say, right, that is
a good selling line let's get that in, that's a bad selling line, so
let's get rid of it rather than keeping it on the shop floor.

(Rachel, Trading Manager, Store B, The Supermarket)

Store managers had to combine their analytical skills with local
'know how'. Thus, making judgements in the course of dealing with
specific tasks formed an important aspect of workplace learning. The
evidence collected in this case study indicated that despite recent
moves further to shift the locus of control of the stock management
system upwards to Head Office, there was still scope for store
employees to intervene in the process. Importantly, while the symbol
gun was perceived as an artefact of control of the stock management
function, it could also be used to adjust stock levels, particularly in
relation to fresh produce. Fresh food could only be displayed for
limited periods, so the scope for creating and reducing waste was
high. In principle, orders for fresh products were automatically
generated, but designated managers were given the opportunity to
alter or cancel them using the symbol gun. The device enabled users
to view the quantities of lines that were scheduled to come into the
store, how much of these lines were currently in stock and their rate
of sale (what quantities were usually sold). Based on this information,
a local decision could be made to override the system, as this store
manager's comment illustrates:

So, what it's got on it [the symbol gun] is it's got your stock
controls, your orders, availability, stock counting. They've all got
various functions. The one we're going to use is 'view orders'.
The majority of the time I don't need to amend it, but sometimes
I do . . . Now, I've got 26 coming in, I've got 37 in stock and I'm
selling roughly 35. So I would look to order, I would say, two
of those. So to adjust the order, press Y.

(Grace, Store Manager, Store B, The Supermarket)

Although the research data indicated that increasing centralization
of stock management limits local managers' discretion, it also created
potential learning opportunities. If store managers, for example, had

the capacity to negotiate with Head Office, then it was possible for orders to be adjusted to meet local conditions even when the system was apparently inflexible. In the following extract, a Trading Manager explained that it was possible to arrange an alteration in an order relating to Minimum Presentation Levels (MPL) of bottled water – a product not usually available for adjustment – if he made a phone call to Head Office and explained why a change was needed:

> You can phone them up. You can tell them the reason why you're doing it and why you need it done, and they'll change it over the phone for you ... They can do it instantly for you, just a flick of a switch ... So you phone up head office, head office will send a message to your systems and say ... increase the MPL, and then the next time your order generates, it will increase the order by well two-fold, three-fold, depending on what the MPL is. So, and then that'll send a message to the depot saying well they've ordered eight cases instead of four now, and then the depot will send you eight cases.
>
> (Adam, Trading Manager, Store D, The Supermarket)

The capability to interact with Head Office in this way required: knowledge about which product orders can be adjusted; knowledge of what method to use and whom to call; and how to express the problem and provide convincing reasons why adjustment is needed. Put another way, tacit, analytical, negotiation and social skills were all needed. This example raises the questions of how consistently such skills were available among store management teams, and whether the company realized the extent of the knowledge and skills employees needed to identify and address stock problems effectively.

Our focus on workplace artefacts, such as the symbol gun and the planogram, has shed light on the extent to which employees are able to exercise discretion in relation to stock control and presentation. In relation to stock ordering, it emerged that discretion to adjust orders was available and was evidenced by the exercise of informed judgements by the relevant staff. It also emerged that lines normally perceived as non-adjustable could be changed if employees possessed sufficient knowledge about how the system worked and had the necessary interpersonal and negotiation skills. The symbol gun, then, was a Janus-like device which, on the one hand, acted as an instrument of Head Office control over stock management in local stores, but, on the other hand, could enable store managers to intervene in the system by using it to adjust orders of particular sorts of goods. In addition, the symbol gun acted as a boundary object, in the sense that the information it contained was utilized by two broad constituencies, comprising store and Head Office staff. In relation to stock presentation, however, there was little, if any, scope for staff to depart from the text represented in the planogram. The apparent absence of discretion over stock layout and display had closed down an area of participation and had restricted the nature of the store as a learning environment.

Conclusion

In this chapter, we have drawn on our case study evidence to illustrate the important role that artefacts of different kinds play in facilitating, impeding and controlling learning in the workplace. We do not regard artefacts as inert or neutral resources. They are 'creatures' of the productive systems in which they are located. Their role and purpose may be determined by forces external to the organizations and workplaces in which they are used. They may be generated in the Head Offices of an organization and distributed throughout its various layers. They may emerge as a result of everyday workplace activity. They have different meanings for their various users and those meanings may change over time. Some artefacts take on the function of boundary objects and act as catalysts and tools for mediation between networks, as portrayed in CHAT. In the case of supermarket retailing, the symbol gun certainly played this role, but the human agents involved differed in terms of whether they saw that mediation as a source for discretion or for vertical control (cf. Figure 8.3). Moreover, the example of the Trading Manager who was able to draw on his prior learning, experience and social capital to achieve an adjustment in the quantity of a 'locked down' product line reinforces the finding in our automotive case study that the reification of workplace procedures and resources does not inevitably lead to standardized and homogeneous workplace practices. The contribution of the Working as Learning Framework (WALF) here is the insight that productive systems comprise a balance of constraints and opportunities whose outcomes are often unintended and difficult to predict.

In the case of the automotive companies, the implementation of programmes to prove 'competence' to customers and owners – parties positioned vertically above and horizontally later in the productive system – introduced an externally generated artefact (the NVQ) into the workplace. This triggered the repositioning of some everyday workplace artefacts as resources for the excavation and accreditation of expertise, which, in turn, led to the creation of yet other artefacts. The companies differed, however, in their approach to the NVQ itself. This resulted in the curtailment of an essentially expansive process in Green Company, where existing artefacts shed their newly found identity and the newly created professional discussion became part of the historical 'sediment' of the shop floor. For Brown Company, however, the NVQ initiative was regarded as one element of a substantial process to change the way work was organized and increase skill levels across the plant. The tutor pack lived on as a symbol of this long-term vision, even though the initial accreditation driver for introducing the NVQ had been superseded by a programme of multi-skilling.

In this chapter, we have signalled the importance of using artefacts as a lens for understanding the workplace as a learning environment. We have also challenged perspectives that strongly emphasize the role of artefacts as instruments by which the centre creates and sustains long-distance control over members of its network and those that conceive artefacts as neutral mediators of relations between groups. In our view, locating artefacts as important elements in dynamic and indeterminate productive systems helps avoid these shortcomings. Such a perspective is central to the Working as Learning Framework.

Chapter 9

Bringing working and learning together

Introduction

Throughout this book, we have presented a variety of evidence to illustrate the Working as Learning Framework (WALF) outlined in Chapter 2. In this concluding chapter, we bring together the different elements of our argument. This shows how our framework offers a new contribution to: methodological approaches to the study of working and learning; theories of workplace learning; and policy formulation in the field of skills and workforce development. The chapter also discusses the implications for the future of research in this field.

The project on which this book is based took place over almost five years. During that time, interest in the relationship between working and learning continued to grow within research, policy-making and practitioner communities across the world. Yet, despite a great deal of activity and a substantial body of high quality research evidence, our understanding of that relationship has tended to remain as separate pieces of a large and daunting jigsaw puzzle. In this book, we provide what we believe to be the first substantive attempt to put those pieces together to form an integrated picture of the ways in which learning and work relate to each other. The development of our argument has evolved through the detailed and extensive fieldwork we conducted across the public and private sectors of the UK economy, through building on existing theories and concepts from the research literature, and through debating our ideas with many people over the course of the project. This latter point is significant because the issues we discuss in this book are vitally important to people's lives, to the organizations in which they work, and to local, regional and national prosperity.

In Chapter 2, we presented a new conceptual and analytical framework, the Working as Learning Framework. It comprises the inter-related concepts of: productive systems; work organization; and learning environments and territories. We argued that the productive system perspective challenged existing approaches to the analyses of learning and work which tend to focus attention at the level of a single workplace, organization, or specific groups of workers. This enabled us to identify, illuminate and examine the nature of the social relationships involved in the creation and delivery of goods and services at all levels, within, out(with) and beyond the different sites of activity. By both mapping and developing an understanding of the productive systems within which our case studies operated, we were able to contextualize the second and third concepts of our framework. Thus, the way work is organized and the level of discretion afforded to, taken up and shaped by workers in our case studies resulted from the interplay between the social relationships in the different structures and stages of the productive system. It is through this contextualized understanding of the employment relationship, the ways in which jobs are designed and executed, and the nature of worker involvement, that we can better explain the way workplaces operate as learning environments.

It is our contention that, by applying the Working as Learning Framework, we are able to show how each learning environment comprises a dynamic interplay between processes generated within workplaces and those emanating from wider structures and stages of the productive system. These shift, change and re-organize, like the shapes in a kaleidoscope. This dynamic complexity overrides conventional notions held by some policy-makers, researchers and practitioners that the differences between workplace learning environments can be accounted for by fixed variables such as sector, size and product market. More researchers are asserting that employee characteristics, dispositions and biographies are also important influences, but, in seeking to demonstrate the power of individual agency, they can lose sight of the contextual factors. Our argument is that all these factors are clearly important and relevant, but that, in themselves, they represent only some of the phenomena that, together, comprise a complex social world. It follows, therefore, that if certain phenomena are studied in isolation and/or extracted from their context, they will burn as individual candles, while the rest of the world remains in darkness. Moreover, by privileging certain phenomena, we begin to formulate incomplete and potentially misleading accounts of the worlds to which they belong. Examples of this would be relying solely on the views of senior managers about the introduction of high performance/involvement work practices to claim that levels of employee autonomy had increased, or relying entirely on individual employees' biographies to explain why employees are more or less likely to engage in learning.

We now turn to a more detailed consideration of the book's central argument. At certain points, we refer to case studies that formed part of our overall study, but are not represented in the individual chapters. In this way, we provide a 'gateway' to the research results that we have not been able to present elsewhere in the book due to space constraints.

Investigating working and learning

One of the key challenges for researchers who study workplaces is balancing the need to spend time absorbing and collecting data about the dynamics of the everyday hustle and bustle, while also standing back in order to see how that hustle and bustle is constituted. As we have shown throughout the book, we used a range of research methods to excavate the constituents of workplace activity. Although using a mixed method approach has become more common in social science research, the majority of studies of workplace learning, and, indeed, of work-related training and employer' skills strategies, still tend to rely on questionnaire surveys and interviews. The preponderance of these two methods indicates that researchers regard individual employees (of whatever level) as the key focus of their inquiries. Researchers working in the tradition of Cultural Historical Activity Theory (CHAT) use a strategy of intervention and work with groups and teams (sometimes from different organizations) to co-construct new ways of working (see, *inter alia*, Engeström 2001). An example of this is the study by Daniels *et al.* (2007) of professionals from a range of agencies (e.g. social services, police and schools) who have the responsibility of jointly preparing education and care plans for young people at risk of social exclusion or with special educational needs. Although CHAT demands that researchers take account of the cultural and historical underpinnings of particular workplaces, their attention is focused at the micro level. Indeed, CHAT researchers themselves become part of the very microcosm (one of the team) they are investigating.

A significant influence on our early thinking about how to construct a methodological approach came from the fields of 'situated learning', labour process theory, and the sociology of work, where ethnographic methods, such as participative and non-participative observation, have been used to enable researchers to feel closer to or even part of the workplace. This enabled Darrah (1996), for example, to illuminate how workers developed much of their knowledge and skills through what he called the 'unacknowledged curriculum' operating inside the factories he studied in the US. Ethnography is, of course, a highly demanding approach, both in terms of time and resources. When done in the purest sense (as in Darrah's case), the researcher becomes an employee of the organization being studied (see also Beynon 1973; Burawoy 1979). Similar to the CHAT approach, full immersion on this scale necessarily places ethical and pragmatic constraints on the researcher. By becoming part of a team, researchers build up a relationship of trust with their co-workers and sacrifice their sense of distance in order to maintain that trust.

From our previous experience of conducting research in workplaces (Fuller *et al.* 2003; Fuller and Unwin 2004; Felstead *et al.* 2005a), we were very aware that the forces that shape the ways in which people work and learn, originate and exist both within and outside the workplace. While highly focused studies at the micro level provided us with important insights, we knew that this misses the bigger picture. In Chapter 8, we discussed our impressions of the way supermarket staff were interacting with a centralized stock ordering and management system. Our close observations of managers using the hand-held 'symbol guns' as they checked the amount of goods on the shelves led us to formulate a story of deskilling in which machines controlled from a distance had replaced human discretion and judgement. As we showed in that chapter, however, once we had learned more about how the system worked and, crucially, developed a much more nuanced understanding of the interplay between head office and the local stores, we were able to gather evidence of the ways in which store staff could and did exercise a degree of discretion in overriding the system. The 'symbol gun' itself became transformed from being a rigid tool to a vehicle through which managers could apply their knowledge and make informed decisions. The 'planogram', however, offered no such opportunities for discretion in determining store layout. In essence, we had begun to look both within and beyond the micro level of the supermarket, and, crucially, to investigate the different layers of the productive system of supermarket retailing.

By using the metaphor of the 'Russian doll', we developed a variegated and non-linear methodological approach (Unwin *et al.* 2007). To see inside the doll and, therefore, to appreciate its full meaning and beauty, you have to first expose each of the internal dolls, and then put them back together to re-establish the complete object. By conceptualizing our case studies in this way, we devised ways of moving both vertically and horizontally between and along the different axes of the productive systems we were investigating. As discussed in Chapter 1, we referred to this as a 'research shuttle' approach to data collection. Sometimes, as in the case of the exercise to music (ETM) instructors discussed in Chapter 5, we began a case study by zooming in on a specific group of individuals based in different workplaces, while in other case studies the research began with meetings at senior management level (as in the case of sandwich manufacturing discussed in Chapter 7).

The 'research shuttle' approach enabled us to investigate the different layers of the productive system. It also played an important role in exposing the power relations that characterize all sectors of the economy. Although the concept of a 'sector' is problematic given the porous boundaries of the economy and the shifting definitions of occupational categories, it has come to have a common usage, acting as a shorthand for ease of navigation round the different types of employment and production that constitute a country's economic landscape. In many industrialized countries, governments use a sector-based approach as part of their economic policy (see Sung *et al.* 2006). In the UK, this has been happening since the mid-1960s, but in the last 20 or so years, government-sponsored sector bodies have become the vehicles for channelling public funding to employers to stimulate training and other workforce development strategies (Payne 2008; Keep 2006). These bodies have joined other organizations (some with much longer and more independent histories), such as professional bodies and employer forums, that seek to represent their sectoral interests to government and the general public both at home and abroad. In addition, there are various regulatory agencies that exist to protect the consumer and serve the public interest. We saw how, for example, in Chapter 8, the automotive sector is governed by very tight quality assurance controls to protect public safety, and in Chapter 7 we noted the role of a range of regulatory bodies in the sandwich making industry.

Currently, the UK government's key sector bodies are the Sector Skills Councils (SSCs). Part of their remit is to facilitate greater employer participation in publicly-funded initiatives to raise the skill and qualification levels of the workforce (Keep 2006). At the same time, the trade unions and the Trades Union Congress (TUC) have also been given government funding to lead on some initiatives (such as the introduction of Union Learning Representatives in workplaces) and to build partnerships with employer-led bodies. Critics of the unions' decision to play this role argue that they are now in the grip of a government's skills agenda that has no place for revitalized trade unionism (McIlroy 2008; Hollinrake et al. 2008). In England, reference is now made to a 'learning and skills sector', encompassing all the education and training institutions, sector agencies and other bodies that have some remit for improving the nation's skills capacity (see, inter alia, Hodgson et al. 2008). It could be argued that this is a clear manifestation of agency power. What was once a collection of disparate bodies jostling for the right to serve and influence employers has itself become a many-headed bureaucratic hydra, which, in turn, devours part of the funding intended for the 'real' economy.

The devolution of power to Scotland, Wales and Northern Ireland (see, inter alia, Birrell 2008; Cook and Clifton 2005) is enabling the Scottish Parliament and Welsh and Northern Ireland Assemblies to diverge from England, to some extent, in terms of policy-making related to skills, lifelong learning and labour markets (see Keep 2008; Felstead 2009). Some agencies, however, such as the SSCs and the UK Commission for Employment and Skills (UKCES), have a UK-wide remit. While the number of agencies who play, or might potentially play, a role in any organization's productive system varies, all productive systems will have some connection (however tenuous) to one or more of the bodies within their orbit. They, therefore, play an important role in the structure of production in both the public and private sectors of the economy. In Chapter 8, for example, we noted that the use of National Vocational Qualifications (NVQs) in the automotive sector had been supported by government-funded adult training initiatives, and in Chapter 4 we showed how the decision in England to combine services for children was affecting the way the work of health visitors was being reconfigured. As we write this book, further changes are being made to and proposed for the funding and delivery of initiatives related to workforce development and skills more generally across the UK. Policies, like politicians, come and go, and sometimes change is merely a cosmetic exercise, leaving the underlying structures and cultures in place. We have learned, however, that researchers concerned to understand the nature of workplace learning, must keep abreast of the changing policy landscape, otherwise they may overlook important factors that penetrate the workplace from outside its walls.

In relation to our project, agency power asserted itself when we tried to use some of them (including a trade union) to gain access to employers in sectors where we had few contacts or where we were uncertain as to which employers might be willing to allow us access. In the majority of cases, the agencies we approached were very helpful indeed. However, in two instances, we were prevented from pursuing case studies when agencies withdrew their initial (and very strong) commitment to act as gatekeepers to organizations in their sectors, which we would have struggled to access on our own. This experience provided a valuable insight into the roles played by, and the power of bodies that sit within, a productive system, yet operate at a considerable distance from the companies and individuals creating goods and services. It also alerted us to be wary of making assumptions about how agencies might react to our presence. For example, the reliance that some trade unions and the TUC itself now have on government funding (as discussed by McIlroy 2008) may mean they will not, necessarily, be sympathetic to researchers who ask searching questions about this relationship and the effectiveness of government policies in this area.

The power relations that lie within and help shape productive systems are manifested in many forms. Again, our methodological approach alerted us both to the different sources of power embedded within our case studies and to the sources of power comprising the outer layers of their productive systems. In Chapter 6, for example, the introduction of European Union legislation in relation to contract research staff in universities was the catalyst for change in the work-ing patterns, career trajectories and identity formation of researchers in the case study university. By way of contrast, power relations in the software company, also discussed in Chapter 6, were manifested in two ways. First, power rested in the daily engagement between the software engineers and the company's corporate customers. The engineers learned through this engagement how to view the customer as a partner in the co-construction of innovative solutions and ideas for new products. Second, power rested in the trust that the employees had in the fairness of the performance-pay system, a trust that appears to have underpinned the strong sense of community and the very low rate of staff turnover. In Chapter 5, the key source of power in the working lives of the ETM instructors lay with the global company controlling the pre-packaged products they used to deliver classes to their clients. The location of control, however, was not so clear-cut in Chapter 3, where we explored the battle for the control of knowledge between the specialists in back office departments and staff in the contact centre.

Our understanding of the differentiated nature of power relations within productive systems was also developed through two case study settings in hairdressing and hospitality involving organizations run as franchises within large, national chains. We have reported these case studies in detail elsewhere (see Lee *et al.* 2007; Kakavelakis 2008). In the case of hairdressing, our research focused on four high street hairdressing salons in England which operate as franchises of two hairdressing chains. Franchisees were required to conduct their businesses within strict parameters laid down by the franchisor organization, including adherence to employment policies, product use and sales, use of promotional and marketing materials, staff demeanour and salon presentation. Hence, they were typical of 'business format franchises' that operate in many parts of the service sector (see Felstead 1991 and 1993). Vertical controls operated not only through bureaucratic structures, but also via company norms surrounding salon culture, particularly with respect to customer service. Although, during interviews, franchisees spoke of their involvement in company decision-making, via formal procedures such as meetings and focus groups, the organization of both companies was largely 'top-down'. By thoroughly investigating the nature of the power exercised by the franchisor, we were able to trace its impact on the learning environment of the franchised salons. This enabled us to reveal how, despite the individual hairdressers' stylists' commitment to learning, their development of new skills and knowledge was confined within restricted and tightly controlled parameters laid down by the franchisor.

In the case of hospitality, we carried out research in restaurants belonging to a chain with several hundred outlets across the UK. When it was established in the mid-1990s, the company aimed to bridge the gap between fast food and traditional restaurants. It prided itself on its management style, which has allowed it to maintain the 'family' atmosphere of its early days and for which it has achieved national recognition. Constructing the 'family' atmosphere represented a deliberate attempt to address the perennial issue of high labour turnover common in the sector. The research literature on hospitality tends to argue that 'McDonalized' chains of restaurants (often referred to as 'service factories') rely on tight bureaucratic controls to ensure consistency of service and product (Lashley and Taylor 1998). In the case of the company we researched, however, we found that it managed to deliver standardization by employing a form of cultural control, emphasizing the notions of 'family and fun' interspersed with a paternalistic discourse and a set of associated practices. The emphasis on the family ethos was supported by a number of management practices that differentiated the company's approach from the 'command and control' style of management usually found in service factories. The exercise of power through the productive system of this company appeared, therefore, to challenge the homogeneous narrative that typifies the hospitality literature.

In conclusion to this section, we would stress that our methodological approach became much more than a set of decisions about how to collect data. Our starting point for the study was to go beyond the standard questions about how people learn in workplaces by locating learning within the broader context and political economy of work in contemporary society. Our methodological contribution has been to show that the forces that shape workplace learning cannot all be found in the workplace. By exposing and examining those forces, we will begin to build much clearer explanatory models of how workplace learning occurs, what it comprises, and how it is shaped by and shapes both productive activity and the lives of all those engaged in it.

Positioning the Working as Learning Framework

The importance we place on putting workplace learning in context has, of course, been stressed by other researchers (see Chapter 1). In this section, we will argue that our contribution has been to develop a means for achieving that goal, both theoretically and empirically. In the previous section (and exemplified by all the chapters of this book), we discussed the ways in which our analytical framework can be used by researchers as an empirical tool to excavate the relationship between working and learning more deeply and across a much larger canvas. From a theoretical perspective, the Working as Learning Framework has enabled us to advance understanding in three areas that are central to the conceptualization of 'context' as applied to workplace learning:

- the vertical and horizontal interdependencies that comprise productive systems;
- the levels of discretion afforded and created by different forms of work organization;
- the nature of workplace learning environments.

In the course of applying the Working as Learning Framework, we have highlighted the relationship between employees' position in the productive system and the ways in which their knowledge is developed, privileged and managed. This has emerged in the writing of this book through the iterative process of preparing the chapters and making cross-comparisons between them. It is to the ways in which our thinking concerning the framework has developed and become consolidated since completing the fieldwork that we now turn.

As we discussed in Chapter 2, by placing so much importance on the concept of the productive system, we will no doubt be criticized for being overly deterministic and allowing structural concerns to dominate. Billett (2004: 110), for example, argues that workplaces are learning spaces in which 'individuals learn through experiences that are mediated by both the contributions of workplaces and individuals' agency'. He also uses the term 'affordances' when referring to the different conditions in workplaces that serve to facilitate learning. Throughout our work, we have acknowledged the important contribution of Billett and researchers such as Hodkinson and Hodkinson (2004a and 2004b) and Evans et al. (2004) who place stress on the power of individual agency (see also Billett and Pavlova 2003). For example, in Chapter 5 we saw how ETM instructors with contrasting experiences and backgrounds responded to the same learning environment in different ways. In Chapter 4, it was apparent that the distinctive and personal learning experiences of three 'old timers' was crucial to the emergence and development of new ways of working among a group of health visitors.

We have also been influenced by Goffman's (1959) research into 'impression management', which he described as the 'way in which the individual in ordinary work situations presents himself [sic] and his activity to others, the ways in which he guides and controls the impression they form of him, and the kinds of things he may not do while sustaining his performance before them' (Goffman, 1959: xi). Building on Goffman's work, researchers such as Witz et al. (2003) and Bolton (2004) have investigated the extent to which these impressions are created, explicitly or implicitly, by others. Thus, while individual employees certainly play a key role in shaping their own image at work, it is clear that there is considerable corporate interest in the management of employee performance, particularly in service industries. In Chapter 5, for example, we showed how the once 'freestyle' image of ETM instructors is being fashioned into a globally choreographed performance to ensure consistency of service wherever they are employed. The type of products and services that an organization provides will, therefore, influence, create, sustain and/or change the way individual workers think about themselves and the way they are seen by others (see Felstead *et al.* 2007c and 2009b for a fuller discussion of these issues).

As we said in the introduction to this chapter, both the labour process and sociology of work traditions have always been concerned to explore how workers resist and reshape the tasks and roles they are given. Our case studies contain detailed depictions of the ways in which employees, from across the economy, take up or react against the 'affordances' for learning they encounter. However, the concept of 'affordances' is too opaque and benign to have real purchase if it is to be used to explain how workplace learning occurs. As it stands, it implies something about structures and procedures, but it is ethereal rather than substantive. Furthermore, it is a benign concept that floats free of a political economy conceptualization of work. It tends to say much more about individuals and much less about the structural characteristics against and within which their agency is constituted.

The analytical power of the Working as Learning Framework, however, is that it combines the concepts of productive systems, discretion in relation to work organization, and learning environments. This approach allows us to provide a much more holistic and integrated account of how learning and work relate to each other. It also allows us to monitor changes and trace their effects through the structures and stages of productive systems. Thus, the Working as Learning Framework reflects the dynamism that characterizes all workplaces. During the time we spent carrying out fieldwork in the case study organizations, we witnessed considerable change in their fortunes. In the case of one of the automotive companies we were surprised it survived as a business for the length of our project. By using the concept of the productive system, we were able to examine the nature of the managers' and employees' responses in the various organizations to turbulence and change. For some, this represented an opportunity to take risks and to involve employees more in discussions about how to respond. For others, the response came in the form of a reduction in levels of discretion given to employees and a retreat away from innovative solutions.

As we discussed in Chapter 2, a key building block for the Working as Learning Framework was Fuller and Unwin's (2004) 'expansive-restrictive continuum' and the associated concept of 'learning territories'. This provided a starting point for considering how we might analyse the learning environments we encountered in our fieldwork. Both concepts stress the importance of context, but by bringing them together with the concept of productive systems, we have been able to strengthen their analytical purchase. As a result, the role of agency becomes much more strongly anchored in the social relations of both production and human interaction. This can be seen in Chapter 4, which documents attempts by a group of health visitors to re-engineer part of the productive system that they felt restricted their learning opportunities. It can also be seen in Chapter 8, where individual employees in supermarket retailing and automotive manufacturing utilize workplace artefacts to develop and make visible skills and knowledge that would otherwise remain hidden.

This brings us to another area in which our framework makes a new contribution. There is a considerable literature that addresses the role of knowledge in the economy, in work, in innovation, and in organizations. There is a strong social-constructivist tradition that views all knowledge in relation to work as being contextual or 'situated', whereas the social realist tradition differentiates between knowledge types, arguing that some knowledge transcends context (see Fuller *et al.* 2006; Young 2004). This battle is at the heart of the so-called academic–vocational divide in which knowledge of subjects (or disciplines) such as physics and mathematics is held to have greater objective currency than context-specific knowledge acquired in the workplace. More recently, attention has shifted away from knowledge as a static entity to the more active process of 'knowing'. Knowing is viewed as practice in a particular organizational context, which entails interaction with the world, something that affords the acquisition and use of knowledge. Cook and Brown (2005) argue for recognition of the value of these distinct epistemologies as the interplay between knowledge and knowing can generate new knowledge and new ways of knowing.

These debates have profound implications for the way knowledge is developed, valued and managed in workplaces and throughout productive systems. They also challenge the often simplistic assumptions made by teachers and trainers that knowledge acquired off-the-job can be transferred in a straightforward manner to the workplace without any intervening processes of support and recontextualization (see, *inter alia*, Eraut 2004; Tuomi-Grohn and Engeström 2003). Eraut (2004: 221) stresses the importance of considering knowledge within its context and 'locating knowledge in space and time'. Our ethnographic study of a five-day off-the-job training course for commission-based sales staff working in the leisure industry, for example, underlines this point (Kakavelakis *et al.* 2008). This aptly illustrates the difficulty of transferring knowledge, skills and practices from the classroom to the workplace. Here, difficulties of recontextualization arose because of workers' unease about using the 'hard sell' tactics they were taught in their daily practices.

We make two specific contributions to the debate. First, through our case study evidence, we are able to show that while both academic forms of knowledge ('know what') and those characterized as 'know-how' are valued in different ways by different workplaces, their strength comes from the place their possessors occupy in the productive system. In our case study of sandwich making (see Chapter 7), for example, we showed that there were considerable differences in the experiences and career trajectories of staff engaged in new product development. These differences were related to the final destination of the product and, in particular, the role of the retailer in controlling the early stages of production. In Chapter 3, the position of departmental specialists in a local authority was gradually being diluted as their knowledge was recontextualized and appropriated by staff in the contact centre. In Chapter 4, the health visitors, who were trying to create an identifiable 'community of practice' in order to expand and concentrate on using their specialist knowledge, were being pressurized to spend their time conducting the routine tasks of weighing and immunizing babies because of their relationship with doctors and their spatial location in doctors' surgeries.

The second way in which we can make a contribution to the issue of knowledge relates to the dominant conceptualization of the 'knowledge worker' as someone who has control over their career trajectory and nature of work by virtue of being knowledge-rich. In Chapter 6, we showed the difference between the ways in which two types of 'knowledge worker' were being managed and supported by their respective organizations. The software engineers benefited from being part of a productive system that placed considerable emphasis on the nurturing of young talent for the benefit of the overall community of practice. Furthermore, the company's corporate status gave it a position within a productive system which had a very compressed vertical structure. The engineers expressed the view that they were part of an 'intelligent' community, which valued their knowledge and trusted them to make decisions. As a result, they displayed a sense of confidence in both their current position in the company and their future trajectory, which they conceptualized in terms of personal growth within a commercially successful context. In contrast, the contract researchers displayed considerable anxiety, and in some cases, anger about their current and future positions. They felt their knowledge was being devalued through the expectation that they could work across disparate projects and even disciplines. They worked within an organization (a university) that sits within a productive system that has become increasingly state-managed and highly regulated. The health visitors in Chapter 4 can also be cited here as posing a challenge to the 'knowledge worker' concept, given their position in a productive system even more complex than that of higher education.

In our study of the construction sector, we were given insights into how some productive systems do not necessarily support genuine collaboration or knowledge-sharing between parties (see Bishop *et al.* 2008 for a fuller account). During the 1990s, government-commissioned reports on the British construction sector (Latham 1994; CTF 1998) highlighted low levels of client satisfaction, poor health and safety records, high accident rates, under-investment in research and development, budget overspends, late project delivery and a 'crisis in training' (CTF 1998: 7). The sector was characterized by ingrained patterns of work organization and 'adversarial' forms of contracting, in which contractors at each point in the production process tried to exploit each other whenever possible. This created a hostile and litigious environment that militated against more strategic and co-ordinated modes of project management. The proposed solution to this problem was a move towards more collaborative forms of working, and associated practices such as 'partnering'. These 'new' modes of project and supply chain management – already popular in manufacturing and engineering – are focused on forming closer relationships with clients and (some) suppliers in order to facilitate the delivery of the construction project to time, budget and specification. The stage was set, therefore, for the building of more genuine collaboration, knowledge-sharing and the organic formation of what Engeström *et al.* (1997) call self-organizing 'knots'.

Our case study findings show, however, that the essential fabric of the productive system in construction militates against collaboration and undermines collective learning. Decades of conflict and mistrust, alongside a reward structure that in many cases encourages cynicism and exploitation, all contribute to an unfavourable environment for co-operation and knowledge sharing. With the best will (and skill) in the world, attempts to move towards collaborative working and 'knot-working' may struggle in construction, due to the culture and structure of the industry, and the fact that there are still tangible rewards for working against rather than with other parties. It is also questionable whether an environment 'which is frequently characterized by one-off contracts and short-term gain is capable of supporting a concept which is based on mutual trust and long-term collaboration' (Beach *et al.* 2005: 612). This is the reality of work in a productive system with a long history of adversarial relations. Yet this is precisely the environment in which moves towards collaborative, co-configured models of work organization and collective learning must be contextualized.

The advocates of more co-configured, collaborative modes of working in construction and manufacturing settings claim that they require and promote heightened levels of skill and knowledge transfer (see, *inter alia*, De Vilbiss and Leonard 2000; Cheng *et al.* 2004). We would argue, however, that these theoretical models do not adequately take into account the historical, cultural, social and economic contexts within which such practices must operate. In the construction industry, for example, the wholesale adoption of such (unfamiliar) ways of working entails a fundamental cultural and structural shift that cannot happen overnight. Not only are new skills and attitudes required, but traditional working practices and incentive mechanisms need to be transformed. Thus, the barriers to co-configured, collaborative forms of working and learning in the construction industry are formidable.

The Working as Learning Framework provides the means by which researchers, policy-makers and practitioners can formulate better questions about what constitutes and drives workplace learning. In addition, it provides the means for testing ideas to improve the conditions for growing, nurturing and sustaining learning at work. In the final section of this chapter, we discuss the applicability of the framework for policy and practice, and present ideas for further research.

Implications for policy, practice and research

Throughout the world, skills policy is still heavily influenced by the metaphor of 'learning as acquisition' (Sfard 1998; also see Chapter

1). The result is that government-funded initiatives are frequently aimed at increasing the levels of certified skills (through formal qualifications). This places little or no emphasis on helping employers reconfigure the way they organize work, but instead concentrates solely on getting more individuals qualified. This, in turn, creates pressure on the sectoral bodies, training providers and trade unions who receive government funding, for they too are judged by qualification-led targets. Wolf *et al.* (2006: 557) argue that this has led to the ironic situation in which many businesses in the UK are 'approached by "cold-call" providers who offer to deliver and assess training, free, with minimal involvement by the employer' in order 'to provide a personal development initiative rather than a commercial one'. This separation of skill development from business need or context has long been reflected in the machinery of government in England, where departments of education have tended to have responsibility for the organization and funding of vocational education and training provision. Departments of work, on the other hand, have been responsible for welfare benefits and pensions, and departments for trade and industry have looked after business growth and innovation. In the UK, from 1995 to 2001, education and employment were brought together in an attempt to achieve more 'joined-up policy-making', but this was short-lived.

By viewing working and learning as conjoined phenomena in the ways we have explained in this book, employers could be helped to develop workforce development plans that are embedded in their business strategies. Furthermore, ways could be found to help employers learn from each other about the small/realistic steps they can take to enable them to develop more expansive forms of learning environments in which employees would be afforded the discretion to make decisions and judgements based on their experience and expertise. However, findings from the Skills Surveys carried out in the UK show that despite the rise in skills (measured in a variety of ways) between 1992 and 2006, there was a marked decline in the level of discretion levels exercised at work (Felstead *et al.* 2007d: 120–32). As Green (2006) has argued, employers and governments need to ensure that, in the light of increased levels of certified skills in the workforce, they pay attention to the quality of jobs to ensure that people are able to work at the appropriate level. The more capability an individual has, the more discretion they are likely to crave.

The case study evidence presented in this book indicates that – regardless of the sectoral context, type of organization or grade of employee – learning at work plays a major role in the development of skills and work-related knowledge. From his research on small businesses in the UK, Kitching (2008) argues that the prevalence, diversity and significance of workplace learning calls for a reappraisal of government strategies on skills. It is time to take a much closer look at what is going on within workplaces to identify the factors that facilitate such learning. We know from research that many employers in the UK lack the management and general business skills to take their organizations forward. It follows, too, that these employers also struggle to design appropriate workforce development strategies, particularly if they too have only ever worked in restrictive environments. By using the Working as Learning Framework presented in this book, we argue that it should be possible to create practical models to help employers, employees and the agencies that support them to find ways of reaping greater benefits from everyday workplace activity.

We have seen through the case study evidence that the nature of and access to learning across and within different sectors of the economy are dependent upon a range of factors that are closely interconnected. This requires that stakeholders take a much more holistic approach to the development of strategies designed to improve and expand workplace learning. This includes looking beyond the workplace to the structures and stages of production within which economic activity takes place. This dynamic and turbulent context also demands that much more attention needs to be paid to the pressures on employees at all levels as they endeavour to engage in and apply their learning. Ultimately, then, the arguments presented in this book build towards the most important challenge of all; namely, improving learning by reorganizing and improving work.

Our case study evidence has shown the variety of learning that occurs as part of, or is stimulated by, everyday work activity. In Chapter 8, we discussed how learning can be stimulated and improved by the intelligent use of workplace artefacts and the collapsing of internal boundaries to allow employees with different skill sets and experiences to work together. The resources for learning lie all around in the workplace and in the wider productive system, but they need to be mobilized in order to play their part in supporting the sharing and creation of ideas. All work involves and generates learning, but this is not always harnessed and recognized. Too many workplaces (across the public and private sectors of the economy) consider learning as an 'event', as a specially constructed phenomenon, and, at worst, as something separate from work itself. By seeing *working as learning*, we begin to look at workforce development and organizational performance through a very different lens. If organizations could develop a much deeper understanding of the productive system they inhabit, they could begin to forge a stronger identity and, hence, have greater confidence to challenge ways of working that hold them back.

Throughout this book we have cited a number of previous research studies in the field of workplace learning and related topics. Given the strength of the field and the continued growing international interest from policy-makers and practitioners, as well as researchers, there is considerable scope to be more ambitious in terms of the scale, scope and design of projects. We need projects with a greater longitudinal dimension and much greater effort to bridge the gap between qualitative and quantitative methodologies. Most importantly, we need to build projects that deliberately aim to examine working and learning from an interdisciplinary perspective. It is no longer good enough to study learning at work as a purely psychological or sociological phenomenon. Nor is it good enough to try to isolate the impact of learning on productivity and performance as if learning was a distinct, concrete variable that can be easily slotted into an equation.

Being ambitious is, of course, an easy phrase to write, but the effort involved in mounting and securing funding for the type of research projects we believe are necessary to further advance our understanding of work and learning is considerable. In Chapter 1, as part of a discussion about the methodological approach used in our research, we discussed what we have referred to as the 'politics of access', and earlier in this chapter we returned to a further discussion of our technique of the 'research shuttle'. Although we did, indeed, spend considerable amounts of time negotiating access to workplaces and to various layers of the productive systems we were investigating, we were constantly heartened and surprised by the willingness of organizations to invite us in and to open doors into their world. This willingness reflects a desire to talk about organizational issues and to create time to reflect on those issues away from the daily fire fighting that engulfs many organizations. The door is open, therefore, for a much more collaborative engagement between researchers and workplaces in which the former can play an active role in facilitating dialogue within organizations in order to reveal how improving workplace learning can be achieved.

Bibliography

Abbott, P. and Sapsford, R. (1990) 'Health visiting: policing the family', in Abbott, P. and Wallace, C. (eds) *The Sociology of Caring Professions*, Basingstoke: Falmer Press.

Akgün, A.E. and Lynn, G.S. (2002) 'New product development team improvisation and speed-to-market: an extended model', *European Journal of Innovation Management*, 5(3): 117–29.

Aldridge, F., Tuckett, A., Felstead, A., Fuller, A., Jewson, N., Unwin, L. and Kakavelakis, K. (2007) *Practice Makes Perfect*, Leicester: National Institute of Adult Continuing Education.

Alvesson, M. (2001) 'Knowledge work, ambiguity, image and identity', *Human Relations*, 54(7): 863–86.

Anderson, P. (1999) 'Special Issue: application of complexity theory to organization science', *Organization Science*, 10(3): 216–32.

Appelbaum, E., Bailey, T., Berg, P. and Kalleberg, A. (2000) *Manufacturing Advantage: Why High-Performance Work Systems Pay Off*, Ithaca: Cornell University Press.

Ashton, D. and Sung, J. (2002) *Supporting Learning for High Performance Working*, Geneva: International Labour Organization.

Austin, R. and Devin, L. (2003) 'Beyond Requirements: Software Making as Art', *Software*, 20(1): 93–5.

Bain, P. and Taylor, P. (2000) 'Entrapped by the "electronic panopticon"? Worker resistance in the call centre', *New Technology, Work and Employment*, 15(1): 2–18.

Bakker, M., Leenders, R., Gabbay, S.M., Kratzer, J. and Van Engelen, J. (2006) 'Is trust really social capital? Knowledge sharing in product development projects', *The Learning Organization*, 13(6): 594–605.

Barber, J. (2003) 'The informally trained mechanic: skill acquisition in the workplace', *Journal of Vocational Education and Training*, 55(2): 133–48.

Barber, J. (2004) 'Skill upgrading within informal training: lessons from the Indian auto mechanic', *International Journal of Training and Development*, 8(2): 128–39.

Barlow N. and Chatterton P. (2002) 'Improving competitiveness of companies in the UK automotive sector', *Industry and Higher Education*, 16(5): 315–19.

Barrett, R. (2001) 'Labouring under an illusion? The labour process of software development in the Australian information industry', *New Technology, Work and Employment*, 16(1): 18–34.

Barrett R. (2005) 'Myth and reality', in Barrett R. (ed.) *Management, Labour Process and Software Development: Reality Bytes*, London: Routledge.

Batt, R. (1999) 'Work organization, technology, and performance in customer service and sales', *Industrial and Labor Relations Review*, 52(4): 539–64.

Batt, R. (2000) 'Strategic segmentation in front-line services: matching customers, employees and human resource systems', *International Journal of Human Resource Management*, 11(3): 540–57.

Beach, K. (2003) 'Consequential transitions: a developmental view of knowledge propogation through social organisation', in Tuomi-Grohn, T. and Engeström, Y. (eds) *Between School and Work, New Perspectives on Transfer and Boundary Crossing*, London: Pergamon.

Beach, R., Webster, M. and Campbell, K. (2005) 'An evaluation of partnership development in the construction industry', *International Journal of Project Management*, 23: 611–21.

Beckett, D. and Hager, P. (2002) *Life, Work and Learning: Practice in Postmodernity*, London: Routledge.

Belt, V. (2000) 'Women, social skill and interactive service work in telephone call centres', *New Technology, Work and Employment*, 17(1): 20–34.

Besley, T. and Peters, M.A. (2005) 'The theatre of fast knowledge: performative epistemologies in higher education', *Review of Education, Pedagogy, and Cultural Studies*, 27: 111–26

Beynon, H. (1973) *Working for Ford*, London: Allen Lane.

Billett, S. (2002) 'Critiquing workplace learning discourses: participation and continuity at work', *Studies in the Education of Adults*, 34(1): 56–67.

Billett, S. (2004) 'Learning through work: workplace participatory practices', in Rainbird, H., Fuller, A. and Munro, A. (eds) *Workplace Learning in Context*, London: Routledge.

Billett, S. (2006) 'Relational interdependence between social and individual agency in work and working life', *Mind, Culture and Activity*, 13(1): 53–69.

Billett, S. (2007a) 'Exercising self through working life: learning, work and identity', in Brown, A., Kirpal, S. and Rauner, F. (eds) *Identities at Work*, Dordrecht: Springer.

Billett, S. (2007b) 'Including the missing subject: placing the personal within the community', in Hughes, J., Jewson, N. and Unwin, L. (eds) *Communities of Practice: Critical Perspectives*, London: Routledge.

Billett, S. and Pavlova, M. (2003) 'Learning through working life: self and individuals' agentic action', *International Journal of Lifelong Education*, 24(3): 195–211.

Billingham, K., Morrell, J. and Billingham, C. (1996) 'Professional update: reflections on the history of health visiting', *English Journal of Community Health Nursing*, 1(7): 386–92.

Birecree, A., Konzelmann, S. and Wilkinson, F. (1997) 'Productive systems, competitive pressures, strategic choices and work organization: an introduction', *International Contributions to Labour Studies*, 7: 3–17.

Birrell, D. (2008) *'Devolution and quangos in the United Kingdom: the implementation of principles and policies for rationalisation and democratisation'*, Policy Studies, 29(1): 35–49.

Bishop, D., Felstead, A., Fuller, A., Jewson, N., Kakavelakis, K. and Unwin, L. (2008) 'Constructing learning: adversarial and collaborative working in the British construction industry', *Learning as Work Research Paper No 13*, Cardiff: Cardiff School of Social Sciences, Cardiff University.

Bloor, M. and McIntosh, J. (1990) 'Surveillance and concealment: a comparison of techniques of client resistance in therapeutic communities and health visiting', in Burley, S. and McKegany, N. (eds) *Readings in Medical Sociology*, London: Routledge.

Boer, H., Gersten, F., Kaltoft, R. and Nielsen, J.S. (2005) 'Factors affecting the development of collaborative improvement with strategic suppliers', *Production Planning and Control*, 16(4): 356–67.

Bolton, S.C. (2004) 'Conceptual confusions: emotion work as skilled work', in Warhurst, C., Grugulis, I. and Keep, E. (eds) *The Skills That Matter*, Basingstoke: Palgrave Macmillan.

Boreham, N. (2002) 'Work process knowledge in technological and organizational development', in Boreham, N., Samurçay, R. and Fischer, M. (eds) *Work Process Knowledge*, London: Routledge.

Boreham, N., Samurçay, R. and Fischer, M. (2002) (eds) *Work Process Knowledge*, London: Routledge.

Braverman, H. (1974) *Labor and Monopoly Capitalism: The Degradation of Work in the Twentieth Century*, New York: Monthly Review Press.

Brinkley, I. (2006) *Defining the Knowledge Economy*, London: The Work Foundation.

Brint, S. (2001) 'Professionals and the "knowledge economy": rethinking the theory of postindustrial society', *Current Sociology*, 49(4): 101–32.

Brocklehurst, N. (2004a) 'The new health visiting: thriving at the edge of chaos', *Community Practitioner*, 77(4): 135–9.

Brocklehurst, N. (2004b) 'Is health visiting "fully engaged" in its own future well-being?', *Community Practitioner*, 77(6): 214–18.

Brown, P. and Hesketh, A. (2004) *The Mismanagement of Talent: Employability and Jobs in the Knowledge Economy*, Oxford: Oxford University Press.

Brown, P., Green, A. and Lauder, H. (2001) *High Skills: Globalization, Competitiveness and Skill Formation*, Oxford: Oxford University Press.

Burawoy, M. (1979) *Manufacturing Consent: Changes in the Labor Process Under Monopoly Capitalism*, Chicago: Chicago University Press.

Burch, D. and Lawrence, G. (2005) 'Supermarket own brands, supply chains and the transformation of the agri-food system', *International Journal of Agriculture and Food*, 13(1): 1–18.

Burchell, B., Deakin, S., Michie, J. and Rubery, J. (eds) (2003) *Systems of Production: Markets, Organisations and Performance*, London: Routledge.

Butler, P., Felstead, A., Ashton, D., Fuller, A., Lee, T., Unwin, L. and Walters, S. (2004) 'High performance management: a literature review', *Learning as Work Research Paper No 1*, Leicester: Centre for Labour Market Studies, University of Leicester.

Byrne, D. (1999) *Complexity Theory and the Social Sciences*, London: Routledge.

Callaghan, G. and Thompson, P. (2002) '"We recruit Attitude": the selection and shaping of routine call centre labour', *Journal of Management Studies*, 39(2): 233–54.

Callon, M. (1986) 'Some elements of a sociology of translation: domestication of the scallops and fishermen of St Brieuc Bay', in Law, J. (ed.) *Power, Action and Belief: A New Sociology of Knowledge?* London: Routledge and Kegan Paul.

Callon, M. (1991) 'Techno-economic network and irreversibility', in Law, J. (ed.) A *Sociology of Monsters: Essays on Power, Technology and Dominance*, London: Routledge.

Callon, M. (1994) 'Is science a public good?', *Technology and Human Values*, 15: 395–424.

Campbell, D. (2007) 'Mothers miss a "friend" as health visitors decline', *The Observer*, Sunday 15 April.

Carey, M. (2003) 'Anatomy of a care manager', *Work, Employment and Society*, 17(1): 121–35.

Carmel, S. (2006) 'Boundaries obscured and boundaries reinforced: incorporation as a strategy of occupational enhancement for intensive care', *Sociology of Health and Illness*, 28(2): 154–77.

Chaiklin, S. and Lave, J. (eds) (1993) *Understanding Practice: Perspectives on Activity and Context,* Cambridge: Cambridge University Press.

Cheng, E., Li, H., Love, P. and Irani, Z. (2004) 'A learning culture for strategic partnering in construction', *Construction Innovation*, 4: 53–65.

CIPD (2004) *Training and Development 2004: Survey Report*, London: Chartered Institute of Personnel and Development.

CM Insight (2004) *The UK Contact Centre Industry*, London: Department of Trade and Industry.

Coats, D. (2004) *Efficiency, Efficiency, Efficiency: The Gershon Review – Public Service Efficiency and the Management of Change*, London: Work Foundation.

Colley, H., Hodkinson, P. and Malcolm, J. (2003) *Informality and Formality in Learning: A Report for the Learning and Skills Research Centre*, London: Learning and Skills Research Centre.

Collins L.H. (2002) 'Working out the contradictions: feminism and aerobics', *Journal of Sport and Social Issues*, 26(1): 85–109.

Connolly, M.P. (1980a) 'Health visiting 1850–1900: a review', *Midwife, Health Visitor and Community Nurse*, 16(7): 282–85.

Connolly, M.P. (1980b) 'Health visiting 1900–1910: a review', *Midwife, Health Visitor and Community Nurse*, 16(9): 375–78.

Cook, P. and Clifton, N. (2005) 'Visionary, precautionary and constrained "varieties of devolution" in the economic governance of the devolved UK territories', *Regional Studies*, 39(4): 437–51.

Cook, S.D.N., and Brown, J.S. (2005) 'Bridging epistemologies: the generative dance between organisational knowledge and organisational learning', in Little, S. and Ray, T. (eds) *Managing Knowledge*, 2nd edn, London: Sage.

Cortada, J.W. (1998) *Rise of the Knowledge Worker*, Boston MA: Butterworth-Heinemann.

Cowley, S. (1996) 'Reflecting on the past; preparing for the next century', *Health Visitor*, 69(8): 313–36.

Craig, P. and Smith, L.N. (1998) 'Health visiting and public health: back to our roots or a new branch?', *Health and Social Care in the Community*, 6(3): 172–80.

Crossley, N. (2004) 'The circuit trainer's habitus: reflexive body techniques and the sociality of the workout', *Body and Society*, 10(1): 37–69.

CTF (1998) *Rethinking Construction: The Report of the Construction Task Force* (The Egan Report), London: DTI.

CVCP (1996) *A Concordat to Provide a Framework for the Career Management of Contract Research Staff in Universities and Colleges*, London: Committee of Vice-Chancellors and Principals.

Daniels, H., Leadbetter, J. and Warmington P., with Edwards, A., Brown, S., Middleton, D., Popova, A. and Apostolov, A. (2007) 'Learning in and for multi-agency working', *Oxford Review of Education*, 33(4): 521–38.

Darrah, C.N. (1996) *Learning and Work: An Exploration in Industrial Ethnography*, London: Garland Publishing.

Davies, C. (1988) 'The health visitor as mother's friend: a woman's place in public health, 1900–1914', *Social History of Medicine*, 1: 39–59.

Davis, C. (1995) *Gender and the Professional Predicament in Nursing*, Buckingham: Open University Press.

De Vilbiss, C.E. and Leonard, P. (2000) 'Partnering is the foundation of a learning organization', *Journal of Management in Engineering*, July/August: 47–57.

Delin, J. (2001) 'Keep in step: task structure, discourse structure, and utterance interpretation in the Step Aerobics workout', *Discourse Processes*, 31(1): 61–89.

DeNora, T. (2000) *Music in Everyday Life*, Cambridge: Cambridge University Press.

DeNora, T. and Belcher, S. (2000) '"When you're trying something on you picture yourself in a place where they are playing this kind of music" –

musically sponsored agency in the British clothing sector', *Sociological Review*, 48(1): 80–101.

Department of Health (2007) *Facing the Future: A Review of the Role of Health Visitors,* Department of Health: London.

DfES, DTI, HM Treasury and DWP (2003) *21st Century Skills: Realising Our Potential – Individuals, Employers, Nation,* Cm 5810, London: HMSO.

Dingwall, R. (1977) 'Collectivism, regionalism and feminism: health visiting and English social policy, 1850–1975', *Journal of Social Policy*, 6(3): 291–315.

Dingwall, R. (1983) 'In the beginning was the work . . . Reflections on the genesis of occupations', *Sociological Review* 31(4): 605–24.

Dingwall, R. and Robinson, K. (1990) 'Policing the family? Health visiting and the public surveillance of private behaviour', in Gubrium, J. and Sankar, A. (eds) *The Home Care Experience: Ethnography and Policy,* Newbury Park, CA: Sage.

Drucker, P. (1959) *Landmarks of Tomorrow: A Report on the New 'Post-modern' World,* New York: Harper and Row.

Drucker, P. (1969) *The Age of Discontinuity,* New York: Harper and Row.

Dunn, J. (2006) 'What's in your lunchbox?', *Food Manufacture*, 81(2): xvi-xvii.

Edwards, P., Sengupta, S. and Tsai, C-J. (2007) 'Managing work in the low-skill equilibrium: a study of UK food manufacturing', *SKOPE Research Paper No 72,* July, Oxford: ESRC Centre for Skills, Knowledge and Organisational Performance.

Elias, N. (1978) *What is Sociology?* London: Hutchinson.

Engeström, Y. (1994) *Training for Change: New Approach to Instruction and Learning,* Geneva: International Labour Office.

Engeström, Y. (2000) 'Activity Theory as a framework for analyzing and redesigning work', *Ergonomics*, 43(7): 960–74.

Engeström, Y. (2001) 'Expansive learning at work: toward an activity theoretical reconceptualization', *Journal of Education and Work*, 14(1): 133–56.

Engeström, Y. (2004) 'The new generation of expertise', in Rainbird, H., Fuller, A. and Munro, A. (eds) *Workplace Learning in Context,* London: Routledge.

Engeström, Y., Brown, K., Carol Christopher, L. and Gregory, J. (1997) 'Co-ordination, co-operation and communication in the courts: expansive transitions in legal work', in Cole, M., Engeström, Y. and Vasquez, O. (1997) (eds) *Mind, Culture and Activity: Seminal Papers from the Laboratory of Comparative Human Cognition,* Cambridge: Cambridge University Press.

Engeström, Y., Engeström, R. and Vähäaho, T. (1999) 'When the center does not hold: the importance of knotworking', in Chaiklin, S., Hedegaard, M. and Jensen, U.J. (eds) *Activity Theory and Social Practice,* Aarhus: Aarhus University Press.

Eraut, M., Alderton, J., Cole, G. and Senker, P. (1998) 'Learning from other people at work', in Coffield, F. (ed.) *Learning at Work*, Bristol: Policy Press.

Eraut, M. (2000) 'Development of knowledge and skills at work', in Coffield, F. (ed.) *Differing Visions of a Learning Society: Research Findings, Volume 1*, Bristol: The Policy Press.

Eraut, M. (2004) 'Transfer of knowledge between education and workplace settings', in Rainbird, H., Fuller, A. and Munro, A. (eds) *Workplace Learning in Context*, London: Routledge.

European Foundation for the Improvement of Living and Working Conditions (2002) *Quality of Work and Employment in Europe: Issues and Challenges*, Luxembourg: Office for Official Publications of the European Communities.

Evans, K., Hodkinson, P. and Unwin, L. (2002) (eds) *Working to Learn: Transforming Learning in the Workplace*, London: Kogan Page.

Evans, K., Hodkinson, P., Rainbird, H. and Unwin, L. (2006) *Improving Workplace Learning*, London: Routledge.

Evans, K., Kersh, N. and Sakamoto, A. (2004) 'Learner Biographies: exploring tacit dimensions of learning and skills', in Rainbird, H., Fuller, A. and Munro, A. (eds) *Workplace Learning in Context*, London: Routledge.

Felstead, A. (1991) 'The social organization of the franchise: a case of "controlled self-employment"', *Work, Employment and Society*, 5(1): 37–57.

Felstead, A. (1993) *The Corporate Paradox: Power and Control in Business Franchise*, London: Routledge.

Felstead, A. (2007) 'How "smart" are Scottish jobs? Summary evidence from the Skills Surveys, 1997–2006', *Futureskills Scotland Expert Briefing*, Glasgow: Futureskills Scotland.

Felstead, A. (2009) 'Are jobs in Wales high skilled and high quality? Baselining the *One Wales* vision and tracking recent trends', *Contemporary Wales*, 22(1): forthcoming.

Felstead, A. and Gallie, D. (2004) 'For better or worse? Non-standard jobs and high involvement work systems', *International Journal of Human Resource Management*, 15(7): 1293–316.

Felstead, A., Jewson, N. and Walters S. (2005a) *Changing Places of Work*, Basingstoke: Palgrave Macmillan.

Felstead, A., Fuller, A., Unwin, L., Ashton, D., Butler, P. and Lee, T. (2005b) 'Surveying the scene: learning metaphors, survey design and the workplace context', *Journal of Education and Work*, 18(4): 359–83.

Felstead, A., Bishop, D., Fuller, A., Jewson, N., Lee, T. and Unwin, L. (2006) 'Moving to the music: learning processes, training and productive systems – the case of exercise to music instruction', *Learning as Work Research Paper, No 6*, June, Cardiff: Cardiff School of Social Sciences, Cardiff University.

Felstead, A., Fuller, A., Jewson, N., Kakavelakis, K. and Unwin, L. (2007a) 'Grooving to the same tunes? Learning, training and productive systems in the aerobics studio', *Work, Employment and Society*, 21(2): 189–208.

Felstead, A., Fuller, A., Jewson, N., Unwin, L. and Kakavelakis, K. (2007b) *Learning, Communities and Performance: Evidence from the 2007 Communities of Practice Survey*, Leicester: National Institute of Adult Continuing Education.

Felstead, A., Bishop, D., Fuller, A., Jewson, J., Unwin, L. and Kakavelakis, K. (2007c) 'Performing identities at work: evidence from contrasting sectors', *Learning as Work Research Paper, No. 9*, Cardiff: Cardiff School of Social Sciences, Cardiff University.

Felstead, A., Gallie, D., Green, F. and Zhou, Y. (2007d) *Skills at Work, 1986–2006*, Oxford: ESRC Centre for Skills, Knowledge and Organisational Performance.

Felstead, A., Gallie, D., Green, F. and Zhou, Y. (2008) 'Employee involvement, the quality of training and the learning environment: an individual-level analysis', *SKOPE Research Paper No 80*, June, Oxford: ESRC Centre for Skills, Knowledge and Organisational Performance.

Felstead, A., Jewson, N., Fuller, A., Kakavelakis, K. and Unwin, L. (2009a) 'Establishing rapport: using quantitative and qualitative methods in tandem', in Townsend, K. and Burgess, J. (eds) *Method in the Madness: Research Stories You Won't Find in a Textbook*, Oxford: Chandos Publishing, forthcoming.

Felstead, A., Bishop, D., Fuller, A., Jewson, N., Kakavelakis, K. and Unwin, L. (2009b) 'Mind the gap: personal and collective identities at work', *Studies in the Education of Adults*, 41(1):forthcoming.

Fenwick, T. (2004) 'Learning in portfolio work: anchored innovation and mobile identity', *Studies in Continuing Education*, 26(2): 229–46.

Ferguson, L. (1996) 'Sharing in practice: the corporate caseload', *Health Visitor*, 69 (October): 421–23.

Fernie, S. and Metcalf, D. (1998) *(Not) Hanging on the Telephone: Payment Systems in the New Sweatshops*, London: Centre for Economic Performance, London School of Economics.

Fevre, R., Gorad, S. and Rees, G. (2001) 'Necessary and unnecessary learning: the acquisition of knowledge and "skills" in and outside employment in South Wales in the 20th century', in Coffield, F. (ed.) *The Necessity of Informal Learning*, Bristol: Policy Press.

FIA (Fitness Industry Association) (2003) *Winning the Retention Battle: Reviewing Key Issues of UK Health and Fitness Club Membership Retention*, London: FIA.

FIA (Fitness Industry Association) (2008) *The State of the Industry: 2008*, London: FIA.

Field, J. (2005) *Social Capital and Lifelong Learning*, Bristol: Policy Press.

Field, J. (2006) *Lifelong Learning and the New Educational Order*, 2nd edn, Stoke-on-Trent: Trentham Books.

Fox, A. (1974) *Beyond Contract: Work, Power and Trust Relations*, London: Faber.

Frazis, H., Gittleman, M. and Joyce, M. (2000) 'Correlates of training: an analysis using both employer and employee characteristics', *Industrial and Labor Relations Review*, 53(3): 443–62.

Frazis, H., Herz, D.E. and Horrigan, M.W. (1995) 'Employer-provided training: results from a new survey', *Monthly Labor Review*, May: 3–17.

Freedman, E., Patrick, H., Somekh, B., McIntyre, D. and Wikeley, F. (2000) *Quality Conditions for Quality Research: Guidance for Good Practice in the Employment of Contract Researchers in Education*, Southwell: British Educational Research Association.

Frenkel, S., Tam, M., Korczynski, M. and Shire, K. (1998) 'Beyond bureaucracy? Work organization in call centres', *International Journal of Human Resource Management*, 9(6): 957–79.

Frenkel, S.J., Korczynski, M., Shire, K.A. and Tam, M. (1999) *On the Front Line: Organization of Work in the Information Economy*, New York: Cornell.

Froud, J., Haslan, C., Johal, S. and Williams, K. (2000a) 'Restructuring for shareholder value and its implications for labour', *Cambridge Journal of Economics*, 24(6): 771–91.

Froud, J., Haslan, C., Johal, S. and Williams, K. (2000b) 'Shareholder value and financialization: consultancy, promises, management moves', *Economy and Society*, 29(1): 80–110.

Fuller, A., Unwin, L., Felstead, A., Jewson, N. and Kakavelakis K. (2007), 'Creating and using knowledge: an analysis of the differential nature of workplace learning environments', *British Educational Research Journal*, 33(5): 743–59.

Fuller, A. and Unwin, L. (2003) 'Learning as apprentices in the contemporary UK workplace: creating and managing expansive and restrictive participation', *Journal of Education and Work*, 16(4): 407–26.

Fuller, A. and Unwin, L. (2004) 'Expansive learning environments: integrating organizational and personal development' in Rainbird, H., Fuller, A. and Munro, A. (eds) *Workplace Learning in Context*, London: Routledge.

Fuller, A., Ashton, D., Felstead, A., Unwin, L., Walters, S. and Quinn, M. (2003) *The Impact of Informal Learning at Work on Business Productivity*, London: Department of Trade and Industry.

Fuller, A., Hodkinson, H., Hodkinson, P. and Unwin, L. (2005) 'Learning as peripheral participation in communities of practice: a reassessment of key concepts in workplace learning', *British Educational Research Journal*, 31(1): 49–68.

Fuller, A., Kakavelakis, K., Felstead, A., Jewson, N. and Unwin, L. (2008) 'Learning, knowing and controlling "the stock": the changing nature of employee discretion in a supermarket chain', *Learning as Work Research Paper No 12*, Cardiff: Cardiff School of Social Sciences, Cardiff University.

Fuller, A., Unwin, L., Bishop, D., Felstead, A., Jewson, N., Kakavelakis, K. and Lee, T. (2006) 'Continuity, change and conflict: the role of knowing in different productive systems', *Learning as Work Research Paper No 7*, Cardiff: Cardiff School of Social Sciences, Cardiff University.

Fuller, A., Unwin, L., Felstead, A., Jewson, N. and Kakavelakis K. (2007) 'Creating and using knowledge: an analysis of the differential nature of workplace learning environments', *British Educational Research Journal*, 33(5): 743–59.

Gallie, D., Felstead, A., Green, F. and Zhou, Y. (2009) 'Teamwork, productive potential and employee welfare', *SKOPE Research Paper*, Oxford: ESRC Centre for Skills, Knowledge and Organisational Performance, forthcoming.

Garrick, J. and Boud, D. (1999) (eds) *Understanding Learning at Work*, London: Routledge.

Gastrill, P. (1994) 'A team approach to health visiting', *Primary Health Care*, 4: 10–12.

Gereffi, G. (1994) 'The organization of buy-driven global commodity chains: how US retailers shape overseas production networks', in Gereffi, M. and Korzeniewicz, M. (eds) *Commodity Chains and Global Capitalism*, Westport: Praeger.

Gereffi, G. (1999) 'International trade and industrial upgrading in the apparel commodity chain', *Journal of International Economics*, 48: 37–70.

Gereffi, G. and Korzeniewicz, M. (1994) (eds.) *Commodity Chains and Global Capitalism*, London: Praeger.

Glucksmann, M. (2004) 'Call configurations: varieties of call centre and divisions of labour', *Work, Employment and Society*, 18(4): 795–811.

Glucksmann, M. (2008) 'Transformation of work: "ready-made" food and new international divisions of labour', paper presented at the Spring 2008 Seminar Series, Cardiff School of Social Sciences, Cardiff University, 1 May.

Goffman, E. (1959) *The Presentation of Self in Everyday Life*, London: Penguin.

Green, F. (2006) 'Skills and job quality', in Porter, S. and Campbell, M. (eds) *Skills and Economic Performance*, London: Caspian Publishing.

Green, F. (2008) 'Leeway for the loyal: a model of employee discretion', *British Journal of Industrial Relations*, 46(1): 1–32.

Grimshaw, D., Lloyd, C. and Warhurst, C. (2008) 'Low-wage work in the United Kingdom: employment practices, institutional effects, and policy responses', in Lloyd, C., Mason, G. and Mayhew, K. (eds) *Low-Wage Work in the United Kingdom*, New York: Russell Sage Foundation.

Grugulis, I., Warhurst, C. and Keep, E. (2004) 'What's happening to "skill"?', in Warhurst, C., Grugulis, I. and Keep, E. (eds) *The Skills That Matter*, London: Palgrave.

Guerrier, Y. and Adib, A. (2003) 'Working at leisure and leisure at work: a study of the emotional labour of tour reps', *Human Relations*, 56(11): 1399–417.

Hager, P. (2004) 'The competence affair, or why vocational education and training urgently needs a new understanding of learning', *Journal of Training and Development*, 56(3): 409–34.

Hager, P. (2004) 'The conceptualization and measurement of learning', in Rainbird, H., Fuller, A. and Munro, A. (eds) *Workplace Learning in Context*, London: Routledge.

Hager, P. and Butler, J. (1996) 'Two models of educational assessment', *Assessment and Evaluation in Higher Education*, 21(4): 367–78.

Hall, E.J. (1993) 'Smiling, deferring, and flirting: doing gender by giving "good service"', *Work and Occupations*, 20(4): 452–71.

Harley, B., Allen, B.C. and Sargent, L.D. (2007) 'High Performance Work Systems and employee experience of work in the service sector: the case of aged care', *British Journal of Industrial Relations*, 45(3): 607–33.

Harvey, M., Quilley, S. and Beynon, H. (2002) *Exploring the Tomato: Transformations of Nature, Society and Economy*, Cheltenham: Edward Elgar.

Hennessy, T. and Sawchuk, P. (2003) 'Worker responses to technological change in the Canadian public sector: issues of learning and labour process', *Journal of Workplace Learning*, 15(7–8): 319–25.

Heritage, J. and Lindstrom, A. (1998) 'Motherhood, medicine and morality: scenes from a medical encounter', *Research on Language and Social Interaction*, 31(3) and (4): 397–438.

HM Treasury (2004) *Releasing Resources to the Front Line: Independent Review of Public Sector Efficiency*, London: HM Treasury.

HM Treasury (2006) *Prosperity for All in the Global Economy – World Class Skills*, London: HMSO.

Hodgson, A., Spours, K. and Steer, R. (2008) 'All change for the learning and skills sector?', *Journal of Education and Work*, 21(2): 115–31.

Hodkinson, H. and Hodkinson, P. (2004a) 'Rethinking the concept of community of practice in relation to schoolteachers' workplace learning', *International Journal of Training and Development*, 8(1): 21–31.

Hodkinson, P. and Hodkinson, H. (2004b) 'The significance of individuals' dispositions in workplace learning: a case study of two teachers', *Journal of Education and Work*, 17(2): 167–82.

Holgate, J. (2005) 'Organizing migrant workers: a case study of working conditions and unionization in a London sandwich factory', *Work, Employment and Society*, 19(3): 463–80.

Hollinrake, A., Antcliff, V. and Saundry, R. (2008) 'Explaining activity and exploring experience – findings from a survey of union learning representatives', *Industrial Relations Journal* 39(5): 392–410.

Houston, A.M. and Clifton, J. (2001) 'Corporate working in health visiting: a conceptual analysis', *Journal of Advanced Nursing*, 34(3): 356–66.

Hughes, J. (2008) 'The high-performance paradigm: a review and evaluation', *Learning as Work Research Paper No 16*, Cardiff: Cardiff School of Social Sciences, Cardiff University.

Hughes, J., Jewson, N. and Unwin, L. (2007) (eds) *Communities of Practice: Critical Perspectives*, London: Routledge.

Hunter, N. (2007) 'Where is the UK sandwich market going?', *Sandwich and Snack News*, February, 103: 12–15.

Hyett, E. (2003) 'What blocks health visitors from taking on a leadership role?', *Journal of Nursing Management*, 11: 229–33.

ILO (International Labour Organization) (1999) *Decent Work: Report of the Director-General*, London: International Labour Office.

Jackson, C. (1994) 'Strelley: teamworking for health', *Health Visitor* 67: 28–29.

Jewson, N. (2007) 'Cultivating network analysis: rethinking the concept of "community" within "communities of practice"', in Hughes, J., Jewson, N. and Unwin, L. (eds) *Communities of Practice: Critical Perspectives*, London: Routledge.

Jewson, N., Unwin, L., Felstead, A., Fuller, A., Kakavelakis, K. (2008) '"What is the vision for this profession?" Learning environments of health visitors in an English city', *Learning as Work Research Paper No 14*, Cardiff: Cardiff School of Social Sciences, Cardiff University.

Jones, P., Comfort D. and Hillier, D. (2006) 'Anti-corporate retailer campaigns on the internet', *International Journal of Retail and Distribution Management*, 34(12): 882–91.

Kakavelakis, K. (2008) 'Family metaphors and learning processes in a restaurant chain', *Learning as Work Research Paper No 18*, Cardiff: Cardiff School of Social Sciences, Cardiff University.

Kakavelakis, K., Felstead, A., Fuller, A., Jewson, N. and Unwin, L. (2008) 'Making a sales advisor: the limits of training "instrumental empathy"', *Journal of Vocational Education and Training*, 60(3): 209–21.

Kalleberg, A.L., Marsden, P.V., Reynolds, J. and Knoke, D. (2006) 'Beyond profit? Sectoral Differences in High-Performance Work Practices', *Work and Occupations*, 33(3): 271–302.

Kaplinksy, R. and Morris, M. (2001) *A Handbook for Value Chain Research*, report prepared for the IDCR.

Keep, E. (2006) 'State control of the English VET system – playing with the biggest trainset in the world', *Journal of Vocational Education and Training*, 58(1): 47–64.

Keep, E. (2008) 'A comparison of the Welsh Workforce Development Programme and England's Train to Gain', *SKOPE Research Paper No 79*, May, Oxford: ESRC Centre for Skills, Knowledge and Organisational Performance.

Keep, E. and Mayhew, K. (1999) 'The assessment: knowledge, skills, and competitiveness', *Oxford Review of Economic Policy*, 15(1): 1–15.

Keep, E., Mayhew, K. and Payne, J. (2006) 'From skills revolution to productivity miracle – not as easy as it sounds?', *Oxford Review of Economic Policy*, 22(4): 539–59.

Kelsey, A. (2000) 'The making of health visitors: an historical perspective part 1', *International History of Nursing Journal*, 5(3): 44–50.

Kersley, B., Alpin, C., Forth, J., Bryson, A., Bewley, H., Dix, G. and Oxenbridge, S. (2006) *Inside the Workplace: Findings from the 2004 Workplace Employment Relations Survey*, London: Routledge.

Kessler, I., Bach, S. and Heron, P. (2006) 'Understanding assistant roles in social care', *Work, Employment and Society*, 20(4): 667–85.

Kinsey, J. and Ashman, S. (2000) 'Information technology in the food supply industry', *Technology in Society*, 22(1): 83–96.

Kirkpatrick, I. and Hoque, K. (2006) 'A retreat from permanent employment? Accounting for the rise of professional agency work in UK public services', *Work, Employment and Society*, 20(4): 649–66.

Kitching, J. (2008) 'Rethinking UK small employers' skills policies and the role of workplace learning', *International Journal of Training and Development*, 12(2): 100–20.

Kjaernes, U., Harvey, M. and Warde, A. (2007) *Trust in Food: A Comparative and Institutional Analysis*, Basingstoke: Palgrave Macmillan.

Kleiner, M. (2000) 'Occupational licensing', *Journal of Economic Perspectives*, 14(4): 189–202.

Knights, D. and McCabe, D. (2003) 'Governing through teamwork: reconstituting subjectivity in a call centre', *Journal of Management Studies,* 40(7): 1587–619.

Knights, D. and McCabe, D. (1998) 'What happens when the telephone goes wild?: staff stress and spaces for escape in a BPR telephone banking work regime', *Journal of Management Studies*, 35(2): 162–74.

Knuth, D. E. (1974) 'Computer programming as an art', *Communications of the ACM*, 17(12): 667–73.

Konzelman, S., Wilkinson, F., Crayo, C. and Aridi, R. (2006) 'Global reproduction of national capitalisms: the cases of Wal-Mart and IKEA', in Elsner, W. and Hanappi, H. (eds) *Varieties of Capitalism and New Institutional Deals*, Cheltenham: Edward Elgar.

Korczynski, M. and Ott, U. (2004) 'When production and consumption meet: cultural contradictions and the enchanting myth of customer sovereignty', *Journal of Management Studies*, 41(3): 575–99.

Lashley, C. and Taylor, S. (1998) 'Hospitality retail operations types and styles in management of human resources', *Journal of Retailing and Consumer Services*, 5(3): 153–65.

Latham, M. (1994) *Constructing the Team: Final Report of the Government/ Industry Review of Procurement and Contractual Arrangements in the UK Construction Industry – The Latham Report*, London: HMSO.

Lave, J. and Wenger, E. (1991) *Situated Learning: Legitimate Peripheral Participation*, New York: Cambridge University Press.

Law, J. (1986) 'On the methods of long-distance control: vessels, navigation and the Portuguese route to India', in Law, J. (ed) *Power, Action and Belief: A New Sociology of Knowledge?* London: Routledge and Kegan Paul.

Law, J. and Hassard, J. (1999) (eds) *Actor Network Theory and After*, Oxford: Blackwell.

Lee, T., Fuller, A., Ashton, D., Butler, P., Felstead, A., Unwin, L. and Walters, S. (2004) 'Workplace learning: main themes and perspectives', *Learning as Work Research Paper No 2*, Leicester: Centre for Labour Market Studies, University of Leicester.

Lee, T., Jewson, N., Bishop, D., Felstead, A., Fuller, A., Kakavelakis, K. and Unwin, L. (2007) 'There's a lot more to it than just cutting hair, you know: managerial controls, work practices and identity narratives among hair stylists', *Learning as Work Research Paper No 8*, Cardiff: Cardiff School of Social Sciences, Cardiff University.

Leidner, R. (1993) *Fast Food, Fast Talk: Service Work and the Routinization of Everyday Life*, Berkeley: University of California Press.

Livingstone, D. and Sawchuk, P. (2003) *Hidden Knowledge: Organised Labour in the Information Age*, Aurora, Canada: Garamond Press.

Lloyd, C. (2005) 'Training standards as a policy option? The regulation of the fitness industry', *Industrial Relations Journal*, 36(5): 367–85.

Lloyd, C., Mason, G. and Mayhew, K. (eds) (2008) *Low Pay in the United Kingdom*, New York: Russell Sage Foundation.

LSC (2007) *Train to Gain – A Plan for Growth*, Coventry: Learning and Skills Council.

Luhmann, N. (1993) *Risk: A Sociological Theory*, New York: de Gruyter.

Lynch, L.M. and Black, S.E. (1995) 'Beyond the incidence of training: evidence from a national employers survey', *National Bureau of Economic Research Working Paper No 5231*, August, Cambridge, MA: National Bureau of Economic Research.

Lynch, L.M. and Black, S.E. (1998) 'Beyond the incidence of employer-provided training', *Industrial and Labor Relations Review*, 52(1): 64–81.

MacDuffie, J.P. and Kochan, T.A. (1995) 'Do U.S. firms invest less in human resources? Training in the world auto industry', *Industrial Relations*, 34(2), April: 147–68.

Maguire Smith, J. (2001) 'Fit and flexible: the fitness industry, personal trainers and emotional service labor', *Sociology of Sport Journal*, 18: 379–402.

Malone, M. (2000) 'A history of health visiting and parenting in the last 50 years', *International History of Nursing Journal*, 5(3): 30–43.

Marks, A. and Lockyer, C. (2005) 'Professional identity in software work', in Barrett, R. (ed.) *Management, Labour Process and Software Development*, London: Routledge.

Marshall J.N. and Richardson, R. (1996) 'The impact of "telemediated" services on corporate structures: the example of "branchless" retail banking in Britain', *Environment and Planning A*, 28(10): 1843–58.

Marsick, V. and Watkins, K. (1990) *Informal and Incidental Learning in the Workplace*, New York: Routledge.

Mason, G. and Wagner, K. (2002) *Skills, Performance and New Technologies in the British and Automotive Components Industries*, London: DfES.

McIlroy, J. (2008) 'Ten years of New Labour: workplace learning, social partnership and union revitalization in Britain', *British Journal of Industrial Relations*, 46(2): 283–313.

Mennel, S. and Goudsblom, J. (eds) (1998) *Norbert Elias: On Civilization, Power and Knowledge*, Chicago: University of Chicago Press.

Mikkola, J.H. and Skjøtt-Larsen, T. (2006) 'Platform management: implication for new product development and supply chain management', *European Business Review*, 18(3): 214–30.

Mintel (2004) *Leisure Centres and Swimming Pools*, London: Mintel International Group.

Mintel (2005) *Health and Fitness Clubs, Special Report*, April 2005, London: Mintel International Group.

Monopolies and Mergers Commission (1988) *Collective Licensing: A Report on Certain Practices in the Collective Licensing of Public Performance and Broadcasting Rights in Sound Recordings*, Cm 530, London: HMSO.

Mutch A. (2002) 'Actors and networks or agents and structures: towards a realist view of actor-network theory', *Organization*, 9(3): 477–96.

Nijhof, W.J. and Nieuwenhuis, L.F.M. (eds) (2008) *The Learning Potential of the Workplace*, Rotterdam: Sense Publishers.

Nonaka, I. and Takeuchi, H. (1995) *The Knowledge-Creating Company: How Japanese Companies Create the Dynamics of Innovation*, Oxford: Oxford University Press.

OECD (2005) *Promoting Adult Learning*, Paris: Organisation for Economic Co-operation and Development.

OECD (2007) 'Lifelong learning and human capital', *OECD Policy Brief*, July, Paris: Organisation for Economic Co-operation and Development.

OST (1998) *Research Careers Initiative Report, October 1998*, London: Office of Science and Technology.

Osterman, P. (1995) 'Skill, training, and work organization in American establishments', *Industrial Relations*, 34(2): 125–46.

Payne, J. (2008) 'Sector skills councils and employer engagement – delivering the 'employer-led' skills agenda in England', *Journal of Education and Work*, 21(2): 93–113.

Payne, J. and Keep, E. (2005) 'Promoting workplace development: lessons for UK policy from Nordic approaches to job redesign and the quality of working life', in Harley, B., Hyman, J. and Thompson, P. (eds) *Participation and Democracy: Essays in Honour of Harvie Ramsay*, Basingstoke: Palgrave.

Peckover, S. (2002) 'Supporting and policing mothers: an analysis of the disciplinary practices of health visiting' *Journal of Advanced Nursing*, 38: 369–77.

PIU (2001) *In Demand: Adult Skills in the 21st Century*, London: Performance and Innovation Unit, Cabinet Office.

PPL (2004) *Seventy Years of PPL*, London: Phonographic Performance Limited.

Quintas, P. (1994), 'Programmes innovation? Trajectories of change in software development', *Information Technology and People*, 7(1): 25–47.

Rainbird, H., Fuller, A. and Munro, A. (eds) (2004) *Workplace Learning in Context*, London: Routledge.

Reich, R. (1991) *The Wealth of Nations*, London: Simon and Schuster.

Rhys, G. (2004) 'The motor industry in an enlarged EU', *The World Economy*, 27(6): 877–900.

Roberts, G. (2002) *SET for Success: The Supply of People with Science, Technology, Engineering And Mathematics Skills – The Report of Sir Gareth Roberts' Review*, London: HM Treasury.

Robinson, H., Hall, P., Hovenden, F., and Rachel, J. (1998) 'Postmodern software development', *The Computer Journal*, 41(6): 363–75.

Rowe, A., Hogarth, A., Teager, M., Brocklehurst, N., English, G., Cox, S. and Yates, J. (2003) 'Modernising health visiting and school nursing practice: an account of the PHAAR programme in central Derby', Derby: University of Sheffield and Central Derby PCT.

Salter, B. and Tapper, T. (2002) 'The external pressures on the internal governance of universities', *Higher Education Quarterly*, 56(3): 245–56.

Sassatelli, R. (1999) 'Interaction order and beyond: a field analysis of body culture within fitness gyms', *Body and Society*, 5(2): 227–48.

Sawchuk, P. (2006) '"Use-value" and the re-thinking of skills, learning and the labour process', *Journal of Industrial Relations*, 48(5): 593–617.

Sayers, J. and Bradbury, T. (2004) '"Let the music take your mind": aesthetic labour and "working out" to music', paper presented at the *Work, Employment and Society* Conference, UMIST, 1–3 September.

Scarborough, H. and Swan, J.A. (eds) (1999) *Cases in Knowledge Management*, London: Institute of Personnel Development.

Sfard, A. (1998) 'On two metaphors for learning and the dangers of choosing just one', *Educational Researcher*, 27(2): 4–13.

Sharma, U. and Black, P. (2001) 'Look good, feel better: beauty therapy as emotional labour', *Sociology*, 35(4): 913–31.

SkillsActive (2004) *Working in Fitness 2004*, London: SkillsActive.

SMMT (2002) *Strengthening the Supply Chain: Improving The Competitiveness of the UK's Automotive Components Sector*, London: Society of Motor Manufacturers and Traders.

Speed, S. and Luker, K.A. (2006) 'Getting a visit: how district nurses and general practitioners "organise" each other in primary care', *Sociology of Health and Illness*, 28(7): 883–902.

SSDA and Automotive Skills (2004) *Sector Skills Matrix 2004*, London: Sector Skills Development Agency.

Star, L. (1989) 'The structure of ill-structured solutions: boundary objects and heterogeneous distributed problem solving', Working Paper, Department of Information and Computer Science, University of California, Irvine.

Stasz, C. (2001) 'Assessing skills for work: two perspectives', *Oxford Economic Papers,* 53(3): 385–405

Strategy Unit (2002) *In Demand – Adult Skills in the 21st Century – Part 2,* London: Strategy Unit, Cabinet Office.

Streeck, W. (1989) 'Skills and the limits of neo-liberalism: the enterprise of the future as the site for learning', *Work, Employment and Society,* 3(1): 89–104.

Stroud, D. and Fairbrother, P. (2006) 'Workplace learning: dilemmas for the European steel industry', *Journal of Education and Work,* 19(5): 455–80.

Sung, J., Raddon, A. and Ashton, D. (2006) 'Skills abroad: a comparative assessment of international policy approaches to skills leading to the development of policy recommendations for the UK', *Research Report 16,* Wath-upon-Dearne: Sector Skills Development Agency.

Symonds, A. (1991) 'Angels and interfering busybodies: the social construction of two occupations', *Sociology of Health and Illness,* 13(2): 249–64.

Taylor, P. and Bain, P. (1999) 'An assembly line in the head: work and employee relations in the call centre', *Industrial Relations Journal,* 30(2): 101–17.

Taylor, P. and Bain, P. (2006) '"A very different (non)-economic space"? Emergency call centre workers – a reply to Glucksmann', paper presented to the 24th International Labour Process Conference, School of Management, Birkbeck College, London, 10–12 April.

Taylor, P. and Bain, P. (2007) 'Reflections on the call centre – a reply to Glucksmann', *Work, Employment and Society,* 21(2): 349–62.

Taylor, S. and Tilley, N. (1989) 'Health visitors and child protection: conflict, contradictions and ethical dilemmas', *Health Visitor,* 62(9): 273–75.

Tether, B. (2000) 'Who co-operates for innovation within the supply-chain, and why? An analysis of the United Kingdom's Innovation Survey', *Centre for Research on Innovation and Competition, Discussion Paper No 35,* Manchester: University of Manchester.

Torrance, H. (2007) 'Assessment *as* learning? How the use of explicit learning objectives, assessment criteria and feedback in post-secondary education and training can come to dominate learning', *Assessment in Education,* 14(3): 281–94.

TUC (2007) *Time to Tackle the Training Divide,* London: Trades Union Congress.

Tuomi-Grohn, T. and Engeström, Y. (eds) (2003) *Between School and Work: New Perspectives on Transfer and Boundary Crossing,* Amsterdam: Pergamon.

Tuomi-Grohn, T. Engeström, Y. and Young, M. (2003) 'From transfer to boundary crossing between school and work as a tool for developing vocational education: an introduction', in Tuomi-Grohn, T. and Engeström, Y. (eds) *Between School and Work, New Perspectives on Transfer and Boundary Crossing,* London: Pergamon.

Twinn, S. (1993) 'Principles in practice: a re-affirmation', *Health Visitor,* 66(9): 319–21.

Unwin, L., Felstead, A., Fuller, A., Bishop, D., Jewson, N., Kakavelakis, K. and Lee, T. (2007) 'Looking inside the Russian doll: the interconnections between context, learning and pedagogy in the workplace', *Pedagogy, Culture and Society*, 15(3): 333–48.

Unwin, L., Fuller, A., Bishop, D., Felstead, A., Jewson, N. and Kakavelakis, K. (2008a) 'Exploring the dangers and benefits of the UK's permissive competence-based approach: the use of vocational qualifications as learning artefacts and tools for measurement in the automotive sector', *Learning as Work Research Paper, No. 15*, Cardiff School of Social Sciences: Cardiff University.

Unwin, L., Felstead, A., Fuller, A., Lee, T., Butler, P. and Ashton, D. (2008b) 'Worlds within worlds: the relationship between context and pedagogy in the workplace', in Nijhof, W.J. and Nieuwenhuis, L.F.M. (eds) *The Learning Potential of the Workplace*, Rotterdam: Sense Publishers.

van der Valk, W. and Wynstra, F. (2005) 'Supplier involvement in new product development in the food industry', *Industrial Marketing Management*, 34: 681–94.

Villosio, C., Di Pierro, D., Giodanengo, A., Pasqua, P. and Richiardi, M. (2008) *Working Conditions of an Ageing Workforce*, Luxembourg: Office for Official Publications of the European Communities.

Vygotsky, L.S. (1978) *Mind in Society: The Development of Higher Psychological Processes*, Cambridge, MA: Harvard University Press.

Wallace, C. and Eagleson, G. (2000) 'The sacrificial HR strategy in call centres.' *International Journal of Service Industry Management*, 11(2): 174–84.

Warde, A. (1999) 'Convenience food: space and timing', *British Food Journal*, 101(7): 518–27.

Warhurst, C., Grugulis, I. and Keep, E. (eds) (2004) *The Skills That Matter*, London: Palgrave Macmillan.

Wenger, E. (1998) *Communities of Practice: Learning, Meaning and Identity*, Cambridge: Cambridge University Press.

While, A.E. (1987) 'The early history of health visiting: a review of the role of central government', *Child Care Health Development*, 13(2): 27–36.

Whitfield, K. (2000) 'High-performance workplaces, training, and the distribution of skills', *Industrial Relations*, 39(1), January: 1–25.

Wilkinson, F. (1983) 'Productive systems', *Cambridge Journal of Economics*, 7(3/4): 413–29.

Wilkinson, F. (1998) 'Co-operation, the organisation of work and competitiveness', *ESRC Centre for Business Research, University of Cambridge, Working Paper No 85*, Cambridge: Department of Applied Economics, University of Cambridge.

Wilkinson, F. (2002) 'Productive systems and the structuring role of economic and social theories', *ESRC Centre for Business Research, University of Cambridge, Working Paper No 225*, Cambridge: Department of Applied Economics, University of Cambridge.

Williams, G., Blackstone, T. and Metcalf, D. (1974) *The Academic Labour Market,* Amsterdam: Elsevier.

Winship, J. (2006) 'The British sandwich industry fact file 2006', *Sandwich and Snack News,* April, 97: 10–12.

Winterbotham, M., Shury, J., Carter, K. and Schäfer, S. (2008) *National Employers Skills Survey 2007: Main Report,* Coventry: Learning and Skills Council.

Witz, A., Warhurst, C. and Nickson, D. (2003) 'The labour aesthetics and the aesthetics of organization', *Organization,* 10(1): 33–54.

Wolf, A. (1995) *Competence-Based Assessment,* Buckingham: Open University Press.

Wolf, A., Jenkins, A. and Vignoles, A. (2006) 'Certifying the workforce: economic imperative or failed social policy?', *Journal of Education Policy,* 21(5): 535–65.

Wood, S., Holman, D. and Stride, C. (2006) 'Human resource management and performance in UK call centres', *British Journal of Industrial Relations,* 44(1): 99–124.

Young, M. (2004) 'Conceptualising vocational knowledge', in Rainbird, H., Fuller, A. and Munro, A. (eds) *Workplace Learning in Context,* London: Routledge.

Index